Modern India's Economy
Two Decades of
Planned Growth

Wilfred Malenbaum

Wharton School of Finance and Commerce
University of Pennsylvania

Charles E. Merrill Publishing Company
A Bell & Howell Company
Columbus, Ohio

Merrill's Economic Systems Series
William P. Snavely, Editor

International Standard Book Number: 0-675-09760-6

Library of Congress Catalog Card Number: 72-165986

Printed in the United States of America

1 2 3 4 5 6 7 8 9 10 — 78 77 76 75 74 73 72 71

Editor's Foreword

The Merrill Economic Systems Series has been developed to meet three clearly recognized needs. First, it is designed to provide greater flexibility and broader coverage in formal economic systems courses. To do so, the series contains a core volume and ten books covering individual countries. The core volume presents an analytical discussion, placed in historical perspective, of the major types of systems. The individual country-study volumes, written by outstanding scholars and specialists on the country, provide illustrations of the nature and operation of various systems in practice. The ten countries included in the initial series illustrate a wide range of economic systems. Those who are involved with the systems field will find it possible to choose from this extensive selection those particular country-study volumes which fit most effectively their own individual courses. As the series is expanded to include additional countries the flexibility of choice will become even greater.

The second important need which this series is designed to meet is that for collateral reading in various social science courses. Those who teach principles of economics, introductory political science, comparative government, or general social studies courses, will find excellent possibilities for assigning individual volumes for greater in-depth study of particular areas. Each book has been prepared as an entity in itself and can therefore profitably be studied either individually or as part of a more comprehensive program.

Finally, this series will provide a stimulating introduction to different economic systems for the interested reader who is concerned about this subject of major contemporary importance.

William P. Snavely

Preface

The poor nations of the world can achieve higher rates of economic expansion in the 1970's than they did in the 1960's or the 1950's. But such goals, as in the United Nations' new Development Decade, will require more than continuation and expansion of the types of programs associated with past development achievement in these lands. Twenty years and more of planned and stimulated development activities have not uncovered an assured path for more rapid growth during the new decade. The United Nations emphasizes the need to seek new insights and hypotheses on the growth process; the new tasks require new models and strategies, new programs and tools. In the past the pre-eminent role in growth was given to new investment inputs, particularly from the more developed world; their contributions are now judged casual and unpredictable. The new efforts need to reflect a new concern with people in the poor lands and with their broad participation in the development process. Development programs can now embody a new precision based on study of the actual experience in the poor lands themselves; they must embody the vigor of populations committed to progress.

Modern India provides decisive evidence of an evolution in development policy, program and promise. Two decades back, India pioneered new development activities for long-static poor nations. In any event, among these lands it was India that first prepared and published a comprehensive five-year development plan in a longer-term perspective. India formulized the program's dependence on new investment with explicit provision for the level and the gain from capital inflows from abroad. India established a planning commission in the high echelons of government, with the Prime Minister himself as its chairman. Jawaharal Nehru was a charismatic leader with broad popular support in India and with high prestige throughout the world. There was confidence that the Indian effort would achieve its growth objectives in India and also serve the cause of accelerated development in many other poor countries.

v

Two decades of planned growth brought fundamental changes in India's development posture. In the third plan period it became clear that economic programs were not in step with reality; new directions in planning were needed. These were to emerge during a hiatus in the plan sequence — from April 1, 1966 through March 31, 1969. The planning commission was reconstituted in 1967 — enough so to provide a new commission for the first time in its nearly twenty years of existence. But the new fourth plan has not yet set India on a clear path of economic expansion. Indeed, for almost two years into late 1970, Prime Minister Indira Gandhi — Nehru's daughter — had to formulate development policy and program through a government with a tenuous parliamentary base. Her stated objective, economic progress shared broadly by the people of India, found limited support either in the fourth plan itself or in the legislative party structure through which basic development decisions and actions had to move. The special election of March 1971 testified to the wide gap between popular and party aspirations in recent years. Now the Prime Minister's government is assured of a firm political base for its operations; it is in a position to support its policies by legislative actions at state and national levels.

New directions for development actions have yet to be announced. An entirely new planning commission will be led by an experienced minister of Cabinet rank, with a record of outstanding achievement in past ministerial posts. Mrs. Gandhi will seek development goals directed to both greater growth and more equal distribution of national product. Development theorists and practitioners have increasingly favored policy orientations based on the interdependence of these two goals. Current doctrine also puts heavy emphasis on the role of national leadership in the development process. The present setting for India's economic growth must therefore be judged auspicious indeed. Into this organizational and philosophical structure can now be fit specific policies and programs suited to India's development needs, aspirations and capabilities. This means development activity that has been tested in the actual experience of India's planned growth over past decades.

The present study offers an interpretation of this past record, both the continuity of development from the early 1950's and the influence of the new agriculture and the new industrial orientation of the past five to six years. The analysis points to the gains for India's growth from a new employment effort. It outlines the implications of past Indian growth experience for the leadership needs and for the financial aspects of such supplementary labor programs.

In the present Indian setting therefore our analysis of modern India's economy assumes a relevance beyond what was anticipated while the study evolved. It can be significant for India's own course of future development. In the current world development scene, decisive new actions in India may again have pioneer significance for economic growth in other poor lands.

Wilfred Malenbaum

Legend

Rupees (Rs) — currency unit used throughout this study
    $1.00 (U.S.) = 4.76 Rs to June 5, 1966
    $1.00 (U.S.) = 7.59 Rs from June 5, 1966
Crore (Cr) — number unit usually used in India's *Plans*
    1 Cr = 10,000,000
    Rs cr = $2,100,000 to June 5, 1966
    Rs cr = $1,300,000 from June 5, 1966
1950/51—Indian fiscal year April 1, 1950 through March 31, 1951
1951-56—the fiscal years from April 1, 1951 through March 31, 1956

Contents

India in a Developing World

1

The Setting for Development in the 70's

Pursuit of progress in a development-conscious world did succeed in moving economic output ahead of growth of population in the developing nations of Africa, Asia, and Latin America. Over the past 15 to 20 years, output increased by 85 percent and population by 40 percent; per capita incomes rose by almost 2 percent annually. Is this record testimony to a new and revolutionary change in lands whose economies have long been static? Are the poorer lands actually on the road to economic well-being, as were today's wealthy lands 75 to 150 years ago? Recent achievements are below the expectations of a world which since 1950 has focussed its efforts upon economic development in the poor lands. There is also some disquieting evidence that neither the growth of total product in these lands nor the growth of product per person has maintained momentum in the last decade. These rates for all the developing nations together were lower in the 1960's than they were in the 1950's. Persistent increases in product per person, in successive five-year periods, were confined to a handful of countries — Guatemala, Panama, Chile, perhaps Korea and Taiwan — with less than 3 percent of the population of the poor lands.

1

The necessary tasks for economic expansion in the poor countries are still being discovered. Increasingly these tasks have been enmeshed with two basic components of national progress: number of people and amount of food. Shortage of food relative to number of people is scarcely a phenomenon of the present and future alone. The threat and the reality of famine have characterized the history of man. But food and population today seem to be at the core of development problems. This is partly because the entire world is now alert to explosive rates of population growth and to limited expansion in food production in poor lands. Future shortage must therefore take on a large order of magnitude. Partly, however, food and population now receive attention because the world community is intolerant of past solutions that meant widespread famine and starvation.

How effectively do current plans and policies cope with the population-food-growth complex? Control efforts on population are widespread, and some reductions in birth rates are becoming apparent. Yet for all developing lands together the population growth rate may increase at least into the early 1970's. In any event, this overall rate, 2.5 percent in the past few years, is not expected to fall below 2.0 percent during the present century.[1] An appraisal by a Presidential Scientific Advisory Commission, PSAC, published in 1967, expressed doubt that an effective solution was in sight for economic growth and food for these expanding populations.[2] In the PSAC view, all poor nations together showed agriculture growing at an average of 2.7 percent, while their total demand for food was increasing by 3 percent each year. Net imports of foodgrains by these nations, including Mainland China, reached nearly thirty million tons in several recent years. These trends could raise this net deficit to one hundred million tons per year by 1985/86. Imports on this scale can be visualized even with limited provision for expansion in the low level of per capita food consumption in the poor lands.

These analyses did not give extensive consideration to the "green revolution"; the miracle seeds, where there was enough water and

---

[1]See U.N. Population Division, *World Population Prospects, 1965-2000,* December, 1970, pp. 14-15 [Doc. ESA/P/WP 37].

[2]PSAC, *The World Food Problem,* May, 1967. (Referred to as PSAC report.) See especially Vol. I and Vol. II, pp. 165-77. For similar results see the summary appraisal of the Food and Agriculture Organization of the U.N., *Monthly Bulletin of Agricultural Economics and Statistics,* Vol. 17, No. 5 (May, 1968), pp. 104-10. The FAO's new Indicative World Plan (IWP) for agriculture and development starts from a comparable food and population imbalance.

fertilizer, brought a new dynamism into crop output in poor lands. But this began to be apparent only with the 1967 harvests, notably in a few Asian countries. Even today we can only say that the long-term prospects about levels of food output are hopeful here — but scarcely certain.[3] On the other hand, the richer lands would be able to supply foodgrains sufficient to meet the large magnitudes indicated, if there were in fact effective demand for such quantities.

The food supply problem can, in other words, be viewed in terms of domestic agricultural output in the poor lands *and* of their ability to finance purchases from the wealthier nations of the world. For the developing world, food objectives become agricultural product and level of export (or level of foreign aid) objectives.

Economic development programs must bring about more rapid rates of growth; that growth needs to generate relatively more foreign exchange as well as relatively more food output. PSAC recognized both these objectives and gave particular emphasis to the second. For poor lands as a whole it suggested the following annual average growth targets over the years to 1985/86[4]:

Food output	4.0% (2.7%)
Food demand	4.0% (3.0%)
Gross national income	5.5% (4.5%)

It is probable that a 5.5 percent rate of growth of national income will bring with it a 4 percent growth in demand for food,[5] but the larger expansion in food production (from 2.7 percent to 4.0 percent)

---

[3]Two important views expand on both aspects of this statement. See Lester R. Brown, "The Agricultural Revolution in Asia," *Foreign Affairs*, Vol. 46 (July, 1968), 688-98; Clifton R. Wharton, Jr., "The Green Revolution: Cornucopia or Pandora's Box?" *Foreign Affairs*, Vol. 47 (April, 1969), pp. 464-76. The effects of the new agriculture in India are appraised in this book, especially in Chapters 5 and 7, pp. 158-62, 219-21.

[4]PSAC report, Vol. I, p. 22. Percentages in parentheses are PSAC figures on (1966/67) rates of growth in these countries. For 1965-69 the figures in brackets would be somewhat larger for gross national income and for food output. Both these favorable results can be attributed primarily to good harvests after 1967.

[5]In these PSAC projections, total consumption in the developing lands will be well above the levels of 1965/66, about two-thirds of the increase matching population growth and the remainder permitting higher per capita consumption levels. The latter is an essential component of the economic progress assumed over these years. (*Ibid.*, Vol. II, especially pp. 165-77). The rate of growth of national income per capita (y), the per capita income elasticity of demand for food (ε), the rate of population growth (p), and the rate of growth of food demand (f) are directly related: $f = p + \varepsilon y$. With $y = 3.1\%$ (the 5.5% growth of GNP and a 2.4% growth of population) and with $\varepsilon = .52$, f is computed at about 4.0%.

is scarcely an automatic concomitant of such overall growth. The PSAC took the position that a 4 percent growth rate in agriculture in the poor lands was possible, provided "massive efforts" were made. But the Committee was not overly hopeful that the developing nations would look favorably upon an agricultural emphasis in any reformulation of development activities. "Agricultural development has never been a particularly appealing or inspiring national goal; it is politically unglamorous, unrecognized, and unrewarding. It does not raise visions of the twentieth century, the age of technological revolution, in the minds of most people."[6] Nonetheless the last few years have presented new possibilities and perhaps new interest in agricultural expansion in the poor lands. New ways of intensifying output, led by the development of new high-yielding seed varieties for foodgrains—wheat, rice, sorghum, corn, millet—are (in some views) already ushering in an agricultural revolution in Asia and perhaps soon in Latin America and Africa. As indicated, this new direction may make the outlook for the PSAC targets for agricultural growth more hopeful. For the poor lands as a group these targets were exceeded in the favorable crop year of 1967 and again in 1969, although in the last years expansion was notable primarily in South Asia alone.

Many aspects of agricultural growth warrant consideration here, as indeed throughout a study concerned with India's development prospects. But we must first observe that, even with the achievement of the PSAC targets for agricultural output, these lands would still require an annual level of foodgrains imports of some fifty-five million tons by the end of the next 15 years, twice the level of the recent past. Success in agriculture must thus be matched in the poor lands of the world by success in expanding export capacity. In the years since 1950 their share of world exports actually fell from more than one-third to less than one-fifth. This period saw a four-fold expansion in rich-nation exports, attributable for the most part to growth in foreign trade among the world's rich lands. The underdeveloped lands did expand their exports by 80 percent in real terms, and their imports grew even more rapidly. We noted the growth in food imports; development efforts in the poor lands spurred the need for capital goods and intermediate products from abroad. Foodgrains apart, the poor lands must still anticipate expanded imports over the next decades.

---

[6]*Ibid.*, Vol. I, p. 8.

While export prospects for these lands need not be unfavorable, especially if trade among them can be expanded, the course for such growth remains to be plotted. Certainly the conclusions of the second United Nations Conference on Trade and Development (UN-CTAD) in its meetings, held in New Delhi in March 1968, did not present ready paths for this growth. Some form of special financing was involved for at least 60 percent of the foodgrains imports of the poor nations in recent years. When the need for imports of food-grains is of the order of fifty to sixty million tons a year in 1985/86, to say nothing of ninety to one hundred million tons, it is not possible to make straightforward projections for payment arrangements through new export proceeds or new foreign assistance.

The poor lands have of course stressed the importance of indus-trialization and diversification as the route to expanded export po-tential, anticipating a growing capacity to purchase raw materials and agricultural products abroad in exchange for exports that con-tain a rapidly increasing percentage of manufactured goods. Devel-oping nations, like development theorists, usually rest their plans for economic expansion upon their reading of the past experience of today's rich lands. Since the late eighteenth century, nations have actually been making the transition from poverty and stagnation to economic well-being and continuous expansion. Today about 30 percent of the world's people live in nations which have accom-plished this feat. Since 1950, their output has expanded by more than 130 percent and their population by less than 30 percent. Over the past two decades their economies have grown twice as fast per capita as have the economies of the poor lands; they have ex-panded their rate of growth in the 1960's beyond the growth of 1950's. Today's poor lands want to emulate this experience.

However, the situation of the mid-twentieth century is basically quite different from the situation 100 and more years ago. The industrial transition was then being made by a few nations at one time. They were pioneer leader nations, already economically ahead of most of the world's lands; they were anxious to continue to move even further ahead. Their initial growth paths — a phase taking some 25 years — were reasonably staggered. Great Britain domi-nated the early decades of the nineteenth century; Belgium, France, and the United States were important in the middle of that century. These nations were followed by Germany, Sweden, Japan, Russia, and Canada into the first decades of the twentieth century. At any time over these 100 to 150 years, nations with only a very small per-centage of the world's population were embarking on the transition from relative stagnation to progress. Their initial dependence on the rest of the world was small; their capacity to trade, high and increasing. They could count upon significant economic exchange with the rest of the world's nations.

When Britain's economy began to be industrialized at the turn of the nineteenth century, the nation experienced an increased demand for foodstuffs, thus stimulating domestic output in an agriculture which had "modernized" some decades earlier, before the industrial revolution.[7] Especially after the 1830's, abundant food supplies and agricultural raw materials were increasingly available abroad in poorer lands for export to developing nations in Europe, at least when agricultural protection policies in these developing lands permitted the substitution of low-cost imports for their own higher-cost foodstuffs. Agricultural exports from the less advanced lands in America could readily be paid for by the new activities of modernization. Over most of the nineteenth century and even later, the cost of production and delivery and the price of food and raw materials tended to decline relative to costs and prices of their manufactured products. Productivity in overseas agriculture was expanding rapidly; demand for its products tended to be less elastic than for the new products of the new industry in the developing lands. In the small share of the world where economic life was diversifying at a rapid pace, increasing percentages of factor inputs could be devoted to industrialization and the services intimately related to it. Home markets were growing; new output could readily be exchanged for food and raw materials abroad. International trade proferred assistance to developing and other nations.

Current contrasts with the historical picture arise principally from the relative scale of today's effort and from the relative economic status of its participants. Today 70 percent of the world's people are seeking more or less simultaneously and over essentially a single 25 year period — 1950–1975 at first, 1965–1990 now — to make this initial transformation from poverty to the promise of greater well-being. Despite their large share of the world's area and population, they manifest relatively few economic complementarities with the richer lands and in general still fewer among themselves. Their share of world trade has been declining. Apart from producers of petroleum and other major primary goods, their export ratios do not expand. Programs of regional integration, in Central

---

[7]See, for example, Thomas S. Ashton, *The Industrial Revolution, 1760-1830* (London: Oxford University Press, 1948), pp. 1-10.

and South America, in Asia and in Africa, still hold uncertain promise for future increments in the small degree of mutual dependence of member nations.[8] Since they cannot depend on one another for imported foodgrains and agricultural staples in any significant degree, they have to turn to the developed world for such imports. And this has been clearly reflected in mounting food shipments.

The poor lands are not pioneering new technologies and new products for domestic use or foreign trade. Instead their emphasis is on catching up with the rest of the world. In this they count upon the assistance of the developed lands. Development plans have proceeded mostly on the assumption that intensified industrialization efforts are the key to progress and indeed the prerequisite for a subsequent, efficient expansion in food and agricultural sectors. Domestic policies and programs in these poor countries have often favored low levels for food prices and for interest rates — both in order to stimulate precisely such industry-focussed development. The process demands large machinery inputs that must come from the more developed lands; this is also reflected in import patterns of recent years. At best then, success in present development efforts will mean that all of the poor nations, more or less at the same time, will be seeking to turn the trade tide with a very large increase in exports of processed goods to the richer lands. On the whole these would not be new products like those featured in export trade of industrializing countries in the previous century; the exports could only be foreign replacements of familiar products.

Will the poor lands be able to expand their exports beyond imports of needed industrial goods and services to buy some five to eight billion dollars worth of foodgrains each year from the advanced countries? Meaningful answers are not easily found. Trade optimists are hopeful, albeit in a cautious way. They emphasize particularly the possible gains from international trade if growth in the poor lands offered expanding markets among the other poor lands; multilateral transactions might then more easily provide needed food imports. Agricultural specialists who emphasize the wide scope for relatively low-cost agricultural expansion in poor countries tend often to be trade pessimists. We must again stress that the probable solution can involve both agricultural expansion and an increase in foodgrains imports. Opportunities do exist both for mutually ad-

---

[8]Twenty percent of developing nation exports goes to other developing lands; these "own markets" have tended to become less important over the past five years. See U.N. *World Economic Survey, 1967* (New York: 1968), pp. 19-30, 139-41.

vantageous growth in trade and for economically feasible expansion in foodgrains and in other agricultural output. Under present world conditions it seems likely that most poor nations will in fact move in both directions; and that, in particular, new attention will be given to direct means of closing their food gaps. We also note some backing off from the heavy reliance of past years on resource transfers from rich lands to fill domestic needs for food and agricultural products. While foreign aid will continue to play some role on the world development scene, it is now generally appreciated that foreign aid can not provide an assured route for development. Partly this is because of the nature of the real problems of growth (to which we turn often in this study) and partly it is because even high levels of foreign aid spread thinly over the large percentage of the world's people in the developing nations.

For many countries, and certainly for India, it is indeed likely that there will be a new emphasis on agriculture. This is not in the expectation that a modernizing nation can neglect its industrial development. Rather the new approach stresses the role that more rapid expansion in agricultural output can have in achieving more or less the same types of industrial economy goals that have been espoused in past plans. Agriculture has in fact been receiving new and more careful attention over the past five years or so in the development activities of countries throughout the world, and especially in Latin America (notably in Colombia and Chile) and in Asia (China, Pakistan, and India). The explanation for this shift in emphasis varies in the different lands: development experience has prompted new views and insights on appropriate development paths for today's poor lands; the outlook for surplus foodstuffs from the United States has at times seemed uncertain (as in the year 1966/67); experts from the FAO, IBRD, and UN, among others, have stressed such action. The levels and trends in productivity measures such as output per acre tend to be low in poor lands as compared to the richer nations of the world. For all grains, North America's output per acre was 659 kg in 1948–52 and 927 in 1960/61. Comparable figures for Africa were 287 and 318; for Asia, 441 and 542; for Latin America, 450 and 498.[9] In 1963, the average for Japan was 861 kg, for India, 307 kg. Even the low figures in a poor

---

[9]These contrasts between North America and the poorer regions of the world are more marked if comparison is made of output per head of (total) population. See U.S., Department of Agriculture, Foreign Agricultural Economic Report No. 11, Lester R. Brown, *Man, Land, and Food* (November, 1963).

country are themselves averages of a wide range of different yields per acre on a regional, crop, and farm-size basis. Thus in 1960/61 India's average gross value of output per acre was Rs (rupees) 183; for different states the averages ranged from Rs 18 to Rs 509. In three states recently studied differences of 100 percent or more were found in average foodgrains output per acre in neighboring districts. [10]

This situation —low average yields and wide internal differences in yield — gives prominence to two alternative possibilities for agricultural improvement, assuming national policy is committed to this objective. Growth paths for agriculture in poor lands could widen internal yield variations through primary program emphasis on the top, with the rich farmer; or it could narrow yield differences with relative emphasis on the bottom, with the poor farmer. Which path offers the better route to growth is not readily determined. History provides different answers; national programs do lean in one direction or the other, although both policies might be pursued simultaneously in different parts of the same country. The choice obviously has implications that are political as well as economic. The optimum outcome depends on analysis of the actual causes for the observed differences in internal yields per acre of the same crop. It may depend also on the opportunities that exist or can be created for non-farm employment for underutilized agricultural workers, and on other considerations. Operationally, a stipulated target of additional output would probably be easier to achieve through the "top" route, for the richer and better and larger farmers should respond to stimuli more readily. On the other hand, that route could place government publicly on the side of the few and the rich as against the many and the poor in what is usually the largest sector of the total economy. For any given output target the two routes will yield differences in agricultural structure as well as differences in costs. The first will presumably result in fewer active farmers and larger farm units, but it will also isolate a large subsistence sector in agriculture that has slow development prospects at best, that will gradually lose its labor force to other occupations (or to death). The second might retain a larger agriculture, of smaller sized units perhaps, without rapid changes in the number of total agriculturists. But if the program were successful, most of the agricultural units would tend to be economic.

---

[10]Alan Heston, "Variations in Agricultural Growth and Output Between and Within Regions of India," *Asia Survey* (March, 1968), pp. 175-79.

In Japan's development from the close of the nineteenth century at least until recent years, agriculture may have followed essentially the second route. Over the decades government and private agricultural organizations deliberately pursued a policy of bringing the better methods in yield-benefitting practices from the leading regions and farms to all the farmers of the more backward agricultural areas. The range in measures of productivity narrowed progressively throughout the land. Output grew continuously; labor requirements per unit of product in 1960 were one-third or one-fourth their 1890 level. There was, of course, progress near the top, but more than 80 percent of the gain in national yield per man was due to narrowing of the differential between different regions and producers.[11] Only in the last two decades did the pressure from non-agricultural enterprise begin to reduce the supply of labor on the farms at a rapid rate. Over much of the first half of this century Japan maintained a fairly constant level of workers in a prospering agriculture and a vigorous economy.

In what is more nearly the alternative course, the USSR seems to have achieved its agricultural growth through preferential treatment of the better components of the farm economy. The tremendous post-war gains in Russian agricultural output were associated with reductions in the number and increases in the size of collective farms. Similarly, in the parallel state farm structure, recent policy changes are furthering development of a relatively small number of the better state enterprises. The path for agricultural growth was characterized by uneven treatment within agriculture, by widening differences in the well-being of the farmers.

Finally, Mainland China seems increasingly to be counting upon differential growth in a relatively small part of its agriculture to achieve most of its production goals. Initially about 10 percent of total acreage will benefit from special intensive development programs, involving preferential treatment in supplies of fertilizer, insecticides, improved seeds, water, and beneficial marketing arrangements. Much less is planned for agriculture on the remaining land, from which there is expected to be a gradual displacement of labor (as well as acreage). Most of China's agriculture promises to remain traditional and backward for a long time, while the nation's agricultural output goals are being achieved by a relatively small part of the total agricultural establishment.

With regard to democratic India, official views on agricultural improvement have long favored the proposition that gains in agricul-

---

[11]These facts are from John J. Dall, Jr., "Agricultural Development: Japan, A Case Study" (Ph.D. dissertation: University of Pennsylvania, 1968).

ture must spread widely among farmers over the nation. Emotional, cultural, and political considerations prompted this approach, more than did economic considerations. The official economic rationale for industrialization did not mesh readily and easily with an official emphasis on rural uplift and village development throughout India. India's development philosophy over the past plans actually favored some redistribution of income toward rural areas and the poorer farmers. In very recent years, however, there is evidence that India's new interest in agricultural expansion may be shifting toward the first alternative, to progress through the "top," through the rich farmer.

Development today sets a new place for agriculture in the programs of national growth in poor lands. Agriculture is certainly receiving new attention in India's current development activities. This policy, its development plans, and its actual achievement record will in considerable measure guide the evolving structure of India's economy — and of India's polity and society as well.

The Importance of India

In the context of food : people : growth relationships, India's experience in the past two decades corresponds broadly with that of the developing lands taken together. Population growth has been at a somewhat higher rate (2.5 percent); total income, at a lower rate (3.8 percent). Foodgrains output may have averaged almost 3 percent in annual growth and food demand, 3.5 percent. India alone imported nine to ten million tons of grain in each of the years from 1965 through 1967; continuation of these trends would raise the annual deficit to thirty-five million tons in 20 years. Even optimistic estimates of India's export possibilities do not encompass payments for an import expansion of this size.[12] Rather, India's new fourth plan extends a pattern that began to emerge in the past three (interplan) years: agriculture receives a high development priority.

With such action India could again assume a lead role in the world's development efforts, as it did in the world of the early 1950's. That was when rich nations of the West were becoming aware of how great were the economic inequalities among nations politically equal in the United Nations. They became acutely aware of the truth that, aside from a relatively small part of the world's

---

[12]See, for example, G.O.I. Planning Commission, *Notes on Perspective of Development: 1960-61 to 1975-76* (April, 1964), pp. 157-69. Subsequent official publications suggest lower levels for exports by the end of this period. This matter is discussed in this book in Chapter 6, pp. 189-92 and Chapter 7, pp. 223-25.

population in Europe and North America, most people live in nations with very low average standards of living. The Colombo Plan, an Australian-initiated effort modeled on the U.S.-sponsored Marshall Plan, invited nations of Asia in 1950 to formulate programs for growth and assistance. India alone, among eight underdeveloped Asian nations which joined the plan in the 1950–1953 period, was able to present a comprehensive growth scheme — one that was later incorporated in its long-term development perspective.

Very soon after independence India had in fact established a skilled planning staff in a structure formalized by the Lok Sabha, the Parliament of independent India. The Planning Commission was headed by the Prime Minister himself; Pandit Nehru recognized the need to create and to publicize an aura of top priority for the tasks of India's economic expansion. The Commission's administrative and technical personnel had experience in the regular ministries of government. They also had the glow of an elite corps established for a national task of fundamental importance. Both attributes fitted them for their roles as formulators, guides, and coordinators of the development work to be undertaken through the individual ministries. These ministries had the resources and the operational responsibility for creating new facilities and for achieving new levels of efficiency in the economy. The presence of the Finance Minister as a full member of the Planning Commission was evidence of coordination between resource commitment and allocation at the Planning Commission level, and between resource availability and use at the operational ministerial level. Given the representative character of India's parliamentary system on the one hand, and the charismatic person of the Prime Minister on the other, this administrative structure for planning constituted an appropriate action framework for the technical and economic competence assembled in the Planning Commission staff.

Such organization evolved from experience rooted in colonial days. The commission was a continuing entity that could maintain ties at the very highest level of government (the Prime Minister's Office) and still work easily with ministerial "equals" at the Center, with Chief Ministers in the states, and with their staffs.[13] By the time of independence in 1947, the outline for a new Indian economy

---

[13]For a disciplinary analysis of administrative doctrine on the structure and function of the commission see S. N. Eisenstadt, "Bureaucracy, Bureaucratization and Debureaucratization," *Administrative Science Quarterly* (1960), Vol. IV, pp. 302-20; and the basic treatment in J. G. March and H. A. Simon, *Organization* (New York: John Wiley & Sons, Inc., 1958), Chapter 6 in particular.

was emerging, as well as what were argued to be optimal paths for its attainment. India's plans leaned heavily on the new growth literature crowding the professional journals of that time. The Planning Commission of independent India, formally established in March, 1950, had authority, expertness, and flexibility. It was equipped with information, schemes, and policies — and appropriate responsibility. This organizational achievement in itself served to place India as a pioneer in the new field, and as a model of how a nation ought to proceed in setting up its development activity.

The U.S. became involved in this effort from its early years. After the Bengal famine in 1950/51, the large wheat loan of 1951 augured a continuous flow of U.S. assistance, as development loans and grants as well as food assistance. Through 1969 the United States provided over $6,500,000,000 in such loans and grants, some 60 percent of which was in agricultural commodities, primarily foodgrains. The bulk of America's assistance was provided in the form of credits, although interest and repayment terms were below market levels. Increasingly, and partly through the Consortium arrangements of the World Bank, other western lands have provided about three billion dollars in assistance over the past decade, also primarily as loans. Notable here, in descending order of their quantitative participation, have been the United Kingdom, West Germany, Canada, Japan, and Italy, although the Netherlands, Switzerland, Norway, and Sweden were also important contributors, particularly in technical assistance projects associated with Indian industry and agriculture (including fishing).

The World Bank itself began to make loans to India in the very beginning of the first plan. There are now more than two billion dollars outstanding from various credits of that organization and its affiliate, the International Development Association. And while capital assistance from non-communist lands and organizations has frequently paid homage to India's status as the largest democracy in the world, the USSR also associated itself with India's growth effort. Since 1955, communist lands have been important sources of assistance. Total aid agreements with Russia and its European neighbors involve capital assistance in excess of $1,500,000,000, again mostly as credits. Such a world-wide mobilization of twelve to thirteen billion dollars of additional resources for growth is testimony of India's status as a nation and its promise for economic expansion.[14]

---

[14]See this book, Chapters 4 and 7, pp. 96-100, 189-90.

In the 1950's, the contrast between the development efforts of India and China received great attention throughout the world. India sought progress through methods appropriate to an open society. Mainland China was a comparably poor nation and sought progress through the totalitarian methods of a closed society. The two great lands became identified as participants in a classic competition between two alternative paths to self-sustaining economic progress.[15] It is probably true that clear lessons from this comparison are still hard to draw, for new insights continue to emerge. Western democratic nations have been playing a role in helping meet China's needs after the Sino-Soviet schism of 1960. In any event, the ideological basis of the contrast may now be more difficult to draw. Be that as it may, India-China contrasts did play an important part in the western world's interest in the success of India's economic program.

Nonetheless the central role India assumed early on the world development scene rested on more fundamental ground than this ideological contrast. First was the simple quantitative significance of the Indian effort: it encompassed almost one-third of the people of the underdeveloped world. India was an ex-colonial nation. Like so many other new nations, in Asia and Africa especially, India dedicated its efforts to the achievement of levels of economic well-being never attained in its history under foreign rule. Its program was to be a demonstration of the importance of national independence to progress; it was to serve as a lesson for the world on the role of government in the development process. Leaders in an independent state could undertake new investments in appropriate industries and regions, new training facilities to develop appropriate skills, new inducements to inculcate relevant attitudes and motivations among the people, new legislation and policy to encourage the appropriate milieu for growth. An external power represented interests that were at best linked to both homeland and colony. The independent government had no comparable schism.

In addition, it seemed to be clear that India was tackling its development efforts with the skills accumulated by specialists in economic growth. The experience of the past was surveyed, especially the experience of Russia and Japan, the two nations that had most recently made the transformation into "developed nation" status. Lessons from the expert literature of the world were applied with a

---

[15]See Wilfred Malenbaum, "India and China: Development Contrasts," *Journal of Political Economy* (February, 1956), pp. 1-24.

minimum of doctrinal bias. India preferred to speak of its "social-istic path to growth," but its plans recognized the strengths of private activity and the market. Thus at no time did the Indian economy have a public sector where value added was as large rela-tively as that sector now is in the U.S. economy, for example.

Finally the Indian development plan was always an open book, published and broadly distributed, usually as revisions of draft plans that had been circulated long before. Planning was associated with the central groups of Indian leadership in business and govern-ment; India's most senior officials, from the Prime Minister down, were constantly involved in problems of planned growth and devel-opment. University and officialdom seemed to mix readily in devis-ing methods and in appraising possibilities. Plan progress reports appeared frequently, with critical analyses of past efforts and pro-posed changes for subsequent plan years and subsequent plans. It was this openness of India's planning process and development ex-perience that seemed actually to make India a development labora-tory for scholars and practitioners throughout the world.

The Problem of Indian Development

This experience notwithstanding, India's development record has not matched what was expected officially in the plans and popularly in a development-conscious world. By the 1960's it was clear that India was not fulfilling the lead role promised by the early begin-nings. Average growth rates were perhaps 80 percent of expectation. India's food deficit exceeded expectations; India's dependence on foreign assistance including foodgrains grew steadily over three plan periods. Indeed, the orders of magnitude of these shortfalls seemed beyond gradual rectification. In late 1967, in the second year of the fourth plan period, the government decided to call a halt to that plan. Then, after more than a year of interim annual plans, the new fourth plan was begun on April 1, 1969. The three-year hiatus in plans provided India's government and its planning officials an opportunity to appraise India's growth experience and the forces impeding or aiding India's progress. The new plan could thus better serve India's economic expansion.

The causes of limited progress in India, as in other lands, must be discerned in the past record of program and achievement. India's first three plans, as the plans of most other poor nations, assumed that resource shortages were the main cause of economic stagnation and of desultory progress. India was a very low-income nation. Opportunities for increasing per capita output therefore required domestic savings to be supplemented from abroad in order to finance the needed level of investment. The economy simply had to have more resources than it could itself generate; the problem of continuing growth was related intimately to the solution of India's resultant *international* imbalance. The line of argument here is familiar and conventional.

Alternatively, and much less conventionally, there is the view that economic stagnation and desultory growth arise primarily from domestic *internal* imbalances. The nation has resources and potential for expansion, but the laws of economic behavior in the society operate so that growth is casual, if at all. Thus, one might note that India's low-level income and low-level productivity are actually averages of extremes of wealth, modernity, and productivity. India's modern industrial life began in the mid-nineteenth century, when comparable industry was in its infancy in lands like Russia and Japan, now well developed. Throughout a century and more, modern industry grew alongside traditional handicraft and backward enterprises. Even in agriculture itself, India's average yields have long been among the lowest in the world for many basic crops; yet there have always been Indian farmers who produce as much per acre as the best farmers anywhere in the world. India's agricultural scientists pioneered new strains of rice and sugar cane, and these were at times applied more effectively in foreign lands than they were at home. In banking, in finance, in transportation, and in a wide range of professional services, India was at once a most modern nation and a practitioner of inefficient and costly production by traditional methods. Despite the sophistication of India's banking system, the early establishment of a central (reserve) bank, and the growth of organized mobilization of personal savings, India has remained a nation where moneylenders flourished, where economic activity was not fully monetized, where considerable investment was made outside the money economy.

In other words, on the economic front, poverty, backwardness, traditionalism did prevail; yet wealth, modernity, progress were also familiar to Indians. Similar diversities are found in the political, social, and cultural aspects of Indian life. Sophisticated parliamentary governments in New Delhi and in state capitals contrast with autocratic domination of the electorate in districts and villages. Modern patterns of life, foreign music and art, modern technical education, advanced science and medicine all flourish, but in narrow compass. The split is manifest even within the individual, as is so well revealed in a classic description by Pandit Nehru himself: "I have become a queer mixture of the East and the West . . . at home nowhere. . . . I am a stranger and alien in the West. . . . But in my own country also, sometimes I have an exile's feeling."[16]

Persistent coexistence of the modern and the traditional in important parts of the economy is significant for the problem of growth; the efficiencies of the modern and successful in India's past apparently failed to have significant effect upon the backward, traditional, and poor. And this dichotomy persisted even when it seems that the advanced sectors could have gained from greater access to the rest of the economy, to say naught of reverse gains to the traditional and backward. Indeed the improved technical knowledge and the capital resources sought from abroad under the international imbalance view might be available domestically, at least in part. And the transfer to the backward areas from abroad need not be any easier than the transfer from an advanced domestic sector. Limited development in India, one might thus argue, is rooted in the diversity of its overall poverty. The core problem is, in fact, to uncover and overcome the forces that deter economic adjustment, that prevent the spread of economic gains.

Two such diverse views on the basic causes of non-growth bring different prescriptions for dealing with stagnation; in any event there may be a need for different approaches in different parts of poor nations. The first view emphasizes new capital and the allocation of capital to provide improved economic balance. This may make sense primarily for the modern sector — modern industry, transport, and services, as well as more advanced parts of agriculture. Within and among these activities, which involve not more than 20 percent of India's working population, additional capital may be able to spread its influence and stimulate total output and both capital and labor productivity. With the second, the internal view, a program must cope with the lack of competitiveness that permits persistent coexistence of vigorous modern sectors and very large traditional sectors. It must therefore concentrate action directly on those forces in the latter sectors which inhibit greater domestic internal interdependence. Such action would also benefit India if it were accompanied with a capital program for the modern sector; even on its own it holds the promise of effectiveness. On the other side, an emphasis primarily focussed on capital will not provide

---

[16]Jawaharlal Nehru, *Toward Freedom*, (New York: The John Day Company, 1941), p. 353.

stimulus to forces for narrowing the internal gaps. Whatever use is made of new capital, greater interdependence will require special government efforts to encourage change and modernization in the traditional, backward, poorer parts of the nation.

The appropriate lines of new development action in India may therefore be quite different from the lines past plans have empha-sized. India's approach to planning did in fact stress the importance of increased participation of the citizenry in the process of economic expansion. The main tool here was the greater identification of the people of India with an indigenous as against a foreign government. This is a positive force, but in itself it was not likely to provide a powerful stimulus for narrowing long-prevailing gaps between poor and rich, traditional and modern, within the economy. To this same end the official programs also stressed the role of the public sector. Here again the emphasis was placed principally on the expansion of public enterprise in modern industry, while the basic need is public action to bring change to the traditional parts of the economy as a spur to greater internal integration.

The new fourth plan does emphasize agriculture and expanded export proceeds in line with the food-population-growth interrela-tionships mentioned in the opening pages of this chapter. As the actual plan evolves, its difference from past efforts may actually be manifest in the way the official action deals with internal cleavages and with the participation of the less advanced groups in the nation. Nowhere can this attempt be more clear than in public action with respect to agriculture. In our terms, this new program could con-centrate on progress through the rich farmer, or through most farmers — a choice of fundamental importance to India's economy and society.

We shall develop these possibilities later in this study. First, how-ever, we deal with India's inheritance from the time before indepen-dence and before India's modern plans (Chapter 2); we then turn to the official programs for growth (Chapter 3). The results of these official efforts over the past 15 to 20 years are appraised (Chapters 4 through 6) in the light of the pre-independence structure of the economy. The concluding chapter summarizes pertinent doctrine for India's old strategy of growth and for what may be its new strategy. It is thus possible to provide a basis for assessing India's new plan in the perspective of development over the next few plans. Here too we discuss the specific contribution of India's new govern-ment to development achievement. In many of its aspects, India's long experience with development actions can offer insights and even guides to the promise of development in poor lands throughout the world.

The Economy
At Independence

2

The Base Structure

In the early independence years the government of India created an administrative structure for national planning. Its task was to bring to fruition the government's determination to have the Indian economy grow rapidly and continuously. From the start, development programs centered on a high rate of capital formation. Investment levels were to exceed domestic savings for several plans, thanks to net inflows of capital from abroad. Expanding rates of income growth plus a program to assure a positive gap between marginal and average rates of savings meant an increasing degree of national self-financing. In addition, there were progressive efforts to improve the allocation of capital in the successive plans so that the goals of output and of self-sustaining growth would be attained as efficiently as possible. Mathematical models, input-output analyses, and commodity balances played increasingly important roles in plan delineation and consistency. Attention was focused on determining "the right amounts of new capital for the right places."[1] On the other hand the plan authorities did anticipate that the

---

[1]The official plan program over these years is discussed later in Chapter 3.

nation's 400,000,000 people would be spurred to greater individual and social achievement simply because of their release from colonialism. India's parliamentary democracy asserted its commitment to human values and social justice; these socialistic goals were also to help stir a vigorous popular effort for progress.

The new government set out to uncover the actual economic structure underlying the poverty and stagnation of the Indian economy. In August, 1949, a National Income Committee was established to provide an expert documentation of the macrostructure of India's national poverty.[2] The committee's estimates were princi-

TABLE 1.   National Income in 1950/51

Source	Amount (Rs billions)	Labor Force (millions)	Output per worker (Rs thousands)
Agriculture and related activities	48.9	103.6	0.5
Mining and factory establishment	6.2	3.7	1.7
Small enterprises	9.1	11.5	0.8
Railways and communications	2.2	1.4	1.6
Banking, insurance, other commerce and transport	14.7	9.7	1.5
Professional and liberal arts	4.7	6.4	0.7
Governmental services (administration)	4.3	3.9	1.1
Domestic service	1.3	2.9	0.4
House property	4.1		
Net domestic product (factor cost)	95.5		
Net income from abroad	−.2		
Net national product (factor cost) (= national income)	95.3	143.2	0.67

Source: G.O.I. Ministry of Finance, National Income Committee, *Final Report*, 1954, p. 108.

[2] *The First Report of the National Income Committee* was issued in April, 1951, by the Ministry of Finance. It provided preliminary estimates for 1948/49. The *Final Report* appeared in February, 1954, and presented data for three years: 1948/49 (revised), 1949/50, and 1950/51. National product reports are prepared annually in the National Income Division of the Central Statistical Organization in the Cabinet Secretariat. These annual reports are now (since August, 1967) available on a revised series basis from 1960/61. See *Brochure on Revised Series of National Product for 1960-61 to 1964-65,* August, 1967, issued by the Central Statistical Organization.

pally on output account rather than expenditure; they did not provide figures for the level of capital formation. Still, reasonably firm orders of magnitude became available for India's national product by industrial origin. The proximity of the census dates permitted roughly comparable figures on labor force. Now it could be seen how "underdeveloped" India was and how the country might achieve a state of industrialization and progress.

As shown in the committee's *Final Report*, India's national income in 1950/51 was Rs 95,300,000,000, some $20,000,000,000 at the official exchange rate of that time (Table 1). More than 50 percent of the income was produced in agriculture and associated activities (fishing, forestry). Factories contributed 6.5 percent, well below the 9.6 percent created by cottage industries and handicrafts. The share of trade, transport, and commerce was almost 18 percent and the share of other services about 11 percent. Nearly 75 percent of India's labor force worked in agriculture, less than 3 percent in factory enterprises and mining. The various trade, transport, and service activities provided livelihood for more than 15 percent of the work force. The National Income Committee also separated total output between all kinds of small enterprises (largely household activities) and large ones. Of the 76.5 percent of national income that could be categorized in this way, 65.8 percent and 10.7 percent fell into these two categories respectively. India was clearly a land where labor was the predominant factor of production; where this was most true, output per man was very low. Product per worker averaged Rs 665 per year throughout the nation. Since there were on the average more than 1.5 non-workers for every member of the labor force, annual income per person was about Rs 260, or $55. In agriculture and domestic services the average was significantly below the national level. On the other hand, factory enterprise, railway service, and white collar work in financial institutions and in government provided an average product per worker which was 50 to 150 percent above that figure.

These new data offered dramatic illustrations of the need for economic growth in India. They highlighted modern types of economic activity, where capital and skills made men more effective. The new India had to have more industry and modern services. These important goals could now be made specific, and the planners could devise schemes for their efficient attainment. Expanded imports would undoubtedly be needed, at least initially. To help appraise India's trade and payments position, the Reserve Bank of India (a central bank established in 1935) brought together the results of its studies of India's international trade and payments. Comprehensive estimates of India's international accounts during 1948-51 thus became available in the early plan years[3]. These showed that in the pre-plan period imports and exports were each around 5 percent of national income and were in a fair degree of balance in 1950/51, the last pre-plan year. India usually ran a surplus on international service account; in 1950/51 this assured a net *outflow* of capital from India.[4] But in a developing land this situation would obviously be altered. Imports of capital goods would expand markedly and India would become a significant net importer, at least for some years. Moreover, more than 60 percent of India's exports were in three traditional products—tea, cotton and jute manufactures—where foreign demand was considered to be relatively inelastic with respect to income changes. New industrial products, in growing volume, were therefore seen as the obvious export goods for a developing India. In any event, this early publication of the Reserve Bank provided facts that in turn permitted the projection of meaningful figures for international trade and service accounts over plan years.

Reports from the *All-India Rural Credit Survey*, initiated in 1951 and again by the Reserve Bank, also began to appear during the first plan.[5] These provided a comprehensive view of rural India, beyond what is suggested by the study's title.[6] The *Survey* portrayed the familiar image of poverty, debt, and ignorance, but it also recognized a social "overdevelopment" that complemented economic underdevelopment. A religion-based system of social and personal values and relationships prescribes the scope for important economic activities. While the distinguished Committee of Direction for the new study was particularly concerned with the expansion of credit cooperatives, the reports actually sounded a planning alert: the tasks of growth go beyond merely growth in modern industry

---

[3]Reserve Bank of India (R.B.I.), *India's Balance of Payments 1948–51*, Bombay, 1953. Actually, component materials for this period were presented and analyzed in issues of the R.B.I. *Bulletin* from July, 1949, intermittently through November, 1952.

[4]*Ibid.*, pp. 8-11.

[5]There were three volumes: I, *The Survey Report* (Part 1, 1956, and Part 2, 1957); II, *The General Report* (1954); and III, *The Technical Report* (1956). The second of these received wide distribution in an Abridged Edition released in December, 1955. Specific references below are to that volume.

[6]"— Rural credit . . . is in reality as wide as rural society which means practically as wide as the Indian nation. . . . It embraces all economic activities and purposes as they affect rural society. . ." *Ibid.*, p. 295.

achieved through capital imports and a short-period international account deficit. Rural change must be built upon better understanding of the structure and dynamics of household units with a large subsistence and traditional orientation. This understanding required new research and new analysis. Microanalysis had somehow to become the handmaiden of macroanalysis. What could be done to accelerate change in traditional enterprises — farm, cottage industry, or service venture? Action would require a conscious government effort to alter existing power relationships in rural areas — "the close conformity of association and interests between the subordinate officials of Government and the more powerful elements in the village; . . . the rigidity of caste feeling in conjunction with the power derived from money, land, leadership; . . . the combinations of factors which . . . operate against the interests of the bulk of those who reside in the village . . ."[7] The *Survey* made clear how slow the processes of economic expansion could be.

In the early plans, this *Rural Credit Survey* did not offer an appealing image of the process of growth and of the rural change inseparable from it. The appeal of emphasis on modern sectors was much greater. And in fact all past plans have counted on the spread of industrialization to provide a more or less automatic and straightforward route to rural change. It is ironical to observe the *Rural Credit Survey* now, almost two decades after its appearance,[8] assume importance as a guide for programs of rural development and indeed of overall national progress, after three five-year plans (1951-66) and the preparation of a fourth plan a second time after three annual plans (1966/67—1968/69). What the *Survey* revealed in the 1950's as the growth tasks in India are recognized as core development tasks in the 1970's.

These three basic reports of the early plan period themselves pose the problems of development in India. The simplicity of prescriptions derived from the first two — expand modern sectors and enlarge import surpluses — stands in contrast to the complexity of solutions indicated by the third report in its analyses of the economic and social structure restricting the lives of most Indians.

---

[7] *Ibid.*, pp. 126–27.

[8] By this time, of course, the literature on this subject has multiplied (see below, pp. 142–54). There have been follow-up surveys in selected districts, beginning with data for 1956/57. Finally, there is now the R.B.I., *Report of the All-India Rural Credit Review Committee,* July 30, 1969 (see pp. 217–22 below in Chapter 7).

More than 80 percent of the people live in rural India, and an even larger percentage is dependent in some way upon agriculture for economic well-being. Development programs either cope with problems of change and modernization in this large, essentially traditional sector, or they tend to bypass them. India's development planners instinctively leaned to the first alternative: the large traditional parts of the nation were to become more modern over the course of the plans. By-passing them was obviously inacceptable: it smacked of the enclave-type growth characteristic of colonial exploitation. Yet, this choice notwithstanding, little is known even now about programs that bring rural change and traditional-modern interdependence. The dynamics of subsistence economies is not understood; the relevant tasks are not delineated by the disciplinary bounds of the economist. Development programs have had to cope with motivation for change and the role that economic opportunity plays in behavior patterns of people on the fringe of an economic system, where non-monetized transactions persist as a relatively large percentage of the total value of consumption.

The India of 1948–51 was not simply a poor country. Its national economic behavior was a combination of divergent forces, superimposed more than reconciled. Its large subsistence-oriented sectors display their roots in India's social, cultural, and political past; its relatively small modern sectors emulate the dynamic ways of life in the rich western world outside.

The national income reports of the early 1950's showed an economy still at the low level that had long persisted. Yet it is great oversimplification to infer that the low level represented some economic equilibrium, from which higher levels could be attained simply through the addition of scarce factor inputs beyond India's own ability to provide. It is more realistic to think of the pre-plan economy in a state of economic disequilibrium: the economic opportunities in an imbalanced economy were held in check by counterforces on the social, cultural, and even political fronts. In other words, the dynamics of Indian society did establish an overall equilibrium in pre-plan years as in earlier periods, but it is not the type of equilibrium that moves along some optimum path of growth through the addition of more capital and labor. The Indian economy operated *within* its production frontier. Additional resources from abroad provide some offset to indigenous output potential that the society does not utilize adequately, but they can not make up this domestic gap. Indeed, efforts at replacement may themselves aggravate the domestic disequilibrium; in any event the foreign assistance will not automatically bring growth.

The Low-Level Equilibrium

India did modernize rapidly during the nineteenth century. Commercial agriculture, factory enterprise, railway network, export trade — achievement in these modern dimensions of economic growth may have been greater in India than in Japan, Russia, and even Canada in the last part of that century. But today, these nations far surpass India by modern growth criteria; India now ranks among the world's least developed nations as measured by per capita income. Two broad categories of reasons are usually advanced to explain India's failure to proceed with other early-beginner nations in the modern development process. One is colonial history: foreign rule prevailed through the critical years when the roots for rapid and persistent growth needed to be established and nourished. The other is Hindu life-style: values—and institutions that sustained them—undercut the economic opportunities appropriate to India's human and material endowments.

Literature on these subjects is extensive, distinguished, and controversial.[9] It provides no definitive explanation of India's aborted growth effort. As a dependent of the pioneer nation in modern economic growth, India was helped as well as held back by Britain. Similarly there are too many modern economic achievements in India and by Indians to permit the judgment of incompatibility between Hindu values and modern life. The degree of relevance in each category of reasons differs depending on what aspect of economic change and what time interval are considered.

We note what might be a third view—one that questions whether India's growth was in fact aborted. It stresses the reality of significant economic expansion over the nineteenth century and the fact that development product is now emerging from these beginnings.

---

[9]Most famous perhaps is Max Weber, *The Protestant Ethic and the Spirit of Capitalism* (New York: Charles Scribners' Sons, 1958); and *The Religion of India,* trans. H. H. Gerth and D. Martindale (Glencoe, Ill.: The Free Press, 1958). The modern economic theory effects of the Indian social system are appraised in K. W. Kapp, *Hindu Culture, Economic Development and Economic Planning in India* (Bombay and New York: Asia Publishing House, 1963). Objective treatment of the colonial deterrent can be found in D. H. Buchanan, *The Development of Capitalistic Enterprise in India* (New York: The Macmillan Company, 1934); Michael Kidron, *Foreign Investments in India* (London: Oxford University Press, 1965); and Helen Lamb, "The State and Economic Development in India," in Simon Kuznets, W. E. Moore, and J. J. Spengler, eds., *Economic Growth: Brazil, India, Japan* (Durham, N. C.: Duke University Press, 1955), pp. 464-95. A summary analysis appropriate to the text observations is M. D. Morris, "Values as an Obstacle to Economic Growth in South Asia: An Historical Survey," *Journal of Economic History,* December, 1967, pp. 588–607.

The path of growth may have been longer than for today's developed lands, but the process and the result are essentially the same. Limited data and limited research still prevent careful documentation of this view, but the best record available certainly shows very slow progress over the century to independence, without much evidence of structural change in a modern growth pattern.[10] On the other hand, it is quite clear that India's overall growth record is a composite of very different results in specific regions, sectors, and times. And it is this diversity of actual growth performance, with an overall level never sufficient to spread broadly or to sustain itself for a long period, that is most revealing about the past, and perhaps most significant for the future.

Colonialism and the domestic cultural heritage did not rule out important growth performance. On the contrary, Indian history records unusual entrepreneurial and development achievement. Even today, as in the past, this is often accomplished through skillful combination of the modern need and the traditional form. Nonetheless these advances were not translated into more general gains. A long-sustained broad-based growth process depends upon continuous linkage to other commodities, services, sectors. In India this fundamental spread of the growth process seems to have been blocked. While it is clear that initiating, selective economic activity did occur, it is much less clear that the counterpart response also occurred, at least in sufficiently widespread degree. And this lack may be attributable to India's value system and social structure, as it could also be to the country's dependence on a national leadership persistently ambivalent in its responsibility to *both* India and Britain.

In sum, opportunities for economic change in India impinged on large parts of the population through a barrage of social and religious forces and through active institutions committed to the preservation of forces that served to brake adjustment to a changing world. Marked dynastic changes over many centuries, during more than a thousand years of diverse Hindu rulers and half again as many years of Muslim empires, and even with the advent of the British Raj and indeed of Indian independence itself, have moderated these forces only to a limited degree. The contemporary scene promises significant breakthrough, but it remains true today that economic forces in large parts of rural India still operate in an environment inimical to change and progress.

---

[10]See M. Mukherjee, "National Income," in V. B. Singh, ed., *Economic History of India, 1857-1956* (Bombay: Allied Publishers, 1965), pp. 661–703.

More than 85 percent of India's population and a higher ratio of the rural people adhere to some form of Hinduism. While the commitment is nominal for many individuals, and while the Hindu religion is on the whole a permissive one, the religion limits elasticity in the social and economic adaptations of the people. It is each person's religious duty to fulfill the obligations of a traditional status in his life. The Hindu religion emphasizes categorization — in ideas, in societies, in occupations — through essentially non-competitive ranks structured from high to low. Hinduism does not provide moral pressure for changes in the interrelations of these rankings to encourage social equality, communal homogeneity, and national achievement. It is a remarkable characteristic of Hinduism that these persistent cleavages, promulgated as the natural order of man's affairs in this world, are nonetheless held to be consistent with a universality that reconciles all conflicts. Perhaps this is why Hinduism can be so tolerant of the inconsistencies and conflicts posed by the affairs of India's real world. For traditionalism and modernism coexist without moral recriminations, notwithstanding the persistent economic imbalance and inequality in this coexistence.

Caste distinctions and the ties of the joint family remain strong characteristics of India's social order, again among rural people particularly. On the surface these indigenous attributes of the society are counter to the mobility and flexibility in movement and in ideas that are important in modernizing an economy. For most Indians, especially those involved in economic activities in villages and small towns, caste remains a real-life consideration. To those in high categories it contributes an aversion to manual labor; in the low, it serves to discourage achievement motivation toward higher economic or social status. In some lower castes, energies are diverted to a struggle for progress within the caste structure (*Sanskritization*). In the extended family a hierarchical pattern serves to discourage specialization and the assumption of responsibility on the part of the more able. Rules of average consumption and reward counter the allocative principles of marginalism that optimize satisfaction and outputs in other societies.

Change in Indian Society

The external political and economic forces operative during the decades of British rule and even more during Indian parliamentary rule itself might have been expected to effect a deep penetration of the old social structure. However, while there were adaptations, there was scarcely a groundswell for change. There was no strong

pressure from government, either British or native, to initiate unequivocal and systematic programs for reducing the forces of custom, in rural India particularly. Ambivalence is understandable:
rule that is primarily maintenance of order in a large and diverse
country may be easier with tradition-bound institutions than without them. The reins of central power were more stable if problems
of land and its products were handled through centers of power in
the countryside. *Local* authority was also appealing to caste, family,
and religious hierarchies. The circle was complete; Britain ruled
most Indians through landlords. The Indian Congress, too, found
its leadership role most congenial when Congress could remain
responsive to the rural centers of power, the landed interests. This
was especially true with respect to public policies and programs
concerned with agriculture and rural populations, the predominant
component of India's economy and society. Thus, again to quote
the *Rural Credit Survey,*

> ". . . directions (for change) merely remain on paper, espe-
> pecially where they involve some disadvantage to the more
> powerful in the village. . . . An illusion of implementation (is)
> woven around the reality of non-compliance. . . . This marked
> tendency towards the promotion of an impression of change
> around changelessness, of active obedience to behests around
> stolid resistance to instructions . . . has always to be taken into
> account in assessing the worth of reports that the policies of
> Government have been put into operation in the village."[11]

Cracks in the traditional structure have appeared and are widening. "Westernization" has spread — rapidly perhaps in the years
since independence. Economic industrialization and political demo-
cratization have found new ways to take root through traditional
systems. Thus caste has become a significant component of the
modern political process, not only in rural areas but at state and
national levels also. Caste and faction play western-type pressure-
group roles in elections.[12] Indeed panchayati raj (rule by village
council) has opened new leadership opportunities to lower and
poorer social groups. Greater social mobility in villages has occurred

---

[11] *All-India Rural Credit Survey, op. cit.,* p. 126.

[12] As an illustration, the Yadava Caste has held 42 annual meetings since its
Mahasaba was established in 1924 as a cultural association (to create unity,
reform customs, promote education, and safeguard interests of castemen). It
has become increasingly politicized, as is clear from a recent All-India Conference in 1968, attended by 40,000 Yadavas. See M.S.A. Rao, "Political Elite
and Caste Association, A Report of a Caste Conference," *Economic and Political Weekly (EPW),* Vol. 3, No. 20 (May 18, 1968), pp. 779–82.

with easier transportation and communication, and with new accessibility to education and to non-traditional sources of income. Democracy and the vote thus serve the spread of social change even while new power opportunities strengthen, even rigidify, traditional patterns.

Some aspects of land reform, notably elimination of private intermediaries, may have reduced power differentials among rural social classes. On the other hand, land redistribution schemes have not contributed significantly to any narrowing of rural income differences; indeed, these differences were probably accentuated through other aspects of India's development program (as we shall see in Chapter 5). In the modern life of the city and the factory, new patterns of power retention have been discovered for India's joint family structure. Big business is learning to flourish around the extended family, for example.[13] But the problem has scarcely ceased to exist. Current research yields a variety of insights and outlooks. Thus a comprehensive study of worker adaptation in Jamshedpur, India's oldest steel city and home location of the Tata Iron and Steel Company (TISCO) for more than 60 years, emphasizes the effective merger of modern and traditional habits of life. ". . . It is impressive to observe the resiliency, durability, and flexibility of Indian social institutions like caste and joint family, as well as the adaptability and pragmatism of the individual members of the work force." There has emerged "a pluralistic . . . ethical system: 'class for the city and caste for the village'. . . . There are good grounds for optimism."[14] Conversely, a study of workers in a modern public sector plant in West Bengal concluded on the extent to which "the triads of Indian social institutions, the village, the joint family, and caste are . . . retarding the process of economic development . . . (because of) a value system and behavioural pattern . . . absolutely different from those necessary to make the technological system productive . . . ."[15]

---

[13]For some specific material and a general analysis, see Milton Singer, "The Indian Joint Family in Modern Industry," in Singer and Cohn, eds., *Structure and Change in Indian Society* (Chicago: Aldine Publishing Company, 1968), especially pp. 433–47. See also M.N. Srinivas, *Social Change in Modern India* (Berkeley: University of California Press, 1967), and D.G. Mandelbaum, *Society in India* (Berkeley: University of California Press, 1970) 2 vols.

[14]From a preliminary report by Michael M. Ames, "Modernization and Social Structure," *EPW* (July, 1969), pp. 1217–24.

[15]G. Chattopadhyay and A. K. Sengupta, "Growth of a Disciplined Labour Force: A Case Study of Social Impediments," *EPW* (July, 1969), pp. 1209–16.

The evidence as a whole certainly indicates the growing influence of modern needs on the traditional order. But the situation remains one where the automatic adaptation and spread of new ideas and methods will continue to lag and falter. As in the case of caste, local government, and perhaps even the joint family, substantive adaptations toward a more modern way of life are often encompassed in the traditional forms. Coexistence of the traditional and modern worlds may thus understate the degree of adaptation already achieved. And future years may well see more rapid change in this regard, particularly if India pursues paths of growth through programs that deliberately encourage the *spread* of economic gains from modern-type activities.[16]

Still, India's past offers ample evidence that economic pressures have been blunted, if not deterred, in the Indian environment. For example, agriculture was dominated by subsistence farmers until about the mid-nineteenth century. Basic foods were produced for direct consumption; at most they moved short distances to local markets. There were, of course, commercial exceptions even in basic foodstuffs. Thus, what is present day India may have been a net exporter of wheat; around 1880, the volume was of the order of one million tons annually, most of which came from what is now (Indian) Punjab. Under the British there was broadening exposure to the outside economic world, bringing advantages to an agriculture geared to cash earnings. Forces for modernization, reinforced by the expanding railway network, pressed upon the prevailing subsistence agriculture.[17] New markets, both in Europe to replace American cotton embargoed in the Civil War and in India with the growth of a modern textile industry, encouraged output for sale instead of for local use. Indian exports of raw cotton to Britain more than doubled in the five years 1860-64. The output of raw cotton increased in the Deccan Districts of Bombay, as did tea in Assam, jute and indigo in Bengal, wheat and cotton in the Punjab colonies. Opium, hides, and skins began to be exported.

The production of commercial crops expanded significantly. Systematic data for all cash crops show more than a doubling of output from 1900 through the time of independence; for British India, growth at comparable rates (close to 2 percent each year) can be

---

[16]See pp. 203–10 below.

[17]In addition to the pressure of external markets, there were pressures from the revised tax revenue system. Where Hindu and Moslem rulers exacted revenue mostly in kind, cash payments became much more important under the British.

traced from 1890/91. Cotton, tea, and groundnuts were notable in this non-foodgrains expansion, the first two products showing very rapid increases until World War I. The data also suggest that in an earlier period, from 1850 to 1860 perhaps, some of these crops, plus indigo, jute, and various oilseeds, were already recording rapid growth.[18]

This modernization process in Indian agriculture revealed a striking contrast. The output of foodgrains may actually have declined absolutely over the half century to independence; at most it remained stationary. The relatively precise estimates available for British India show that *total* crop output expanded by less than 20 percent between 1891–1895 and 1941–1945; production of foodgrains increased by 1 to 2 percent and the remaining agricultural crops, primarily commercial, 90 percent.[19] With the growth of population, India's grain export status gave way; by 1920, perhaps, India was a net importer. Moreover, gains in such productivity measures as output per acre were more or less confined to commercial production, including the Punjab wheat produced for sale to urban areas. Growing use of irrigation and fertilizer as well as improved cultivating practices contributed to some expansion in area and in yield per acre for the commercial products, but there were *declines* in per acre yields for foodgrains. The technical progress in the commercial sectors of agriculture simply did not permeate the more traditional parts of India's agricultural economy. The gains from the new demand for agricultural product and from reduced costs of production did not suffice to penetrate to any major extent the barriers around most of rural India.

There were modernizing forces in industry also. Coal output increased ten times, to one million tons, between 1840 and 1880 — notably because of railways and steamship demand and because of the new accessibility of the Ranigranj fields thanks to the East India Railway. In the 1850's there were beginnings of modern textile production in British companies near Calcutta as well as in Indian companies in the Bombay area. Rail transport expanded rapidly. Industrial, modern, factory employment in India multiplied three times in two decades from 1890 through 1910. Iron and

---

[18]See K. Mukerji, *Levels of Economic Activity and Public Expenditure in India* (Bombay: Asia Publishing House, 1965), pp. 23–35; George Blyn, *Agricultural Trends in India, 1891-1947: Output, Availability and Productivity* (Philadelphia: University of Pennsylvania Press, 1966), pp. 107-18.

[19]From one-fifth of total crop value, commercial crops rose to provide one-third by the time of Indian independence. Blyn, *op. cit.*, pp. 316-17.

steel production was begun in the nineteenth century; a fully integrated modern plant of one million ton capacity was operating in
1911 with Indian ownership and management. There was promise
in the extensive coal and iron ore reserves, both located in relatively
compact areas in the northeast, in Bihar, Orissa, and West Bengal.
Reserves of manganese, bauxite, asbestos, limestone, and mica were
known to exist, and some were already being mined at the turn of
the century. Output in India's modern enterprises grew rapidly
after 1850, encroaching on production in the traditional handicraft
and cottage activities that long dominated the industrial scene. But
the rapid early growth of modern industry was short-lived. It did
not continue beyond World War I and had actually slackened before that war. As in agriculture, so in industry: the modern began
to coexist with rather than replace the traditional. At independence
all industrial production provided one-sixth of total national product and about one-tenth of all employment; the modern component
of industry contributed well under half of all industrial product; it
used less than one-fourth of the workers in all industry. (See Table
1, p. 22.)

The pre-independence government in India did not push aggres-
sively for modernization — a familiar economic drawback of colonialism. Increasingly after 1850, and especially from 1870 at least
until 1922, *laissez faire* on the part of the Secretary of State for India brought what was perhaps a premature end to tariff protection
for Indian industry. British industrial interests at home were not
sympathetic to Indian competition, even on the part of British-
controlled firms; neither did Indian industry receive stimulus from
British purchases of stores for use in India — with very little exception these were imported from England. Many consumer industries,
from candles to paper, as well as coal, iron, and steel, might have
had a different development experience in India were it not for this
British policy.[20] Similarly, the transportation network was geared
to the export possibilities of Indian output more than to its domestic use.[21]

On the other side, British rule did expose India to western and
modern schooling. Traditional families began to educate their children abroad. During the British period, western education took firm

---

[20]A summary account of specific developments and extensive references are
available in S. R. Rungta, *Rise of Business Corporations in India 1851–1900*
(Cambridge: Cambridge University Press, 1970).

[21]For documentation see D. H. Buchanan, *op. cit.*, pp. 181–93; see also
Daniel Thorner, *Investment in Empire* (Philadelphia: University of Pennsylvania Press, 1950), pp. 44–118.

root in India's great universities. The Indian political system provided considerable stability over time and, with the railroads, facilitated internal movement of people and goods through the vast subcontinent. In this environment there emerged modern business communities from a variety of India's religious, caste, subcaste, and regional groups — from Hindu to Parsi and Jew, from Brahman and Vaishya to Shudra and even Untouchable. From traditional backgrounds in rural production, or in trade and credit, business groups emerged to make their mark in modern business and technology, in India, and throughout the world. These strong links to the modern from the traditional certainly aided industrialization and economic expansion. Still, neither the new industries nor the new entrepreneurial groups, nor indeed a government which opened India to the world succeeded in bringing *continuous* industrial expansion. New industry did not spread its products broadly through the land or into the cost structure of other sectors of the economy. Modern industry did not bring rapid urbanization, although it may have offset some loss of urban concentration associated with the decline of princely capitols. This helps explain why new industrial expansion did not bring to the basic food crops the gains from expanded demand and the gains from enhanced productivity in the non-foodgrains crops.

We have seen two broad patterns in agriculture. In one part there were responses to new market opportunities, whether in India or abroad. The other part was not stimulated in any significant way by the growth and diversification of industry. These two components coexisted, just as modern industry found some balance with its traditional counterpart. For in pre-plan India, the progressive and efficient did not set a pattern that caught on to modernize, to replace, or to complement the traditional. The two worlds persisted in an enclave-type of growth. Despite the large number of changes to which India was exposed over the past century — western rule, new land tax structures, new educational systems, new categories of elite groups in public and private life — basic shifts were not engendered in the patterns of economic life. The economy moved little from its low-level output position over the years before independence. Even with a relatively low average rate of population growth in India, total output per capita expanded by less than 50 percent over 100 years, an average growth of about 0.4 of one percent each year. Whatever the beginnings and the potentials in the land, economic growth was not spurred in the century of British rule.[22]

---

[22]See M. Mukherjee, *op. cit.*, pp. 661–703.

The low level equilibrium in the years from 1948 to 1951 continued to represent an average of great differences within the nation. Personal income inequalities, as in other poor lands, tended to exceed those in the wealthy lands.[23] Certain groups in Indian society had incomes, wealth, and ways of personal and professional life with few parallels even in the rich world. There were large regional differences. At the time of India's independence the state of Bihar had average per capita income 40 percent below the national average, even if we exclude from that average the high-income capital region of Delhi; West Bengal was some 40 percent above the average. And the rest of India's states spread throughout that range. Average urban-rural income differences were then close to 2:1. All such differences are but suggestive of the major point: the great diversity *within* averages of income groups, of states, of urban, and especially rural India. Thus

> "In the same area, the best farmers are known to have produced yields per acre several times higher than those produced by average farmers. For instance the average yields of rice per acre in different states vary between 400 and 1200 lbs while the highest yields obtained in crop competitions vary between 3000 and 9000 lbs. Corresponding ranges for wheat are 300 to 1000 and 2500 to 6000 lbs respectively. In fact, while the best in Indian agriculture does not compare unfavorably with the best elsewhere, the difference between the best and the average is much wider in India than in the technically advanced countries. This is both an index of the backward character of Indian agriculture and a measure of its potentiality for development."

> "Take Assam (for example) where large-scale plantations have been developed right in the middle of a peasant farming area. These plantations, which use modern and scientific techniques, do not seem to have any 'demonstration effect' on the neighboring agriculturists. . . . Use of chemical fertilizers and pesticides is very intensive in the plantations but the use made by the farmers of Assam is amongst the lowest in India. . . . There seems to be a chasm between the planters and their neighboring farmers. . ."[24]

---

[23]Thus, see Simon Kuznets, "Quantitative Aspects of the Economic Growth of Nations: VIII. Distribution of Income by Size," *Economic Development and Cultural Change*, Part II (January, 1963), pp. 12–17.

[24]G.O.I., Ministry of Food and Agriculture, S. R. Sen, "The Strategy of Agricultural Development," *Agricultural Situation in India* (January, 1960), pp. 1072–73. Figures cited precede the advent of new wheat and paddy strains to Indian agriculture, but the new crops probably aggravated the internal differences. See below, pp. 158–62.

While this account by a skilled and responsible Indian official provides an important illustration of the limited spread influences and the internal gaps in the economy, it may understate the force of the social, political, and economic heritage that permitted their persistence. The complexities of India's rural structure lie at the core of India's low-level product. Programs that cope directly with the non-economic deterrents to greater equality may well be the essential ingredients for continuous expansion in India's "low-level equilibrium" output.

The Rural Structure

For more than a century, India's agriculture was exposed to pressures and opportunities of an expanding export market, of the changing demands characteristic of a modernizing industry and nation. There was also a shift to the use of cash for payment of rent and tax obligations under the British. It was an environment that pushed the adoption of more commercial types of enterprise by India's farmers. While the network of rural money lenders always provided some buffer between traditional peasant and a modern world of money transactions, this was a costly service. Yet most agriculture by far avoided commercialization; it persisted in the production of goods for local if not direct family consumption.

"The main characteristics of village life are still those of the centuries anterior to British rule," reported a Royal Commission in 1928.[25] Of course there have also been studies and commission reports that stress the precipitous shift from a barter to a cash type of economy in India; there are even reports that attribute "the economic malaise of the agrarian population entirely to (such) external factors as fluctuations in the price of products in the world markets. . ."(!)[26] In fact, however, many villages of India still remain relatively closed. Even after some years of formal planning by state

---

[25]Great Britain, Royal Commission on Agriculture, *Report*, 1928, p. 5

[26]This paragraph draws from the introductory chapters of P. K. Mukherjee, *Economic Surveys in Under-Developed Countries: A Study in Methodology* (Bombay: Asia Publishing House, 1959) especially pp. 1–60. The author stresses the gap between assumption and actuality and the predisposition of Indian specialists even in universities and government to assume away their lack of "familiarity with principles and systems of (India's) agriculture" and "to live with the industrial economics developed in the western conditions." (p. 2) His study focuses on the need for careful farm management and rural economic surveys, beginnings of which first began to be made in India in the mid-1950's. See below, pp. 41–42 and pp. 150–51.

and central governments of an independent India, the country is predominantly agricultural; rural life and the routine of labor are still "organized by custom and tradition." While few studies have been made of the extent of non-cash transactions in India (or in other developing nations) such data as are available for recent years suggest persistence in India of a non-monetized component in rural consumption to the extent of almost 45 percent from 1951 to 1958.[27] Even intensive plan activities did not bring marked reductions in this important index of a subsistence agriculture and way of life.

At independence, India still had a traditional agriculture. For most farmers, techniques of production were on the whole those of many generations past: there were, in 1950, a few hundred tractors in all of India's agricultural operations, involving about sixty-five million rural households. Fertilizer application was lower per acre — less than one-half pound of nitrogen for example — than in any other land in the world. These are measures of the limited productivity of India's agriculture. The unit of ownership — by households — was small: 4.72 acres for all rural households and 6.05 acres for those actually owning land. *Contiguous* holdings were much smaller; on the average there were more than five separate parcels per household. In the early 1950's, fourteen or fifteen million households (22 percent of all those in rural India) owned no land at all. Mostly they provided laborers for agriculture as well as workers in non-farm activities; some may have rented land. Almost 25 percent of all rural households owned less than one acre. In other words, 47 percent of all rural households possessed less than 1.5 percent of all India's cultivated land. On the whole these small owners leased *out* more land than they leased *in*; the chances are that a very large part of this half of all rural households was comprised of laborers; tenancy was not significant.[28] The remaining half (actually some 53 percent) of rural households divided roughly in two: 27.5 percent owned from 1 to 5 acres, 15.4 percent of all cultivated land, or an average of 2.65 acres per household; the remaining 25.5 percent had at least 5 acres or 83.3 percent of all land, an average of

---

[27] M. Mukherjee, "The Role of Transactions in Kind in Developing Economies," *The Review of Income and Wealth*, Series 13, No. 4 (December, 1967), pp. 338–39. These results are reasonably consistent with data for 1955 presented in Wilfred Malenbaum, *Prospects for Indian Development* (London: George Allen & Unwin Ltd., 1962), p. 140.

[28] See G.O.I. National Sample Survey (N.S.S.) No. 10, Eighth Round, July, 1954-March, 1955, *First Report on Land Holdings, Rural Sector*, pp. 14, 34. (Hereafter G.O.I. National Sample Surveys will be referred to by N.S.S. and identifying number.) Also see below, pp. 147–49.

15.15 acres per household. While perhaps 20,000 of these households owned 250 acres or more, India's "large" farmers are the 25 percent or so of the rural households owning at least 5 acres, although this bottom figure varies in the different climatic regions of the country.[29]

For the most part, rural landowners operate their own lands. In the early plan years almost 70 percent of all cultivated land was worked by the 81.4 percent of all rural landowners who did not lease out any of their land. Average holdings for these owners were 5.15 acres, while the holdings of the 16 percent of the rural households who leased out part of their lands (29 percent of total area) were on the whole larger, an average of 10.93 acres, some 60 percent of which they worked directly while the rest was worked by some kind of tenant.[30]

Thus almost 19 percent of rural households are landlords, some exclusively, though most are operators also. In the early 1950's these leased out about 12 percent of the area cultivated in India. In addition a roughly comparable area was leased out by urban or foreign (e.g. Pakistani) landholders. Since the number of these must be very much smaller than the 12,500,000 rural landlord households (19 percent of all rural households), absentee ownership must be in much larger units. In any event, the 24 percent of India's cultivated land under tenancy arrangements served less to help the landless as a cultivator than to *increase* the average scale of farm operation: those who own also tend to lease *in*. Tenancy thus served to lower, in some measure, the percentage of farms *operated* with a total of less than 5 acres. When account is taken of lease arrangements, less than 71 percent of operating units are below 5 acres, although 74.4 percent of *owned* units are in this size category.[31]

These patterns of agriculture pervaded the land in a general way. The average size of owned land is at least twice as large in west and northwest India as in the south, east, and northern regions. In the former areas the 25 percent of households that own the largest farms operate at least 7.5 to 10.0 acres, as against the 5.0 acre low-point for this group in the country as a whole. Tenancy is relatively more important in the west and northwest, and in those

---

[29]N.S.S. No. 10, pp. 14, 34.

[30]In addition 2.65 percent of all landholders leased out *all* their lands (2 percent of India's cultivated area). Mostly these were relatively small holdings which account in great measure for the importance of renting out among owners of less than one acre of land. (*Ibid.*, pp. 20–28.)

[31]*Ibid.*, pp. 29–38.

areas it serves even more to expand the average farm *operation* as against *ownership*.[32]

The striking characteristic of Indian agriculture is of course the limited scale of individual operations. Even the wealthier and the larger farmers — the top 25 percent of all households — had units of a size that were, for the most part, manageable by individuals. And their efforts would encompass more than 80 percent of the total land in farms. Moreover these same farmers dominated India's villages. They served as village officials and arbiters. Presumably they would provide most agricultural employment; they were the prime source of credit for most purposes, including the operation of the smaller farm units. If the large and wealthy farmers were the good farmers, presumably they could assure the spread of improved practices to the very large numbers of small and less advantaged agriculturists. But the large share of land in relatively large agricultural holdings (above 5 acres) on the one hand, combined with the low-yield, limited-progress history in the predominant agricultural product on the other hand, can only mean that on the average the large and wealthy farmers were *not* efficient and productive farmers.

The following account of farm practices on the part of a relatively large farmer in a Mysore village in the early 1950's illustrates this point:

> "He conducts his agricultural operations on a scale which only a very wealthy country could afford. Rather than use proper amounts of seed of good quality and known germinating ability (all available information) the farmer scatters vast quantities of unselected, untested seed. Failing to protect the young plants in the field, he perforce shares his seedlings with every bird, insect, and wild animal that comes around. He heaps his manure and compost outside his door, unprotected from sun and rain. Instead of carefully storing his harvested crop, he places it in his house in clay jars, or worse, on a crudely made stone floor. What the rats don't eat is drilled and powdered by worms and weevils." [33]

---

[32]While these statistics are from Government of India Sample Survey and Labor Enquiry sources, they are best considered approximations and general orders of magnitude. For extensive discussion on them, see Gunnar Myrdal, *Asian Drama* (New York: Pantheon Books, Inc., 1968), (3 vols.), pp. 1029–92. See also below, pp. 147–49.

[33]Alan R. Beals, *Gopalpur: A South Indian Village* (New York: Holt, Rinehart, & Winston, Inc., 1963), p. 78. In his major study of the human and social components of political evolution, Barrington Moore, Jr. characterizes such economic behavior as "still characteristic all over India after seventeen years of Independence." See his *Social Origins of Dictatorship and Democracy* (Boston: Beacon Press, 1966), p. 387. See also below, p. 150.

This scarcely qualifies as a statistical generalization even for the pre-plan years. But it does indicate that the relevant decision-makers in India's agriculture — those owners and operators of most of the land, those on the larger-scale units of operation — were *not* universally impelled to efficient operation. The resource and the output shortages that characterized the poverty of their nation did not impel these entrepreneurs to make the most of the resources available.

Indeed there is impressive evidence that output per acre in Indian agriculture has tended to be *higher* on agricultural holdings of 5 acres or less than on larger holdings. For a large sample of farms (2692 holdings) in six major agricultural regions of India — in Tamil Nadu, Uttar Pradesh, Madhya Pradesh, West Bengal, Maharashtra, and Punjab — and in the production of all the main crops, the *smallest* farm-size category has shown the highest yields. Farms of 10 acres or more generally have yields per acre 20 percent below the average yield of all farms; small farms (5 acres or below) tend to yield more than 20 percent above this average. The differences arise from differences in intensity of cultivation: labor use per acre has been significantly higher on the smaller farms. Observed output per acre increases with additions of labor, other inputs being the same. The lower per acre returns on the larger farms (and hence on most of India's cultivated acreage) are thus a manifestation of underutilization of an available and productive resource.[34] Actually the analysis indicates that other resources, notably land and draft animals on the larger farms, were not being used efficiently because insufficient labor was applied in combination with them. Many farmers on the above-average-size units apparently chose not to add more labor or additional irrigation water, which would also have increased output per acre. Higher physical output per acre would certainly have been accompanied by higher net value per acre. Both labor and water were generally available beyond actual use. Incremental private costs (to say naught of incremental social costs) would have been smaller than increments in value of product at prevailing prices. For reasons that do not seem to be associated with physical resource availability, the economic equilibrium position was not sought by many farmers, *particularly* by the larger agricultural units. The deterrents to output expansion were cer-

---

[34]These data and this conclusion are given by Morton Paglin, "Surplus Agricultural Labor and Development: Facts and Theories," *American Economic Review (AER)*, Vol. 55, No. 4 (September, 1965), pp. 815–34. His results rest entirely upon the extensive farm survey reports conducted in five Indian research centers during 1955–57. In this regard see below, pp. 147–50.

tainly *within* the large and wealthy agriculturists. They are not to be found in the supplies of basic inputs such as land, water, labor —or even capital.

These observations and conclusions run counter to familiar views on the deterrents to agricultural expansion in poor lands like India. At the minimum they underscore the need for a greater policy concern about small units of operation in any program for economic expansion in India.[35] It is true that there has been some criticism of these farm management survey results; they are attributed in part to spurious correlations as well as to differences in soil fertility in small as against large farms.[36] These notwithstanding, the evidence still indicates relative efficiency of agricultural operations on the smaller farms in the early independence years. In any event, it supports the position that India's larger farm units could have achieved greater output and greater income with available technology and with greater use of labor per unit of area.

Increasing the productivity in rural areas has long been a central theme in Indian economic affairs, at least from the time of British rule. The nation abounds with old institutions—some, like the Agricultural College at Allahabad, of great educational and research importance today—founded in a commitment to an improved agriculture. They were pioneered by imaginative and skilled Indians and by foreigners whose names are still identified with agricultural progress in India—H.L.F. Brayne, Sam Higgenbottom, H.C. Mann, and Henry Phips, for example. Great centers of research in agricultural sciences and in agricultural economics have long histories on the subcontinent. However marked their contribution—in technology, in seed varieties and cultivation practices, in economic accounting—gains tended to be dispersed. The record of output and productivity in India would not have been as good without them, but the record is neither one of the steady agricultural growth they sought nor one of agriculture's integration into an expanding economy.

---

[35]This subject has already been posed for other reasons in our opening chapter, pp. 9–11. But its significance to agricultural, social, and political policy in India concerns us again later (pp. 160–62; pp. 219–23).

[36]For such objections see Ashok Rudra, "Farm Size and Yield per Acre," *EPW*, Special Number (July, 1968), pp. 1041–44; C.H. Hanumantha Rao, "A Comment," *EPW* (September 14, 1968), pp. 1413–14, seeks to support the views of Paglin (and others) as summarized in the text above. For a similar conclusion, see J. N. Bhagwati and S. Chakravarty, "Contributions to Indian Economic Analysis: A Survey" *AER*, Vol. 59, No. 4, Part 2 (September, 1969), pp. 38–48.

The potential for significant improvement in agricultural productivity in India has been recognized throughout the years, and continues to be a major assumption of public policy today. It has reasonably firm support in agronomic science and economic analysis: greater output per man and per acre is possible and by and large profitable in any relevant economic accounting. Moreover, such improvement can be made on the basis of technology already used in India and even with seeds known and available in India. For the country as a whole, agriculture is said to suffer from inadequate water supply and from limited supply of capital. Yet supplies of these inputs that are available in India are not used to full capacity and supplies of both can be expanded. Indeed the extent of underutilization of labor and of irrigation ranks high among India's acute current problems. Such are the themes that emerge from appraisals of technical experts over many years. The "best farmers" match performance anywhere, but most farmers, including those who are wealthy and who operate relatively large units, are not driven to such practice. Expansions in yield per acre by 50 percent and more over a 15 to 20 year period have long been considered technologically possible by relatively small changes in production that involve mostly indigenous inputs. Of course much larger increases now appear possible, given the new seed varieties and ample fertilizer and other plant food inputs.[37] These technological possibilities can now be coupled with a thesis of expansion that emphasizes spreading to farms with low output per acre and per man the practices adopted by the better farmers, with respect particularly to the more intensive use of labor in pre-harvest operations.[38]

---

[37]For the comprehensive views of a British expert, including a summary of recommendations made in the British period in India, see William Burns, *Technological Possibilities of Agricultural Development in India*, Lahore, 1944. See also the Ford Foundation's report on *India's Food Crisis and Steps to Meet It*, issued by India's Ministry of Food and Agriculture, April, 1959. There are also the new program possibilities of the green revolution, a matter on which there is already an extensive experience and literature as we shall see in Chapters 3 and 5. (See also the references on pp. 2–4 above.) For more detailed discussion based on village studies in some important states (Uttar Pradesh, Tamil Nadu, and Maharashtra), see Gilbert Etienne, *Studies in Indian Agriculture: The Art of the Possible*, trans. Mothersole and Megan (Berkeley: University of California Press, 1968).

[38]For data and argument on this "catching-up" (caterpillar) theory, see "Asian Agricultural Prospects," a symposium in *Asian Survey*, Vol. 8, No. 3 (March, 1968), pp. 149-205, with articles on Thailand (J.R. Behrman), India (A.W. Heston), Pakistan (C.H. Gotsch), and an interpretation and comparative analysis, "Progress through the Rich or Poor Farmer: Case Studies in Asia" (W. Malenbaum). Also see pp. 145–47 and pp. 219–21 below.

Such was the structure and such were the possibilities for Indian agriculture at independence. The social, religious, and political roots of rural power combined with economic considerations to provide below-optimum economic performance. Dominated by agricultural sources of income, India's national product remained significantly below its potential. India's people were poorer and less well fed than necessary. Persistent retention of traditional types of both technological processes and interpersonal relations provided social and political rewards to the established centers of rural power. And these rewards apparently outweighed the gains that would have accrued to themselves, to the national economy, and indeed to most of the people of India, from the production, distribution, and consumption of higher levels of agricultural output. It may be understandable that little pressure for such a trade-off would exist in a society like rural India's. Less understandable is the acceptance of such a solution by domestic groups with smaller tradition-bound interests.

The record of Indian economic life suggests strongly that the state of agriculture permeates the entire economic structure — much more so than by simply augmenting it. When crop output is large, national output is large. Non-agricultural activity is stimulated whenever agriculturists, who constitute most of India's people, experience abundant harvests. Notwithstanding the price consequences of crop variations for the real value of agriculture's product, gains in total national product tend to exceed, often significantly, the direct change in the real value of agriculture's product.

Pertinent data are not available for pre-independence years, but recent experience is relevant. Favorable crops in 1953/54, 1958/59, 1960/61, 1964/65, and 1967/68 brought corresponding peaks in product in other parts of the economy. With limited agricultural performance (1957/58, 1965/66, 1966/67, for example) total output is sluggish, in whatever other sectors of the economy it originates. Indeed, it is usual for these other sectors, including modern industry, to be highly dependent on the fortunes of agriculture. Agricultural improvement plays a dynamic role in total output. This non-agricultural gain does not depend upon the availability of low-cost grain in urban markets. The benefits that accrue to *urban* economic activity arise from the well-being of the rural areas more than from the availability of rural surpluses at favorable costs. Programs for expanding agricultural output thus have a multiplying effect elsewhere. And this is particularly important for India's modern industry sector.[39] Even during the years of active national development efforts, modern industry in India has needed the stimulus of aggressive demand for its product. Obviously government's development program itself served this purpose, but industry required that this be supplemented by private sector demand stimulated through an expanding agriculture. In these circumstances one would expect industry's leaders to have played active roles in encouraging a more effective agricultural effort — over long years and especially during the recent decades when the record of a faltering performance was becoming more and more clear.

Questions about the incentives for efficient resource use emerge constantly in a careful study of the history of India's economic progress. India at independence should probably not be characterized as a land striving for goals of progress beyond reach, because India's resources were too limited. Rather India was mostly a large traditional economy that lived readily with levels of output well below its potential; it was coupled with a small modern economy that also tended to accept underutilization of available resources. Each of these two components could have benefitted more from the other, but the inducements to interdependence were not compelling. Disequilibria in the economies of the two sectors were offset by reduced returns and dissociation in the modern sector and by the comforts of religion, caste, and family in the traditional parts of the nation. Development programs based principally upon the expansion of investment ratios and on popular excitement with an indigenous leadership could not cope adequately with either component of the economy, to say nothing of the two as one.

At independence there did not exist in India built-in forces striving to generate the massive agricultural change that was key to industrial and national progress. Rural India has a long history of coexistence with modern and dynamic forces, within agriculture and in other sectors of the economy. The new government formulated a pioneering and ambitious development effort, but in large part it rested on the type of growth opportunities long available in India — opportunities that had not served India's overall development achievement, opportunities that had instead widened the internal cleavages between a small dynamic sector and a vast traditional sector. Nor were alternative strategies readily at hand for government to consider and adopt. Insights from the experience of India's

---

[39]This matter is discussed below, pp. 172–75.

own economic evolution were needed, and especially an understanding of what happened over the plan years in India and in the comparable experience of other poor lands. This type of record is only now beginning to become available; appropriate strategy needs to rest on its analysis and interpretation. To this end we first examine the series of official development programs in India.

The Four
Five-Year Plans

3

What Are the Plans?

India's current fourth plan actually began on April 1, 1969, three years after the completion of the third plan in March, 1966. A "draft outline" of a fourth plan had been issued in August, 1966; interim annual programs guided national development activities in the three inter-plan years. While these were formulated in a framework consistent with the 1966 draft outline, they were increasingly influenced by the current position of the economy. For by the end of 1967, it was clear that Indian planning had lost contact with the realities of the Indian situation. A temporary halt was placed upon systematic programming of national growth so that India could take stock of its development effort. With new directions for Indian planning, or at least with new strategies for achieving progress in the original directions, a fourth plan could begin anew. *The Fourth Five-Year Plan, 1969-74: Draft* was in fact released in March, 1969, to guide the course of India's future development.

India's past programs are discussed in this chapter. Only after analyzing these programs and after appraising the actual record of Indian growth under planning will we turn to what could lie ahead, including new directions of the final fourth plan, submitted to the Parliament in April, 1970.[1] It is customary to think of a nation's plans for growth in terms of the scale and composition of net investment, the number and skill of additional workers, the volume and nature of new production. Any discussion of India's past plans must deal with the basic technological and economic relationships among these inputs and outputs. But whatever the structure of the plan —its size, components, relationships—plans become functioning realities in the exercise of economy-building and nation-building through a nation's people, their institutions, and their patterns of life.

We noted how pioneer was India's attempt to convert a poor, relatively static, primarily agricultural and traditional economy to a richer, dynamic, industrial, and modern nation—and to do so in a generation or two. But such a structural transformation may not be possible without a human transformation. People will use new products and services; labor will combine with new machines and processed inputs; man will participate as a decision-making individual. Perhaps such changes in people's activity and in their motivation and attitude will come naturally as a derivative of the program for structural change. On the other hand, "modernization" of people may need to be encouraged through special programs, or even mandated by decree. Planners may anticipate limited change in many people, perhaps in a significant fraction of the total population, at least for a generation or two. Such different possibilities coexist; the actual course of development may need to differ in a nation's regional, functional, and social components. Planners must nonetheless ask themselves what human changes are needed to make structural changes possible, and how these new attitudes, motivations, and activities will in fact come to be. It may even be desirable for the plans to be explicit about those parts of the nation and society that need to be passed over for some time in the rush of progress; this could perhaps ease the eventual solution for such problems as are today posed by Appalachia and the Mississippi Delta in the United States.

In this context, "what are the plans" really poses questions with which few planning commissions have felt able to deal, if indeed they felt it at all necessary to do so. But India's comprehensive and

---

[1] It is convenient to refer to the 1966 draft fourth plan in this chapter along with the past plans. The new plan for 1969–74 is appropriately part of the possibilities ahead. For the most part we reserve it for the observations of the concluding chapter 7.

conscientious planning effort did not neglect the human side of the great transformation. A tradition of democracy and the concern of a socialist state with welfare meant that high priority was given to the involvement and betterment of India's hundreds of millions of people. Each plan dealt at some length with "agricultural laborers, half of them being without land," with "minimum wages for specified areas which represented low-wage pockets," with "the rural housing programmes for village artisans," with "welfare of backward classes, especially of "scheduled tribes and scheduled areas," with problems of youth, women, handicapped, educated unemployed, and many more. Yet all this said and planned, only the art of the possible can be practiced. And in many ways the possible tended to assume that change in structure would in itself carry the main thrust of human change.

India's plans used several approaches to the role of the people in development. There was explicit enunciation of goals of social and material benefits to all from the plan effort. Growth was to expand employment, reduce the unevenness in the distribution of income and wealth, curb the concentration of power, and encourage equal opportunities in a free and open society. Then there was a series of action programs. Social consumption was increased through greater accessibility of all people to education, health care, and indeed subsidized food and subsidized housing. Village government and leadership opportunities were decentralized through community programs and local government (panchayati raj). A major public investment effort sought to hasten total development achievement. It also sought to substitute public for some private enterprises; this could slow down a concentration of power, and in some measure it could replace private profit with social gain.

But in the last analysis it still remained true that most of the human change considered necessary was expected to be a consequence of change in the material structure. Employment became dependent on output expansion to be achieved through investment. Broadened economic opportunities in all parts of the economy and the extension of the market economy were considered to be critical tools that would eventually spread change to all the people. In sum, while some human development programs were planned and implemented as such, the main thrust of India's development activity centered on the Planning Commission's interpretation of what structures were necessary for growth. Perhaps this was unavoidable in implementing development plans in a democratic society, although it is true that mandated change for the people in such centrally controlled nations as Communist China turned out to be an uncertain process. Nonetheless, the net effect of India's course of action for human change may well have contributed more to India's domestic political experiences of the past five to ten years than to actual economic development objectives. But the record is still in process.[2]

The next two sections of this chapter are concerned primarily with the plans' approach to change in the structure of the economy. We then discuss special programs for some of those people who were expected to experience difficulties in responding to the new opportunities provided by structural change. This approach scarcely offers the integration that the double-sided—structure and people—nature of the development process requires. Still it does point up important contrasts in development planning. For, in general, a program orientation toward structural change means a focus on rapid modernization and industrialization. A human change orientation, in contrast, tends to emphasize the gradual shift to more modern ways of life in the backward, traditional parts of the economy and society. Both are essential ingredients of progress, and the fundamental matter is which emphasis will be more effective in linking the focal points of immediate development action with the rest of the economy and society. The answer is not one or the other. To know what the plans are, we need to know what combination of emphasis on the modern and the traditional sectors will be most successful in integrating structural and human changes into a process of continuous expansion for the entire economy.

The General Structure

We turn now to the actual structure of the development program. India's past five-year plans, including the (1966) draft fourth plan, were part of a single long-period perspective of economic growth. Fundamental to them all was provision for a persistent expansion of real capital at a more rapid rate than the expansion in real income: the nation's investment ratio had to increase continuously. The growth of investment would be achieved through a net inflow of resources from abroad—primarily foreign government loans and grants but with some small component of private equity capital —

---

[2]Some specific aspects of the programs for popular change are discussed later in this chapter (pp. 71–75). Program results are appraised throughout the remaining sections of this study.

and through a marginal savings rate that exceeded the average savings rate. Efficient application of new investment plus this continuous expansion in the domestic savings ratio would in due time assure the nation's independence of any significant net inflow of goods and services from abroad. India's growth could then be self-sustaining. In addition, when net investment and savings in India both reached some 15 to 17 percent of national output, the economy would be growing at a rapid enough rate to assure continued expansion of per capita incomes. In this early perspective, and before the promulgation of the 1969 version of the fourth plan, the goal of self-sustaining growth would be achieved comfortably within the first five plans. The additional goal—persistent growth of income per person—was expected by the end of the five-plan span.[3]

In this 25-year period, total net investment in rupees of constant value would increase from Rs 450 crores in the last pre-plan year, 1950/51, eventually to reach Rs 5000 crores in 1975/76, the final year of the fifth plan. From some 5 percent in 1950/51, as indicated in early plan documents, corresponding investment ratios were to grow to 17 percent.[4] New investment per unit of additional income was scheduled to be almost twice as high in the fifth plan as in

---

[3]The "model" for growth is not given explicitly in the plan documents as such, but the basic scheme appears to be a small modification of the Harrod-Domar formulation:

$$Y_{t+1} - Y_t = \frac{I_t}{k}$$

Change in national product (Y) between the year t and the year $t + 1$ equals net investment (I) in year t divided by the incremental capital-output ratio, k. $I_t = S_t + F_t$ where S_t is the total domestic savings and F_t, the total net import surplus. $S_t = S_0 + b (Y_t - Y_0)$, where S_0 is the amount of savings in the pre-plan year and b is the marginal propensity to save out of national income (equal national product).

The parameters k and b are constant, and were given in the first plan as 3.0 and .20 respectively. Base year observations (1950/51) are known: $Y_0 =$ Rs 9000 crores (a *crore* is ten million); $S_0 =$ Rs 450 crores; $F_0 = 0$. Also $\sum_1^5 F_t =$ Rs 800 crores, and this total includes foreign aid, foreign private investment, and the scheduled drawing down of India's sterling reserves (remaining from India's pre-independence contributions in World War II).

This model with these magnitudes yields the macrostructure of the Indian development plan for 1951-1956. As indicated in the text above, the magnitudes were altered for the second and subsequent plans, but the same model pertains.

[4]G.O.I., *Second Five-Year Plan* (1956) (hereafter referred to as "*Second Plan*"), p. 11. Seventeen percent is the ratio given for the last year of the fifth plan in the original long-term perspective.

the first.[5] This marked increase in capital intensity would be particularly manifest in the modern industry sector, with implications
for the enterprise composition of India's new industry and for its
employment-generating potential. Notwithstanding such intensive
capital use, the level of real national income was still expected to
be more than three times as high in the last year of the fifth plan
as it was in the last pre-plan year. On a per capita basis real income
would more than double over this 25-year period; it was to continue
to grow thereafter.

The whole development scheme was characterized by an expanding ratio of investment in the public sector to total investment.
From well under half in 1948-51, and this mostly in infrastructure
like railways, power, and education, the relative importance of
government in new investment was to grow. It was projected at 64
percent of total new investment in the 1966 draft fourth plan.[6]
What is more, along with continued expansion in the basic fields
of communications, power, and irrigation, government was moving rapidly into direct investment in business enterprises—machine
tools, telephones, paper, steel, chemicals, fertilizers, minerals, and a
wide variety of heavy mechanical and electrical machinery. This
new emphasis on directly productive capital formation in the public
sector was a key element in over-all development strategy. It moved
an indigenous government into a position to provide leadership for
all modern economic activity. The promise of profits from enterprise
gave the public sector new financial flexibility in its development
policy. Thus India could project industrial diversification, and in
particular the production of "machines to make machines," in ac-
cordance with its judgment of the national interest and without
private profit restraints. Reduced dependence on imports is thus
built into the structure; in the Planning Commission view, the goal
of self-sustaining growth status could thus be more readily and
more rapidly achieved. Finally, as noted earlier, this new emphasis
also provided a counter to growing concentration of financial and
industrial wealth and power in private hands. Directly productive
investment by government was indeed a major component of India's program to achieve a socialist pattern of society.

---

[5]This actually applies to fifth plan investment compared to what was in fact
achieved in the first plan (as estimated in 1956). These incremental capital-
output ratios are also discussed later. (See pp. 118–20, 137–39, 225–26.)

[6]In the 1969 version of the fourth plan this ratio was set at 55 percent,
which was below any earlier ratios used, at least since the formulation of the
draft second plan in 1955. In the final version of the fourth plan (April, 1970)
the relative importance of public investment seems again to have been expanded, to 60 percent (See Chapter 4, p. 93.)

It was in the middle 1950's that such new directions began to color and form the perspective of Indian growth. The first plan took a somber view of the process. It would be slow, as was the rate of expansion in most of the developed countries in their early years of growth. The first plan sought to implement many of the growth projects—notably the multi-purpose installations at Bhakra-Nangal, Damodar Valley, and Hirakud—that had been in discussion and planning stages under the British for as much as half a century. These basic efforts did offer great promise in irrigation and power, but at a slow pace. While the 1951–56 scheme also gave pride of place in development to capital formation, it was explicit on the need and possibility of popular participation in the growth effort, a subject to which we have already referred. If India's hundreds of millions of people could somehow become excited about the new development effort and about their role in accelerating it, there could be dramatic increases in rural output—in agriculture and small-scale industry—and in national product as a whole, despite the relatively narrow capital base of the development plans. Yet it was realistic to expect that participation would grow slowly, at best. Early planning reflected this expectation of low rates of economic growth over the five years 1951–56—some 11–12 percent, less than 1 percent per person per year.

The second plan took shape in a new optimism generated by India's actual economic performance during 1954 and 1955. A record harvest converted the doldrums of 1952 and 1953 into buoyancy. In 1955 much larger investments seemed feasible for 1956-61 than those seriously questioned less than a year earlier.[7] However specific the mold for a long-term perspective in a sequence of plans, actual economic conditions at the time of plan formulation and the state of optimism or pessimism generated by the national or world environment do influence the numbers assigned to basic parameters in the growth model. Agricultural yield estimates, levels of tax collections, capital coefficients, marginal savings rates—planners' estimates of the future values for all such measures tend to be responsive to these environmental factors.

True, the second plan was a continuation of the first. Yet "overperformance" in output during 1951–56, the enthusiasm engendered by the favorable harvests in the years of second-plan preparation, and new thoughts on the possibilities for rapid industrialization brought greater structural shifts in the new plan than

---

[7]See, for example, the statement of the Finance Minister, C.D. Deshmukh, in the Lok Sabha on December 20, 1954.

were envisaged in earlier projections. Moreover, the second plan was able to give a new scientific precision to the goal of structural change, thanks to the emergence on the Indian scene of a new emphasis on operations research. With such more sophisticated techniques, plan formulations could deal rigorously with composition of investment, as against the earlier restriction to total investment as a whole.

Prof. P.C. Mahalanobis sat in the high councils of the Planning Commission; his famous "four sector model" influenced basic decisions on sectoral investment and output.[8] The actual structure of the second plan turned out to be close to plausible interpretations of the "answers" provided in this model—close enough so that the two could well have common sources.

Under the stimulus of the new methods and of new research data that became available with the Mahalanobis "plan-frame," as well as the stimulus of a generally favorable environment, the incremental capital-output ratio was actually projected at a significantly lower level than in the original perspective. On the other hand, savings ratios embodied in first-plan calculations were now judged too optimistic: the rate of expansion of capital over the 1951–76 perspective was therefore also lowered. Altogether these adjustments meant that the target date for achieving independence of net foreign inflows was moved explicitly to 1975/76, the end of the fifth plan, appreciably later than the date in the original perspective. And the actual level of income per capita at that time was now expected to be lower than in the earlier view.

Several important characteristics of Indian planning first became explicit in the second plan. A specific course of industrialization was charted for the long-term perspective. From an annual average of Rs 160 crores in 1951–56, total net investments in factory establishments, mining, and power were to expand some 17 times to an annual average of Rs 2700 crores (same price levels) in 1971–76;

---

[8]P. C. Mahalanobis, "The Approach of Operational Research to Planning in India," *Sankhyā: The Indian Journal of Statistics,* Vol. 16, parts 1 and 2 (December, 1955), Chapters 1–7. In this formulation investment was divided into four sub-categories: basic investment goods (heavy modern industry), factory consumer goods (light modern industry), household enterprises (agriculture and handicraft activities), and services (including construction). For each of these, two parameters are presented as relevant to the Indian economic position: one (θ) is net investment per engaged person; the other (β) is the ratio of increment of income to investment. Given these and given total national investment, estimates of investment, employment, and net product are derived for each of the sub-categories of total investment. *Ibid.,* pp. 24–37; see also Malenbaum, *Prospects for Indian Development,* pp. 84–90.

modern industry and mining were to grow relative to the total economy. Within modern industry there was to be a decisive (relative) shift away from consumer goods production toward the output of capital goods.

Secondly, in the broad industrial sector, public activity was to grow relative to private activity. From well under half the total in the first plan, the public ratio in factory, mining, and power investment was to exceed 70 percent for the third. And these probably understate the expansion planned in public industry proper since traditional public overhead investments (*i.e.* multi-purpose projects) were to become relatively less important in successive plans. Thus in the second plan itself development expenditures by government in large and medium factory industry alone were to be more than six times those of the first plan years.[9] Broad scope was still provided for additional expansion in the private sector, but its importance was to decline relative to the public sector's. In fact, while government made less than 20 percent of actual new investment in all industry during the 1951–56 years, its ratio was to exceed 60 percent for the second plan years On the other side, government planned to lower the relative importance of its own agricultural investment. Also, it was in the second plan that import substitution assumed a central position, especially in industry. The plan-frame permitted precise computations on this matter, and beginnings were made so that output of machines to make machines could expand vigorously in later plans. It was during 1956–61 that India saw itself embarking on a course of rapid industrialization.

The third plan moved ahead from a methodological point of view. Through the Planning Commission's Perspective Planning Division, a unit closely associated with the Indian Statistical Institute, projections for the 1961–66 years were made on the basis of input-output matrices of the economy. Particular attention was given to the foreign trade effects of plant construction and operation— especially their direct and indirect import effects. With industrialization and import substitution as basic underlying themes of the investment program, all major industries were studied through

---

[9]These figures may understate the percentage expansion planned in *large* enterprises, including mining. Moreover, when the second plan was formulated it was known that public investment in modern industry in the first plan was actually less than 50 percent of what was allocated in that plan. (Rs 55 crores as against 148 crores) The planned expansion was thus all the more striking. See *Second Plan*, pp. 52-53, *Fourth Five-Year Plan, A Draft Outline* (1966), (hereafter referred to as "*Fourth Plan*, 1966 draft"), p. 11. See also Chapters 4 and 6, pp. 91–94, 166–72 below.

commodity balances. These provided measures in some detail of use of each industrial product, including its use as an intermediate input for other products. Each year of the third plan could now be projected with greater assurance that output from new enterprises, as well as imports, would actually become available as needed in appropriate technical balance.

For this plan too there were propositions born of experience. An acute foreign exchange crisis in 1957 prompted a general tightening of exchange restrictions and brought a new appreciation of the basic difficulty of influencing foreign transactions on private account. It also became clear now that the operational course of industrial expansion was not so smooth. Almost from the start modern industrial plants were constructed and went on steam at a slower rate than the plans anticipated. On the other side was the good harvest in 1958/59; by then there already was evidence that the 1961 census would show India's population growing at more than 2 percent each year. This rate was some 50 percent above the 1.3 percent annual average assumed for the first two plans. By 1958 and 1959, it thus was apparent that the third plan years would also require modifications in the basic long-term picture.

It turned out, as we see later, that the third plan in fact suffered major reversals. Preparation of what was to be the original fourth plan took place during 1965 and 1966, years of considerable disillusionment with plan achievement and indeed with the state of the nation.[10] The favorable economic developments of 1964 and early 1965 were short-lived; they had been generated by record harvests in the fourth year of the third plan. In September, 1965, there was war with Pakistan, as there had been with China in 1962. Crop output was very disappointing in 1965/66, and again in 1966/67. Given also the uncertainties about foreign credits, and the reversals and major recessionary conditions throughout the economy, basic decisions on the final fourth plan simply could not be made. The Planning Commission's structure and its top policy personnel were changed in September, 1967, and in December the decision was taken to proceed with development plans on an interim basis for some years. It was announced, we have noted, that the formal plan sequence would be resumed on April 1, 1969, with a new fourth five-

---

[10]Thus the President of India, Dr. Sarvepalli Radhakrishnan, in a broadcast for India's Republic Day (January 25, 1967), observed: "The last year has been the worst since Independence, full of national calamities and human failures. . ."

year plan. By that time realistic adjustments could be made in the earlier draft plan.

In that draft, issued in August, 1966, the Planning Commission sought to compensate for some of the ground lost in the setbacks of the third plan. Thus the annual growth target for national product during 1966–71 was to be at least 7 percent; this was almost twice the average growth rate actually achieved in the years 1951–66. That 15-year average, moreover, exceeded the actual average growth rates of the third plan years. Clearly the draft fourth plan of 1966 was motivated by a conviction that higher rates of growth and of growth-oriented public action were appropriate for India, the record of the past and the rather depressing circumstances at the time notwithstanding. While the interim program for 1966/67 was formulated along with the draft fourth plan, it could not avoid coping with the actual position of the Indian economy at the end of 1965/66. Public outlays were, in fact, planned at significantly lower levels (for 1966/67 and indeed for each of the three interim plan years) than for the draft fourth plan proper. Public outlay for 1966/67 was *below* what was planned and achieved in 1965/66. In the current price levels of the three annual plans, public outlays were Rs 2221 crores, Rs 2246 crores, and Rs 2337 crores respectively for the annual programs 1966/67 through 1968/69. The fourth plan draft had anticipated an annual average of Rs 3200.[11]

In the real situation of the short-period plans, public outlay and investment (and indeed private investment) were projected at much lower levels than the longer-period plan anticipated. Most Indian officials were concerned about resource and foreign trade limitations on India's capacity to invest.[12] In addition, the 1966/67 and 1967/68 plans appeared during a period in which India experienced broad-scale famine for the first time in two decades. It is not surprising therefore that the annual programs stressed agriculture and the output of such industrial products as fertilizer and equipment meant for agricultural use. Interim plans and policy for their implementation reflected an official intention to slow down past rates of expansion of factory capacity as a whole. Efforts were intensified to complete factories in process of construction and to

---

[11]An *Annual Plan* is available for each year, prepared by the Government of India's Planning Commission. They usually appear in published form at the beginning of the pertinent fiscal year or shortly thereafter. (The 1968/69 Plan, for example, was released in July, 1968.)

[12]However, in this regard see Chapter 5, pp. 137–38.

assure the raw materials and intermediate goods inputs for all completed factories, whether these inputs were of domestic or foreign origin. Finally, exports received new encouragement in all three annual plans.

Thus the period since the end of the third plan seems already to provide some evidence of new directions in official policy. The rate of growth of new capital formation was reduced; indeed new investment was actually planned at lower absolute levels. The original preoccupation with creation of new capital was tempered, in some measure at least, with a new concern about the efficiency of use of capital in existence. The weight of real change seemed to be forcing a new emphasis in India's development thinking. In any event these developments of the interplan years, 1966–69, contribute to our analysis of India's plan performance and prospects, a range of problems we examine in later chapters.

Plan Numbers: New Investment, New Product

Such were the main lines of change expected in the structure of India's economy, as revealed in some twenty years of development planning. More correctly perhaps, a single broad scheme for change over five plan periods was interrupted abruptly at the end of the third plan; a shift in new direction may then have begun to emerge. We turn now to a more specific description of the sequence of plans. Since detailed programs are readily available in government publications, we present here (Table 2) summary statistics taken for the most part from the official plan documents. They make the main lines of planned change specific enough for our purpose.

We must first note some interplay between the plan sequence and actual development. Thus each new plan is built on what the planners estimate to be *actual* national income in the last pre-plan year, *i.e.*, the year when the new plan takes its draft form. This income is usually different from what was the *planned* national income of that year. Each column of Table 2 shows an *ex ante* figure for projected national income in the final plan year (row 4.2); this income usually differs from the *ex post*, the actual last pre-plan national income (row 4.1) in the following plan.[13] Similarly, as noted earlier, when actual performance contrasts with what was planned, the constants and coefficients of subsequent plan formulations are usually af-

---

[13]The latter is usually close to what is later recorded as the actual figure for that pre-plan year.

TABLE 2. Important Numbers, India's Plans for Development 1951-1971

	First (1951–56)		Second (1956–61)		Third (1961–66)		Fourth (1966–71) (1966 Draft)	
1.0 Net Investment Total (Rs crores)	3500[a]	100%	6200[b]	100%	10400[c]	100%	21350[d]	100%
1.1 Agriculture (including irrigation)	875	25	1180	19	2110	20	3439	16
1.2 Big industry (including power and mining)	805	23	1810	29	3632	35	8366	39
1.3 Other (small) industry	175	5	270	4	425	4	550	3
1.4 Transportation and communication	775	22	1360	22	1736	17	3460	17
1.5 Other	870	25	1580	26	2497	24	5355	25
2.0 Public/Total Investment Ratio	53.0%		61.%		61.%		64.0%	
3.0 Employment								
3.1 Additional (million persons)	(n.a.)		9.6		14		19	
3.2 Growth in labor force (million persons)	9		12		17		23	
4.0 National Income — Net (Rs crores)								
4.1 Last pre-plan year	8870		10800		14140		15930[e]	
4.2 Last plan year	10000		13480		18460		23900[e]	
4.3 Increase (%)	11.2%		25.0%		34.0%		50.0%	
5.0 Average Net Investment								
(Ratio of national income)	7.4%		10.2%		12.8%		21.4%	
6.0 Average Domestic Savings								
(Ratio of national income)	5.7%		8.1%		9.8%		15.0%	
7.0 Net Imports[f]/Net Investment	21.0%		18.0%		25.0%		32.0%	
8.0 Incremental Capital/Output Ratio	3.1		2.3		2.4		2.7	
9.0 Wholesale Price Levels (1952/53 = 100)								
9.1 Actual average	103.4	(1948/49)	108.1	(1952/53)	142.8	(1960/61)	205.2	(1966/69)
9.2 Used in plan preparation	104.0		100.1		127.5		186.1	(June, 1966)

Source: Insofar as possible, data are from official five-year plan documents, including the Planning Commission's *Perspective of Development* (hereafter by title) (April, 1964) and *Material and Financial Balances* (hereafter *MFB*) (September, 1966). The fourth plan is the 1966 draft.

[a] G.O.I. *First Five-Year Plan* (hereafter referred to as *"First Plan"*) pp. 70, 71 for public investment only. Private investment data are estimates. See Table 3 below, p. 62.
[b] *Second Plan*, pp. 56, 57, provides a basis for estimates shown.
[c] G.O.I. *Third Five-Year Plan* (hereafter referred to as *"Third Plan"*), p. 28.
[d] *Fourth Plan*, 1966 draft, p. 42.
[e] 1960/61 prices (see *MFB*, p. 7)
[f] Total deficit on current international account

fected. We note that the sequence of incremental capital coefficients (row 8.0) persists at a relatively low level; it does not move
markedly upward as was officially projected in the original long-
period scheme.[14] Experience in the first plan yielded an actual incremental ratio appreciably below expectations (2.0 as against 3.0);
in subsequent plans officials tended to maintain the value of this
important parameter within the range of these two estimates. In
like manner, the planned ratio of foreign dependence (row 7.0) does
not fall, despite the expectation in the long-period projection that it
would move fairly rapidly toward zero.[15] Expectations were apparently not being fulfilled—a matter of concern in following chapters
where we analyze actual performance.

Changes in price level since 1950 mean that successive plans are
denominated in rupees of different values, complicating comparison
over time. Table 2 (row 9.2) shows the average wholesale price
levels in which data for each plan were presented. The draft outline
for 1966–71 is thus reckoned in prices substantially above those for
the 1961–66 plan, although certain magnitudes (the national income estimates, for example) are specifically listed in the draft outline as "at 1960/61 prices"; that is, comparable to those used in the
third plan documents. Any attempt at price standardization (use
throughout of 1948/49, 1952/53, or 1960/61 price levels, for example) is apt to have limited value over these years of marked price
and structural changes in the economy. Not only is any single
wholesale price index an inadequate deflator for the different bun-
dles of goods and services included in such items as investment (and
its components) or agricultural output, but also dynamic interrelations in the economy for any period of time are conditioned by the
price level. This is particularly true for the savings and consumption
flows central to a nation's development and so fundamental to India's approach to growth. It is not likely that the data of Table 2
would present a more relevant set of observations and relationships
were all the data somehow converted to a single price base. In any
event no such effort has been made here. However, Table 2 does indicate (row 9.1) the wholesale price level that actually pertained on
the average over each plan period. Juxtaposed with the price level
actually used in each plan (row 9.2), these can prove helpful for
some comparisons in the development program.

We might observe here that the growth of investment called for in
the plans was significantly smaller in real terms than the total fig-

[14]See Malenbaum, *Prospects for Indian Development,* pp. 63–69.
[15]*Ibid.,* pp. 95–99.

ures (row 1.0) suggest. Thus the third plan appears to call for investment expenditure almost 70 percent above the second, and the (1966 draft) fourth more than doubles the investment in the third plan. More appropriate ratios after adjustments for price levels of the plans themselves would show increases of some 30 to 40 percent in the investment of these respective plans. Of great significance also is the effect of prices on the gap between actual and planned total investment. As an example, based on the price ratios of Table 2 (rows 9.1 and 9.2), it might well take more than Rs 11,500 crores during 1961–66 to approximate the real investment in the Rs 10,400 crores of the third plan.

The Development Scheme Itself

The four plans reveal a consistency over time in patterns of investment allocation (rows 1.1–1.5). Agriculture received a progressively smaller proportion of total investment while modern industry's share expanded, and in much larger ratio. In the third plan, these two basic goods sectors were allocated 55 percent of the total net investment, with industry receiving about 75 percent more than did agriculture. For the first time, these two components of total investment cut sharply into the investment ratios allocated to transportation and other services; together all service investment was reduced from 47 percent to 41 percent of the total (rows 1.4–1.5). Within the service categories, however, allocations to government administration and to activities associated with commodity distribution continued to increase.

The investment data (rows 1.0–1.5) combine public and private sectors; the difference in the two components reflects important development policies of the government of India.[16] Thus we again note the expansion in the relative importance of the public sector (row 2.0): 53 percent in 1951–56 to 64 percent for the 1966–71 years of the (1966) draft fourth plan. The two components are shown in sectoral detail in Table 3. For agriculture alone, these data provide public investment ratios which range from 60 percent to less than 64 percent; for modern industry they expand from 47 percent to 71 percent. Indeed, only in transport and communications—always dominated by public activity—and in the trade and services sectors—where notwithstanding rapid expansion of government administrative services as such, output is dominated by individual

---

[16]As we see below, differences in reliability in the estimates of these two components have other less obvious (but also important) development significance. See Chapter 4, p. 96.

service activities—was public investment apparently not expected
to grow in relative importance over the series of plans.

TABLE 3.   Planned Investment Allocations

		First (1951–56)			*Second (1956–61)*		
		Public	Private	Total	Public	Private	Total
1.0	Net Investment Total (Rs crores)	1850	1650	3500	3800	2400	6200
1.1	Agriculture (including irrigation)	525	350	875	780	400	1180
1.2	Big industry (including power and mining)	380	425	805	1190	620	1810
1.3	Other (small) industry	25	150	175	120	150	270
1.4	Transportation and communication	650	125	775	1235	125	1360
1.5	Other	270	600	870	475	1105	1580

		Third (1961–66)			*(1966 Draft)* *Fourth (1966–71)*		
		Public	Private	Total	Public	Private	Total
1.0	Net Investment Total (Rs crores)	6300	4100	10400	13600	7750	21350
1.1	Agriculture (including irrigation)	1310	800	2110	2539	900	3439
1.2	Big industry (including power and mining)	2532	1100	3632	5966	2400	8366
1.3	Other (small) industry	150	275	425	230	320	550
1.4	Transportation and communication	1486	250	1736	3010	630	3640
1.5	Other	822	1675	2497	1855	3500	5355

Sources: *First Plan,* pp. 70-71; *Second Plan,* pp. 56, 57; *Third Plan,* p. 28;
          Fourth Plan, 1966 draft, p. 42; *MFB; Perspective of Development.*

   Labor is, of course, the other major input of the productive process; even in population-rich India, labor supply constitutes an important factor in generating the level of national product, and
particularly so in the large agricultural segment of that product.
Obviously labor supply and employment bear directly on demand
for product; the degree of labor use ties readily into important social and political aspects of economic life. Basic data for size and
employment of the labor force in India are inadequate, but each
plan became increasingly explicit with respect to growth in the labor
force and growth in the demand for labor.[17] During the first plan
years, officials were made very much aware of growth in overt unem-

_____
   [17]This situation changed dramatically with the publication of the 1969 draft
of the fourth plan. See pp. 106-7 below.

ployment. Pressure mounted to create a larger number of jobs with the goal of narrowing the gap between labor force and work opportunities as the economy grew. Still, as rows 3.1–3.2 of Table 2 make clear, economic growth notwithstanding, the plans themselves failed to meet this objective. Successively each expected a larger increase in overt unemployment; almost 20 percent of the growth in labor force could not be matched by jobs, even in the plan documents. The growth schemes that were providing the basis for a self-sustaining national economy over a sequence of five plans were not able to indicate when there might be some balance between growth of employment and employables. For the plans put their emphasis on output expansion; the course of planned structural change did not provide adequately for the human input, at least insofar as employment is concerned. We are again reminded of these two aspects of a modern development effort.[18]

Some expanation has already been tendered for the planned income growth in the successive programs (Table 2, rows 4.1–4.3). The average growth rates shown do not of course represent the planned sequence, again because of differences between performance and plan. With the exception of the 1951–56 period, as we note later on, actual growth rates turned out to be less than those planned. In 1965 it seemed of great importance to the Planning Commission to establish high growth targets in order to make up for the performance lag, or else the official expectations for national income in 1975/76, the end of the five-plan perspective, would have had almost no chance of fulfillment. This accounts for the unusual target rate set in the (1966) draft fourth plan. Here, too, the obvious gap from reality makes the plan numbers of limited relevance to India's development experience.

The mounting investment ratios (row 5.0) reveal the persistence with which accelerated growth was pursued in the framework of India's schemes for structural change, factual achievement apart. The actual sequence, we shall see, differs both because the level of new investment was different from the plans (usually higher) and the average increment in income was also different (generally lower). And perhaps we should again stress the never-never nature of the draft for 1966–71: its planned investment, its planned income, its planned investment ratios were all superseded in interim annual plans (1966–69) where there often was little relationship to the figures of the 1966–71 draft plan. The expectations for domestic savings (row 6.0) were also ambitious. Despite the large marginal

---

[18]See Chapter 3, pp. 47–50, Chapter 4, pp. 117–23; and Chapter 7, pp. 203–10.

savings increases anticipated over the years, the series of plans could not budget a closing of the gap between planned investment and planned domestic savings. It can be seen (row 7.0) that the third plan anticipated a ratio of foreign dependence at a level above the 1951–56 plan. By the fourth plan, self-sustaining status, even at low levels of growth, could not be foreseen within the scope of a five-plan perspective. Uncertainties both of domestic production and of foreign trade and aid undercut the possibility for a favorable forecast of such a balance.

Finally we turn to the parameter that ties new investment to income expansion (row 8.0). The values for this incremental capital-output ratio appear in the plans, but they are not usually discussed in detail. Obviously they relate to (are derived from?) the composition of new investment, and they depend upon some engineering (and possibly some economic) aspects of the lag between new facility construction and the flows of production. The growing emphasis on modernization and industrialization on the one hand and the growing acceptance on the other of a pattern of growth that stresses output before employment, do suggest that this parameter would tend to increase over successive plans; and this expectation was explicit in the first plan document. Nonetheless the sequence of actual plans reveals the persistent use, after the first plan, of a single order of magnitude for this incremental coefficient. We have already suggested some reasons for this, but only an appraisal of the performance record can throw light on the nature and the level of capital coefficients as these are used in the Indian planning schemes. Suffice it to say here that the matter goes beyond the skill and imagination with which Indian officials estimate the output related to a given level of investment: the basic conceptual and analytical aspects of the projected investments themselves are also involved. The estimated magnitudes of investment are so fundamental to India's development schemes that it is surprising there is such limited treatment of them. We return to this important matter below.[19]

----

[19]We note here that India's plans use net investment rather than the more measurable and more operational gross investment. This in itself poses problems, although they are fairly familiar ones. Moreover recent official estimates of actual investment have been shifting away from the net concept with its troublesome depreciation accounts; India's revised national income series are now providing gross income figures. Comparable investment data have not yet been released on an industrial category basis. The point of greater concern here is the *monetized* investment concept of the official plans. See Chapter 4 below, pp. 93–96.

In Table 3 we noted how the public sector's share of new investment gives direction to the total economic effort. Nowhere is this
more fully revealed than in the changing public role in modern
industry. Table 4 shows total investment in the broadest category
of modern industry (*i.e.*, including power and mining) and the
amount to be invested by public authorities at central and state
levels. The rapid growth of this industry sector in the total plan

TABLE 4.   Planned Investment in
                 Modern Industry*

	Total		*Public*	
	*Amount***	*%*ᵃ	*Amount***	*%*ᵇ
First Plan	805ᶜ	23	380	47
Second Plan	1800	29	1190	66
Third Plan	3632	35	2532	70
Fourth Plan (1966 draft)	8366	39	5966	71
Fourth Plan (perspective)	13400	41	(n.a.)	

*Modern industry includes factory establishments, mining and
  power
**In Rs crores
ᵃ Of total planned investment
ᵇ Of total planned investment in modern industry
ᶜ Unofficial estimate

Sources: *First Plan*, pp. 70, 71; *Second Plan*, pp. 56, 57; *Third Plan*, p. 28;
         Fourth Plan, 1966 draft, p. 42; *MFB; Perspective of Develop-
         ment.*

effort and the much more rapid expansion of its public component
emerge clearly, at least as these were planned prior to 1969. The
nation's industrial output was to multiply about 15 times over the
25-year interval, almost two and one-half times as fast as total
output (Table 5). Despite the much more rapid expansion anticipated for the *public* share of industrial investment, ready generalization cannot be made about its product. Given its relatively larger
shares in the power and heavy industry areas, one would expect the
public sector to have, on the average, lower output gains per unit
of investment than would private industry. But no ready separation
can be presented of the public output data in Table 5.

The thrust of public action is well illustrated in Table 6, which
shows how rapid will be the expansion in output from the large
investments in heavy industry. We have seen that India's planning
was able to become increasingly explicit with respect to the output
of capital goods and of intermediate goods. Basic policy on this

TABLE 5.　　Planned Output Expansion in
　　　　　　　　Modern Industry*

	Total output** (percentage increase over 5-year periods)	Share of national product (percentage in terminal year of plan)
First Plan	38[a]	8.6
Second Plan	64	11.4
Third Plan	97	13.8
Fourth Plan (1966 draft)	104	18.0
Fourth Plan (perspective)	61	21.0

*As defined in Table 4
**Based on value added in constant prices
[a]Actual increases; plan estimates not available

Sources: *First Plan*, pp. 70, 71; *Second Plan*, pp. 56, 57; *Third Plan*, p. 28;
　　　　Fourth Plan, 1966 draft, p. 42; *MFB; Perspective of Develop-*
　　　　ment.

matter was formalized by the beginning of the second plan; thereafter policy was built more and more scientifically into specific
targets. The perspective view of the structural change is illustrated
by the three categories of modern industry in Table 6. Where consumer goods output was two-thirds of total net product in 1950/51,

TABLE 6.　　Planned Expansion by Type of
　　　　　　　　Modern Industry*

Industries	*1950/51* Value added (Rs crores 60/61 prices)	*1960/61* Percent- age increase from 50/51	*1965/66* Percent- age increase from 60/61	*1970/71* Percent- age increase from 65/66	*1975/76* Percent- age increase from 70/71
Consumer goods[a]	260.7	62.5	29	49	47
Intermediate goods[b]	89.5	287.0	144	122	70
Machinery[c]	30.9	390.0	180	135	56
Others	3.1	123.0	88	98	59
Total	384.2	141.0	97	104	61

*As defined in Table 4

[a] Mainly food products, textiles, rubber, and leather goods
[b] Mainly paper and wood products, non-metallic mineral products, chemicals, metal and metal products, electronics and electricity
[c] Mainly electrical engineering, transportation equipment, and industrial
machinery

Sources: Data for 1950/51 and 1960/61 are actual figures, as given in
　　　　Fourth Plan, 1966 draft, p. 10; projections for 1965/66-1975/76,
　　　　Perspective of Development, p. 17.

its ratio would decline to one-fifth by the end of the fifth plan (1975/76, in the original perspective). Given the very rapid growth in total industrial output (Table 5), private industry which dominates consumer goods output (and is also important in other categories) was expected to continue to grow.

The more rapid growth of the public sector was to give the lead to the new directions sought by the planners.[20] Industry's structure would change, and an important consequence of this would be India's increased capacity to improve its position on international account. "Steel, machine-building, and the manufacture of producer goods (were to) reduce as rapidly as possible the need for external assistance to purchase (capital) goods and also (were to) permit a broadening of the export base."[21] This import substitution process is again readily illustrated with basic data from the plans. In the late 1950's the Planning Commission anticipated that the new machinery added to the economy in 1960/61 (a value of Rs 850 crores approximately) would be doubled by 1965/66 (a value of some Rs 1700 crores). Table 7 gives an approximation of how the new levels were projected. Where supply is doubled, imports increase by only 25 percent, while domestic output (value added by machine

TABLE 7.   Import Substitution: An Illustration

	(Rs crores)	
	1960/61	*1965/66*
Domestic output		
Value added	150	425
Intermediate goods (approx.)	300	775
Total*	450	1200
Imports (c.i.f.)	400	500
Total Supply*	850	1700

*Exclusive of indirect taxes

---

[20]"In a country aiming at a socialist society, the public sector has progressively to occupy the commanding heights in the economy. The public sector has also to pioneer some of the key but difficult projects where gestation lags are very large . . . but it has succeeded in developing a number of new industrial complexes which are offering new opportunities for the private sector as well." *Fourth Plan,* 1966 draft, p. 11.

[21]*Third Plan,* pp. 65–65. Here it is indicated that, within the 70 percent increase projected in the *total* index of industrial production, there would be the following increases in components of the index: cotton textiles, 18 percent; machinery (all types), 143 percent; chemicals, 150 percent; iron and steel, 160 percent.

industry) expands by the 180 percent shown in Table 6. The simplicity of the illustration should not conceal either the problems of achieving the vast growth in domestic output or the possibilities of very rapid growth in the need for parts and raw materials, *i.e.* the intermediate products where rapid growth in imports could more than offset the reduction in finished machine imports.[22]

These dramatic shifts in the planned structure of the economy rested heavily upon public investment action and on cooperative and complementary private investment and operation. We need to recognize how different are the planned actions in these two components of the official investment data. To start, public investment is planned and controlled essentially through central and state authorities. Governmental budgetary decisions set the stage both for the mobilization of the needed resources and for their expenditure through approved outlays by specific agencies of the nation. Similarly, the allocation of this public investment among sectors of the economy is seen rather directly in the budgeted expenditure plans of the individual ministries and autonomous agencies, at both central and state levels. In effect, estimated magnitudes of public investment, as shown in Tables 2 and 3, can be taken as reasonably firm indicators of what is intended by the public sector.

For private investment, on the other hand, the position is very different indeed. The organized parts of the private sector—corporate and comparable private enterprises that must supply systematic records to various government agencies—do offer a central source for data directly relevant to private investment. But in most plan years these organized components may have contributed less than 25 percent of all private capital formation. Moreover, plans for industrial change in India are formulated so that this part of the private sector is closely attuned to public policy and action on matters of investment and growth. This does serve to provide some basis for making estimates of this big industry private contribution, at least over a period of years. Conversely, the larger part of private investment by far is in small enterprise where there are limited data and indeed very limited understanding of investment behavior. At best there is uncertain knowledge about the large share of private investment outside the big industry category—in agriculture,

---

[22]We return to this in Chapter 6, pp. 186–90. An excellent illustration of these problems in practice can be found in Jack Baranson's *Manufacturing Problems in India: The Cummins Diesel Experience,* (Syracuse, N.Y.: Syracuse University Press, 1967).

small industry, and the many service activities that together dominate the economic life of most of India's people.[23]

In past plans *total* private investment is largely a notional figure, computed as a residual. The calculation starts with an estimate by financial and planning experts of the percentage of national income invested in some base year. We have already seen how important was the familiar 5 percent ratio for all pre-plan investment in determining the total investment magnitudes of the first plan.[24] From this total can be subtracted the reasonably firm estimates of investment projected in the public sector and in the organized private sector. The residual is what the rest of the private sector will invest, according to the plan. If, as seems likely today, the investment ratio in pre-plan years was above 5 percent, this could well have brought about different totals for plan investment.[25]

Limited knowledge of private investment in a large part of the Indian economy is aggravated by the reality, and the persistence, of the phenomenon of non-monetized investment. Part of the reason a country like India has inadequate statistics on capital formation is that an important part of this investment takes the form of inputs of labor for which money is not paid directly. Returns to family labor and to servant labor constitute overhead costs to the enterprise; it is also still not unusual for labor to be paid in kind. Some capital goods in rural areas—like irrigation channels, bunds, houses, and other earth structures—can be built by this labor using tools already available for the farm enterprise. Construction materials include leaves, reeds, mud—not even part of the national product. The non-monetized component was estimated at 23 percent of total investment in 1949/50 on the basis of the first round of the National

---

[23]Important changes in this data situation may be in progress due in large part to the continuing efforts of India's Central Statistical Organization (CSO). Some of this work has now become available. It is unlikely that even preliminary results have yet been incorporated in *past* plan estimates of private investment for the less organized parts of the economy. See also Chapter 4, pp. 86–89.

[24]See Chapter 3, p. 51; footnote 3.

[25]Thus preliminary CSO results suggest a larger total investment during 1951-56 (primarily a larger private investment total) than either the first plan anticipated or subsequent plans incorporated. This may be due to over-fulfillment of investment targets. Alternatively it may be due to inadequate plan estimates for the first plan, perhaps because the normal pre-plan investment ratio was closer to 7 percent than 5 percent. These two interpretations imply very different things for India's development and investment programs. See pp. 100–103.

Sample Survey.[26] Early plan documents were reasonably explicit on their exclusion of this non-monetized investment from the plan numbers. This meant, if the above ratio is used, that they were dealing with only 77 percent of total investment; or, in other words, that actual investment anticipated was to be about 30 percent *above* plan figures. The plans also stated that non-market transactions would be expected to decline as a percentage of total investment as the nation developed. But the matter seems to have received progressively less attention in later plan documents, beginning with the third plan. The official position is thus not at all clear on this aspect of the very nature of plan investment data.

The third plan document anticipated actual private investment for the third plan years at Rs 4100 crores, in contrast to the second plan's Rs 2400 crores.[27] This is a difference of about 70 percent— unless the Rs 4100 crores now encompassed non-monetized investment also, in which case private investment was anticipated to be some 30 percent, or less than half as much, above second plan expectations. This is merely illustrative: similar problems can be cited in other plans. As we noted in Chapter 2, there is no evidence of any significant change over the past 15 to 20 years in the relative importance of non-monetization in the economy. Without any clear delineation of what the investment data represent, there is no certain way of adjusting plan investment estimates on the basis of experience, or of determining measures of capital coefficients. Small wonder there is uncertainty on important aspects of national investment.

The basic numbers and the main data of the plans for India's economic growth in no way separate those parts of the numbers and relationships that pertain for most of India's people. We are struck with the fact that the exciting plan magnitudes and relationships—such as those in Tables 4–7—deal primarily with the modern sector, where governmental and big private enterprises predominate, and where only small percentages of the labor force are apt to be involved over the next decades. On the other hand, if basic problems of growth involve the engineering of direct changes in the larger, more traditional parts of the economy, encompassing most of the nation's workers and people (a possibility to which our attention has been called earlier), the key numbers of our tables provide

---

[26]See M. Mukherjee and A. K. Ghosh, "The Pattern of Income and Expenditure in the Indian Union: A Tentative Study," *Bulletin of the International Statistical Institute,* Vol. 33, Part III, pp. 60–64.

[27]*Third Plan,* pp. 32, 33. See also our Table 3, p. 62.

limited guides for over-all economic development. Official sources tell very little about the numbers and the relationships in those traditional sectors, or about their interdependence with the modern parts of the nation.

The process of development is two-sided. Since human transformation is an essential component of the total process, the familiar material of India's plans may simply fail to deal with India's development needs. Investment data have not even been conceptualized to the point where they tell what is happening to the scale and the nature of important structures in the rural and small-scale sectors which include some 80 percent of all India's population and workers. It seems clear that higher priority is needed for new research tasks directed at discovering relevant investment concepts and their role in income generation, through both structural and human change.

Special Programs: Employment, Welfare

In India's economic development efforts there were, we indicated above, goals and programs directed to the poor and the disadvantaged — and indeed to the many millions of Indians not expected to benefit reasonably directly from the main lines of development progress, at least within the plan perspective. Special programs for the disadvantaged did of course promise gains to the economy as a whole, but while the programs are discussed at length in the plans, they are not generally supported on some cost-benefit basis relative to alternative expenditures that emphasize structural change. On the whole the special programs involve limited outlays; they are not well reflected in key plan numbers like those in our preceding section. The truth is that neither human change nor programs associated with that objective are given much weight in the total development scheme. On the other hand human and social gains fit the philosophical and institutional heritage of the state of India. Certainly, also, India's democratic leaders were aware of their need for the support of India's poor people at election time.

Two aspects of these special programs warrant emphasis. The first is government's attempt to deal *directly* with unemployment and with underemployment in rural areas especially. Here is an explicit exception to the basic scheme of seeking employment gains *indirectly*. The second aspect of interest is the plan for further internal income redistributions to improve the economic well-being of millions of India's families in the lowest range of the personal

income distribution. These special plans were to supplement continuing programs for education, housing, and health—all with some
focus on the less advanced groups. Family planning received increased attention over the plans. This too was expected to have
a differential impact on the well-being of those near the bottom of
the income range, those least affected by the main program of
modernization.

Emphasis on direct employment began with the new community
development effort in 1952, almost at the start of India's plans.
Within ten years or so, the entire nation was to be covered with
rural action programs, of various degrees of intensity. All of the
programs had provision for greater use of local labor, whether in
more intensive agriculture, rural industry, or in social overhead
activities, especially construction. Emphasis shifted over the years
in the degree of program specialization within the villages—agriculture alone, for example, or the entire range of rural life—and
in the center of direction—in Delhi, in the state capitals, or more
locally through panchayati raj. But a direct employment emphasis
persisted through all past plans. Most were budgeted under the
community development schemes. Total community development
outlays were projected at Rs 90 crores, 3.8 percent of the total public outlays for 1951–56; and Rs 200 crores (4.1 percent) and Rs 322
crores (4.3 percent) in 1956–61 and 1961–66 respectively. In January, 1954, community development allocations for the first plan
were multiplied (raised to Rs 300 crores) in an attempt to cope
with a rapid growth of open unemployment in the entire economy.
A broad panoply of village work was to be initiated with these new
resources—all to the end of utilizing more of the man-hours that
were already available, or underemployed, while the labor force was
itself expanding at an increasing rate.

Outside of agriculture a common production effort was undertaken to try to dampen the negative influence of modern industry
upon employment in competing cottage and small-scale industry.
Restrictions on new equipment were put on modern textile plants,
for example, while the growth of their traditional counterparts was
stimulated by subsidies and market advantages. Public outlays for
this purpose increased from less than Rs 1 crore in 1951/52 to more
than Rs 18 crores in the last year of the first plan. They continued
to grow, although total public expenditures for all small industry
remained a relatively small percentage of public outlays. However,
private investment in small industry was expected to surge upward.
The employment generated was expected not only to counter job

losses to modern industry, but actually to be of sizeable (net) magnitude, especially in the handicraft textiles and the cottage food processing enterprises, where more than five million persons were employed in the early plan years.

Increasingly, however, policy began to emphasize labor-intensive activities that were more complementary and less competitive with modern and capital-intensive ventures. By the third plan, considerable attention was given to more urban small industry—bicycles, sewing machines, metal processing—where output could vary directly with expansion of big industry and not inversely, as in the common production programs of earlier plans. On the rural side, rural electrification and industrial estates were stressed. Small beginnings here might constitute cores of new industrial opportunities away from the cities. More striking still was a third plan scheme for rural work cadres, recruited from both the unskilled and the educated unemployed. These people were to be paid a small supplement above maintenance already provided at home; they were to do community- and block-level jobs in irrigation, soil conservation, road development, sanitation. New employment for 100,000 people was to be found during 1961/62, and for some 2,500,000 by 1965/66. A still larger program was originally planned for 1966–71 (1966 draft plan), but with more moderate employment targets: 1,500,000 additional workers by 1970/71. Well under 500,000 new regular jobs had been created by 1965/66—as against the 2,500,000 target. Implementation tasks prompted a more moderate rate of growth for the work cadre program.

Whatever the employment outlook in such direct efforts, the third plan years did bring explicit recognition of the need to mitigate extreme poverty. Expenditure studies in India revealed monthly average consumption of Rs 25 per person in 1960/61. More than half of India's people spent less than Rs 20, the level held to be minimum for living in that year.[28] While plan officials argued that relative income distribution in India was not significantly different from that in other (and even in rich) lands,[29] they were not prepared to infer that substandard consumption would be eliminated

---

[28]This assumes 1960/61 prices and supplements in the form of a housing subsidy and a public health and education program. See Perspective Planning Division, "Perspective of Development: 1961-1976, Implications of Planning for a Minimum Level of Living," August, 1962 (mimeographed). Currently this minimum monthly expenditure would be at least Rs 30 per capita (no less than Rs 1800 per year for a family of five persons).

[29]In the sense that the bottom 40 percent of the population could claim only 15 to 18 percent of total income.

simply through growth in total national income. The main development effort itself might be counted upon by 1975/76 to deal with underconsumption on the part of 30 percent of the population, those in the third through fifth consumption deciles. But it would take many more years for the hard core bottom group (two lowest deciles) to attain an acceptable minimum level of consumption through the main development effort. Hence income transfers were to be initiated; more taxation on the top half of the population would help subsidize consumption by the bottom 20 percent.

However, the theme of assured minimum consumption through direct action was apparently pursued neither into the third plan years, nor in the 1966 draft fourth plan, nor in official statements.[30] Programs for expanding public consumption of education, health, and housing have of course been continued, and some of these offer differential gains to lower income groups. On the whole, however, such differential benefits are not easily measured. Increasingly government has become impressed with the gains from tailoring education to the need for specific skills; health to specific diseases and research needs; housing to specific regional requirements for economic growth. In practice these special programs to achieve specific ends may well bring differential gains to those groups already well ahead.

These employment-oriented and welfare-oriented activities—India's main efforts at direct transformation of people missed by the basic development effort—are enmeshed in a dilemma. There is at once a desire on the part of government for social and human improvement, and at the same time there is government's conviction that direct expenditures to this end are too costly, given the alternative of the major development task of structural change. This has meant that expenditures for social and human ends per se were always kept small, never above 5 percent of total plan outlays, too small *in themselves* to contribute much to employment or well-being. Moreover, programs for development require structural and human progress together. To a limited extent this complementary dimension was pursued in the third plan's small modern industry program, in the work cadres, in expanded public consumption geared to particular structural change problems. In fact, the tasks of growth in a nation with coexisting modern and traditional sectors can be formulated in terms of such complementarities. A dy-

---

[30]But see Chapter 7, pp. 215–17 with regard to this aspect of the new fourth plan. See also *Fourth Plan*, pp. 33–35.

namic modern sector, which is a relatively small part of the total economy, needs demand stimulus from the large traditional part of the nation. Conversely, systematic change in the small-sector areas will be helped by market and resource outlets in the modern areas. In the modern sector there has to be constant concern about absolute costs and about the comparative advantage of modern output; in the traditional, the constant concern is the output potential for products with low opportunity costs that the economy still needs. The dimensions can be mutually supporting. Achievement requires intimate knowledge of the traditional areas of the country; achievement also needs the commitment of officials and a system of leadership recruitment that offers high rewards for performance. Thus when leadership and organization were not made available for the rural cadres program, employment gains lagged and the entire complementary effort lost momentum.

Examination of the major programs for structural change over the past plans emphasizes the importance of new knowledge on the level and pattern of investment in the small-scale sectors of the economy. Change in the traditional sector, with its large share of India's people, is an essential ingredient of the human transformation of over-all growth. Here, as in the matter of plan financing discussed below, we again see that emphasis on the modern sector in over-all growth demands intimate support from programs in the rest of the economy. It takes a development program operating on *both* modern and traditional fronts to achieve the desired goals of industrialization in a growing modern sector. This can provide the traditional sector with immediate and short-run benefits, partly through social consumption and partly through productivity gains, as well as with longer-term progress through closer integration in an increasingly unified and expanding Indian economy.

Financing Investment

Plans for resource mobilization are essential elements of a development program, especially when a nation like India relates its prospects for economic expansion directly to its capacity to raise the level of domestic investment. Net import surpluses are important for investment particularly in the early years of the accelerated growth effort. But an independent nation is neither able nor willing to depend upon foreign lands for extraordinary development financing over any extensive period. To attempt to do so would involve domestic political problems as much as international political accommodations. In the economic area, it might also give rise to large service and repayment obligations, to costs associated with tied transactions or comparable restrictions on use of foreign assistance, to the negative influence of "easy" foreign aid on the nation's "hard" effort to achieve the goal of self-sustaining status. While at least 75 percent of all investment in India was to be domestically financed initially, this ratio was to grow over the plan perspective until essentially the total investment was so financed.[31] Moreover, plan finance apart, a nation that seeks to institutionalize its capacity for continuous economic growth must give high priority to the evolution of a stable and yet elastic structure for domestic resource mobilization and utilization. In the following discussion we focus on the scale and flow of domestic resources for plan finance only. The discussion is based principally upon official plan documents and these are primarily concerned with the mobilization of resources for *public* investment. They provide insights on both the anticipated flow of private resources into public capital formation and the more elusive flow of capital resources into all private investment.

Summary statistics of financing planned for four-five year periods are shown in Table 8. While financing plans need to be closely attuned to actual financing experience, some major themes do emerge. Clearly tax revenues were expected to grow relative to national product. Governmental (central and state) surpluses, on current account and from public business enterprises, were also to increase as a percentage of development outlays in the public sector. Correspondingly, public borrowings from the private sector were to constitute a smaller percentage of these outlays. The image is of an expanding investment effort progressively more self-financing, particularly through the growing surpluses of public enterprises. The seeming hesitation to borrow from the private sector apparently extends to forced borrowing. The plans consciously limited deficit financing,[32] a position often strongly supported in the Ministry of Finance, which emphasized the counter-productivity of inflationary pressures.[33]

---

[31]See above, pp. 56–64, especially Table 2, row 7.0.

[32]In Indian accounts, deficit financing is defined as that surplus (for both central and state governments) of total expenditures over total receipts on capital and current accounts that is financed through drawing down of government's cash balances and through borrowing from the Reserve Bank.

[33]Such caution is reflected in India's top-level endorsement of an early IMF Mission Report, *Economic Development with Stability*, October, 1953. In retrospect, the report and the cautions were somewhat excessive; see below, Chapter 4, p. 103.

TABLE 8.   Major Sources of Plan
Investment Finance*

		First Plan	Second Plan	Third Plan	Fourth Plan 1966 (draft)
1.0	Net Investment: Total	3500	6200	10400	21350
2.0	Public Sector^a	2070	4800	7500	16000
2.1	Surplus: current account	570	800	2260	5375
2.2	Surplus: public enterprises	170	150	550	1345
2.3	Domestic borrowing	(385)	(1200)	(1400)	(2500)
a.	Loans (net)	115	700	800	1500
b.	Small savings (net)	270	500	600	1000
2.4	Other budgetary revenues	135	250	540	1380
2.5	Treasury bills (net)	—	1200	550	—
2.6	Balance (net imports)	810	1200	2200	5400
3.0	Private Sector	1650	2400	4300	7750
3.1	Self financing (small enterprises)	900	1650	3050	5100
3.2	Financing for large enterprise	750	750	1250	2650
a.	Self financing	400	400	600	1165
b.	New sources	200	75	200	360
c.	Loans from government	50	75	150	450
d.	Balance (net imports)	100	200	300	600

*All the data are in RS crores in the price levels of the respective plans. No price adjustments have been made in the table despite the increasing prices in which successive plans are denominated (see Table 2, row 9.2).

^aThe public sector figure refers to outlay rather than investment proper. While this adds a current-account element to these capital items, government had to mobilize the financial resources for total outlays. The two components are shown below:

	Public Investment	Non-Investment Outlay
Plan 1	1850	220
Plan 2	3800	1000
Plan 3	6100	1400
Plan 4 (draft)	13600	2400

Net investment (row 1.0) is equal to rows 2.0 + 3.0 minus this non-investment outlay.

Sources: *Five-Year Plans: First,* pp. 47–68; *Second,* pp. 77–108; *Third,* pp. 93–106; *Fourth,* 1966 draft, pp. 75–91.

The growth of tax revenues was impressive. National and state receipts combined were 6.7 percent of national income in 1950/51 and 14.8 percent in 1965/66.[34] Such elasticity was discovered when the plans began to call for specific supplementary taxes to provide greater surpluses. Indeed increases in such special levies exceeded

[34]Thereafter, in the recessionary conditions of the interplan years 1966–69, the ratio declined to 12.7 percent (1967/68); it had yet to recover its 1965/66 level in 1970/71.

plan expectations, and this encouraged higher expectations the next year or next plan.

Tax receipts expanded in most revenue categories, but indirect levies on commodities and services made by far the greatest strides. The latter now provide 60 percent of total revenues. Domestic excises by states provided 23.5 percent of total (state and central) tax revenues in 1950/51 and 27 percent of the very much larger total revenue in 1965/66. Comparable taxes of the central government jumped from 11.7 percent to 33 percent. While taxes on corporate and personal income increased, their share fell from 27.5 percent of total revenues in 1950/51 to 20 percent in 1965/66. Agricultural income taxes, a prerogative of state governments in India, continued to be of negligible and declining importance as a ratio of all taxes. And finally, land revenues that contributed less than ¾ of 1 percent of tax revenue in 1950/51 provided less than ⅓ of 1 percent in recent years. The main sources of revenue have grown more rapidly than national income; yet the percentage of tax revenues due to direct taxation has been declining. In this sense the revenue structure as a whole tended to become more regressive. The gains in revenue reflect less the built-in elasticity of the tax structure—one that captures differentially the increments of income of wealthier persons—than they reflect the successive additions to rate of excise and to number of goods and services affected—the so-called "buoyancy" of the system. It is a program of revenue expansion that promises future gains at a diminishing rate, more so at least than in an increasingly progressive revenue system.

This growth in total tax revenues was broadly in line with India's expectation to expand surpluses on current account five times over the 1951–66 interval.[35] The plans show combined public surpluses (current and enterprise acounts) sufficient to provide some 20 percent of total outlays in the second plan[36] and more than 40 percent in the draft fourth (Table 8, rows 2.0, 2.1, 2.2). On the other hand, borrowings from the private sector tend to decline relative to public outlays (row 2.3). Such domestic borrowings were meant especially to tap the surpluses of relatively low- and medium-income

---

[35]But there was in fact an *absolute reduction* in this current account surplus, even on a money basis, *i.e.*, without adjusting for price level changes. Outlays for public services grew very rapidly, especially in health, education, transport, and in military items. There were very strong political pressures for salary adjustments to help offset the sharp rise in living costs for the very large numbers of low-wage, unskilled public servants.

[36]Current account surpluses were unusually large in the early 1950's when India's exports and related taxes benefitted from trade expansion associated with the Korean war.

people. Government hoped to divert some of the savings-investment flows from family and small-scale enterprises to the public sector. While "other budgetary revenues" (row 2.4) does include some big-industry deposits (from the Steel Equalization Fund, for example), large-scale private enterprise was expected to contribute to public development activity through taxation more than through loans. Finally, except for 1956–61, when government was very alert to the deflationary developments in some of the first plan years and therefore more inclined to create purchasing power through governmental deficits, programs for borrowing through the issue of Treasury bills were not important in the plans for development finance (row 2.5).

On the private investment side, almost two-thirds of all private investment was expected to be in small-scale activities (rows 3.1 and 3.0). Here self-financing, the direct savings-investment flows within individual enterprises, is of overriding importance. In big business, such direct flows (row 3.2a) were to provide about half the total investment in each plan period (row 3.2). Plans for public borrowing from the private sector notwithstanding, even official projections envisaged that self-financing in all private enterprises together (row 3.1 plus 3.2a) would provide at least 80 percent of the private sector's total investment finance. A predominant part of the private savings used in the private sector was expected to be relatively immobile; most private savings were invested essentially where they were created. Government could anticipate a transfer of private savings to public sector uses through special loan programs and various small savings schemes (row 2.3) only *after* this basic internal and direct movement of savings to investment within the private sector.

Other significant characteristics of the planned flow of investment finance are revealed in Table 9, which indicates the extent to which the public sector planned to use domestic savings, whether as government surpluses or as new borrowings from the private sector. Average use of total savings by the public sector was to move upward over the successive plans (Table 9, row 3.1). In other words, government expected to be able somehow to attract to the public sector an expanding ratio of the increment in total domestic savings. On the average in the four plan periods more than half the *growth* of national savings (row 3.2) was to move into public sector investment. This high expectation was in the plans despite the apparent propensity for direct investment in an economy like India's, where private savings tend to stay where they are generated.

TABLE 9.   The Flow of Private
Savings: Plans*

		First Plan	Second Plan	Third Plan	(1966 draft) Fourth Plan
1.	Domestic savings: total	2600	4800	7900	15350
2.	Used in public sector	1050	2600	3880	8200
3.	Ratios				
	3.1 Average: $\dfrac{\text{Row 2}}{\text{Row 1}}$	40%	54%	49%	53%
	3.2 Incremental: $\dfrac{\Delta\text{Row 2}}{\Delta\text{Row 1}}$	9%	70%	42%	58%

*Rs crores

Source: Computed from Table 8

These plans for greater mobility of domestic savings and for their increasing availability for capital formation in the public sector were hypothesized on growing monetization and commercialization of the economy. Indeed, as the small family unit shifted to a more complete money basis, as big private enterprise expanded the scale and diversity of its operations, and as government's own corporate sector literally multiplied, such expectations were reasonable. Actually, the very effort by government to increase its claim on use of national savings was expected to place greater competitive pressure for these resources on the private sector. This would put a premium on more efficient capital use in private enterprise. Whatever the basic merits of this scheme of public-private competition for funds, its potential rested on increasing the degree of mobility in domestic savings. Today, as throughout the plan years, the bulk by far of India's savings arises in the household, primarily small-scale, part of the economy; corporate and government savings together constitute less than 35 percent of the total in most years. The importance of households in savings and the importance of self-financing in private investment call for a special concern with the actual savings and investment patterns in the private economy if efficient allocation and use of domestic savings are in fact to be achieved. These goals cannot be attained without programs directed to the non-modern parts of the economy—to encourage monetization, to mobilize savings, and to reward efficient capital creation.

The circle is complete: even as development focuses on growth of modern activities, the total scheme for development in India must lean heavily on the traditional parts of the nation. Efficient use of capital there, as efficient use of labor there, is not separable from the task of resource mobilization and use elsewhere in the economy, particularly in the public sector and in modern enterprise in the private sector. Though India's development aims were heavily focussed on these modern parts of the nation, achievement there demanded a major concern with basic changes in the large traditional sectors of the economy.

What Makes the Plans Work?

These programs for structural and human change require coordinated action by governmental agencies and by the private sector's decision makers, large and small. A coherent program emerges because of market forces, interindustry and intraindustry agreement, public-private cooperative arrangements, and governmental decree. Resource mobilization for outlays in the public sector itself involves coordinated action by different governmental entities, and especially by state and by central governments, each operating in reserved areas. Thus agricultural income tax is a state responsibility; income taxes and foreign trade taxes are responsibilities of the center. The national government bears a large share of state expenditures—through repayment of part of the income tax revenue or the excise taxes taken from states by the center. In recent years, 30 to 50 percent of all expenditures in different states were actually met by government in New Delhi. With respect to capital outlays, the center's ratio could be in excess of 90 percent of plan expenditures in individual states. The tasks of planning, of plan financing, and of plan implementation involve collaboration, competition, compromise, conflict, and decree as between these two major levels of government in a federal system. The national plans represent joint compromise positions in which the final decision must reflect the priority position of authorities at the national level, for only at that level can a country total be defined and defended. With respect to implementation, responsibilities are shared differently almost on a project by project basis. Indeed these shares can vary over the course of development of a single project. They are not constant between state and center over a plan, to say nothing of the sequence of plans.

In this area of state-central authority, problems of administration are familiar. Planning for development is essentially an extension of normal federal operations, involving relatively few new principles of resource mobilization and use. Consistent with this, all administrative tasks in a federal system are easier when there is a cohesive central-state political structure. When political parties show markedly different arrays and strengths in state and national governments, all problems of administration, among other problems, are aggravated. Over the sequence of Indian plans, such divergence has become marked only in recent years. Through 1965/66 (more or less), planning authorities could fairly well anticipate plan performance that depended upon state–national collaboration. In the past five years there was much greater uncertainty on this matter with marked and changing differences in the political composition of central and state governments.[37]

Of even more relevance to the main themes of this study are questions posed by the fact that the plans are also financed and implemented by private as well as public parts of the economy. There is little precedent in many countries, and very little indeed in India, for a major involvement on the part of democratic government in the economic conduct of an entire nation in which economic life is generated essentially by private enterprise. In India, the private sector has produced on the average about 90 percent of total output since 1950. Even in recent years, this ratio has exceeded 85 percent. With planning, government now seeks to achieve specific levels and patterns of national investment and output, including, of course, the output from private enterprise. And in this effort the public sector's tools are basically only those of a democratic nation: guidance and inducement, augmented by a limited number of decreed or legislated controls. Use of these tools is specifically geared to the attainment of stated goals and objectives. Since economic goal achievement in a predominantly private economy involves technical knowledge and skills which are mostly found in the private sector, achievement requires cooperation between public and private groups. The greater such joint action in goal determination, in private-public allocation, in establishing inducements and controls, the greater the prospect for efficient operation.

Cooperative activity of this nature is not easily pursued, especially where there is some history of public-private division.[38] Basically, the senior civil servant in India looked down upon the nature and the method of private business activity. The early adoption of a socialist goal for Indian society exacerbated the differences between these two important groups. Beyond this, officialdom can generally have but limited knowledge about the way things can be

---

[37]See Chapter 7, pp. 210–17.

[38]For an appraisal of the new importance now given to internal adjustment and integrating mechanisms see Chapter 4, pp. 119–23.

done in business enterprise, and in particular about the role of profits as a spur to action and about the relationship between profits and the specific goals sought in the plans.

The major devices in India's development tasks have been a series of more or less direct controls: licensing authority for creation of new capacity, allocating authority for scarce goods and services and especially for foreign exchange; price and quota determination for goods and services, including imports and exports. In practically all cases controls involved discussions, if not decisions, by special committees in which the pertinent private sector groups participated. While most of these tools were needed, the programs in successive plans themselves provide testimony of the fact that private action can be projected only from controls that make operational sense to the private entrepreneur. Otherwise plan programs are not implemented, whether (to cite a few illustrations) the goal is the level of savings transferred from the private sector, the scale and variety of steel output, or the volume and structure of imports and exports. Increasingly, direct controls have made room in planning for markets where profits and market shares are incentives to performance.

All this is true for cooperation between big industry and government. But an area of major private–public concern lies outside this component of activity. Most of India's entrepreneurs are in the agricultural and small-scale enterprise parts of the economy. Joint action between public and private entities here presupposes much knowledge that has not been reflected in the plans. In this area official programs simply assumed that some changes in economic and social overhead installations and some new industrial output and opportunities would hasten the achievement of goals for agriculture, and to some extent for other labor-intensive economic pursuits. The plans have not been concerned in realistic detail with the effective operating unit for such change. Indeed relatively little knowledge existed—in the early plan years and even now—on the structure and the dynamics of rural change. Plans could only remain starting points, not programs, for achievement in these areas.

A prerequisite for achievement in this sector is a government with agencies and personnel deeply committed to change in the economic and social life of most Indians, to the human development aspect of the total growth process. This commitment would suffice to call forth new studies, new research, and new directions whenever current efforts appear to falter. Beginnings are only now being made in planning of this kind, and these mostly in programs for the new agricultural revolution, more than in programs for labor-intensive activity as a whole.[39]

Continuing action in rural affairs is of basic concern in the administrative structure and skills of a nation like India. Economic development in India places responsibility for initiating change upon government; such responsibility is not an attribute on which India's bureaucracy was built. The plans seek regularly to improve the competence, efficiency, and responsibility of public personnel. This upgrading is a continuous and long-period process. It was perhaps inevitable that the plans be better on paper than in operation. Administrative capacity for a new and complex effort requires training in skills to be defined and developed. India is still in that stage of delineation.

> ... The first task of the planner is not to do exercises in economic arithmetic, essential as these may be, but to understand the social and political structure of his community. . . . There is hardly a country so underdeveloped that it cannot build factories, hospitals, schools, offices, roads, and even dams, if sufficient [resources,] financial and technical, [are] available to it. All this is 'easy.' It creates an impression of governmental vigour and achieves nothing but the unproductive consumption of scarce resources. The real task of a government's capacity to plan economic development is its success in creating a balanced, self-sustaining, and dynamic productive system, in building up a stable and committed labour force; in training teachers, doctors, nurses, and technicians and providing them with adequate motivations and opportunities; in phasing the provision of the necessary overheads; and in ensuring that expensive collectively-provided benefits, such as irrigation water, are adequately used. All this is difficult, and the most difficult thing of all is the least spectacular but most important: the implanting of development potential in a stagnant, tradition-bound system of agriculture. Compared with this, putting up and even operating a steel mill is child's play.[40]

Plans for modernizing India's economy and society depend inevitably on the nation's capacity to effect growth in agriculture and the rest of the rural economy.

---

[39]See below, pp. 202–3.

[40]A. H. Hanson, *The Process of Planning: A Study of India's Five-Year Plans, 1950–1964* (Oxford: Oxford University Press, 1966), pp. 23–24. Professor Hanson actually wrote "if sufficient foreign assistance, financial and technical, is available to it." In my view the substitution is appropriate and strengthens his point.

Achieved Development: The Input Record

4

Has India been able to mount this development effort — the extent and breadth of new capital inputs, the scale and skill of additional employment, the coordination and imagination of modern leadership? In some measure, development experience always provides a development plan corrective. Thus we have seen the long-term perspective modified through new estimates for capital coefficients, marginal savings ratios, additional tax revenues, or similar adjustments prompted by actual experience. Changes are even made within a plan, when unemployment mounts too rapidly, investment patterns depart from expectations, or private capital responds where public resources were anticipated. Still, real differences remain between plan and record. Mostly these are apparent on the output side; and it is important to ask whether the results of the plans correspond more or less to official expectations. Are goals of national and per capita incomes, of national economic independence, reasonably assured under existing programs and policies? More broadly, is India's development effort keeping the nation on a course of expansion that appears to assure India's economic future?

In this chapter we examine the record of capital and employment inputs and the record of the leadership that converts plan numbers into economic and social reality. Pride of place goes to the level and pattern of investment. This has been the classic deterrent to a poor nation's aspirations for rapid growth. We would therefore anticipate that actual investment would generally fall short of the goals set in the plans. A nation determined to accelerate its rate of economic expansion—to make the most of its relatively scarce capital position —would continue to explore all possible alternatives for improving this status. In any event one would expect persistent and conscientious efforts to record current investment flows and capital formation, in total and in specific components.

New Capital Formation

Investment has always been the core element of India's development schemes. The scale of public and private investment anticipated in successive plans has often been used to characterize the dynamism of the overall development effort: Rs crores 3500, 6200, 10400, and 21350 for the first through (1966) draft fourth plans respectively. This seeming six-fold expansion from the first plan effort is overstated, as we saw in Chapter 3, because the successive plans were denominated in different and generally higher prices. This last was particularly manifest *after* 1960/61, the price year for the third plan, so that doubling (and more) of plan investment between the third and (1966) draft fourth plan is exaggerated. In this section we confine our attention primarily to the record of the first three plans, and hence to a smaller range of price changes. If we convert the first plan investment to a 1960/61 price base, using an (approximate) index of the prices of goods and services in capital formation between 1948/49 and 1960/61, the real level of investment in the third plan was to be some two to two and one-half times that of the first plan as against the triple expansion of the unadjusted plan figures themselves. What actually happened?

The sole series of data for actual investment in India during this period is provided by recent estimates of the Indian government's Central Statistical Organization (CSO), the agency responsible for the official data on national accounts. Only in late 1970 were these accounts extended to encompass consolidated statements on "gross domestic product and expenditure" and "national disposable income and its appropriation." Thus for the first time official data on capital formation and savings — over the years 1960/61–1965/66 only — were published as components of an Indian system of national accounts.[1] The new investment figures had been derived primarily from studies of commodity flows into capital formation, a standard procedure in situations where more direct reporting can not provide sufficiently broad-based sources of information. The CSO estimates benefitted from parallel studies of national savings flows — in the public sector, the private corporate sector, and the household sector. However, neither of these approaches to measurement has yet succeeded in providing adequate estimates of the investment (or savings) in physical assets, including accumulation through non-monetized transactions. These continue to pose major uncertainties in current estimates of capital expansion, although two earlier official publications have been helpful.[2] Particularly important is the underlying research as well as the series of technical papers presented before professional societies by expert members of the CSO staff acting in a personal capacity. These are of special concern here because they provide preliminary estimates from 1950/51 in addition to relevant comparisons of capital formation with important aspects of economic growth over the entire development period from 1950/51.[3]

While *published* CSO data on investment are of very recent date, preliminary and working materials have thus been readily available, especially within the government. On the whole, however, actual investment performance has not been featured in the plans. On occasion these do provide *ex post* estimates of total net capital formation over past plans, but the presentation is not explicit with respect either to source or method of estimation. In particular, plan estimates do not seem to correspond to such CSO estimates as were available in the working papers referred to above. As we indicated in Chapter 3, plan investment data themselves are in a form which

---

[1]CSO, *Estimates of National Product (Revised Series) 1960–61 to 1968–69*, August, 1970. The new consolidated accounts appear on pp. 34–41.

[2]CSO, *National Income Statistics, Estimates of Capital Formation in India 1960-61 to 1965-66*, November 27, 1969 (hereafter "CF-69"); and CSO, *National Income Statistics, Estimates of Savings in India 1960–61 to 1965–66*, November 27, 1969 (hereafter "Saving").

[3]The following are noteworthy: a paper by S. G. Tiwari, B. Kumar, and J. Kumar, presented to the Fourth Indian Conference on Research in National Income and Wealth, in November of 1963 (hereafter "CF-63"); another ("CF-68"), released in 1968, which was an early edition of "CF-69"; S. G. Tiwari, "Some Aspects of Economic Growth in India: 1950-51 to 1964-65," presented at the Sixth Indian Conference on Research in National Income and Wealth, May, 1968 (hereafter "Tiwari"); and R. N. Lal, *et. al.*, "Capital Formation in India, 1950-51 to 1965-66," the Seventh Indian Conference in National Income and Wealth, January, 1970 (hereafter "Lal").

is more useful in model-building than in statistical estimation. Thus, the net concepts of the plans are not readily reconciled with the gross capital formation of actual experience. Similarly the plans articulate sectoral patterns of industry in greater detail than can yet be measured from available materials. Plan preoccupation with monetized investment is not readily reconciled with estimates of savings and capital formation that must accept — only approximately, perhaps — the reality of such economic activity. And, finally, the plans do not offer price data that permit official indication of how a figure on actual investment approximates the real capital formation required in a past plan of Rs 3500, 6200, or 10400 crores. All in all, the Planning Commission documents seem to treat the real data without the concern warranted by the priority status of capital formation in official development doctrine.

Columns (1) and (2), Table 10, provide Planning Commission figures on plan and actual total net investment over the years from 1951/52–1965/66. Also shown [columns (3) and (4)] are the pertinent CSO estimates of actual investment, cumulated in five-year intervals.[4] With the exception of the first plan, post-plan figures [column (2)] exceed plan levels [column (1)], although the difference is relatively small in real terms. But at about the same time, the CSO was providing investment estimates [column (3)] that were significantly larger, in money and in real terms, than the investment targets of the plans. Finally, we note that in the more recent CSO-related data [column (4)], the estimates have been lowered. This is particularly true for the earliest plan period, 1951–56, where the reduction is in excess of 20 percent. The investment data of column (4) are now of the magnitude of those of the plans themselves [columns (1) and (2)].[5]

On this basis one might say that India was able essentially to achieve plan goals for net capital investment. Given the critical importance of these inputs for growth and their relative scarcity in a poor land, this is a significant conclusion from the research on

---

[4]There are also "actual" data on the public-private breakdown over the second plan period. The Rs 6750 crores total is separated into Rs 3650 and Rs 3100 crores for these two parts of the economy (*Third Plan*, p. 59). The corresponding plan figures were Rs 3800 and Rs 2400 crores, for the total of Rs 6200 crores. Thus net public investment was down 4 percent and net private investment up 29 percent as compared with plan totals. (No adjustment for price levels was made in these figures.) See also below, p. 93, footnote 11.

[5]Comparisons in this paragraph are based on the totals of Table 10 adjusted for plan and actual price levels in the respective five-year intervals. See Table 2, rows 9.1 and 9.2, p. 59 above.

TABLE 10.   Total Net Investment:
Some Comparisons[a]

| | Planning Commission | | CSO[b] | |
| | Plan | Actual | | |
	(1)	(2)	(3)	(4)
First Plan	3500	3360	4069	3265
Second Plan	6200	6750	7163	6355
Third Plan	10400	11280	12481	11699

[a]In Rs crores. All estimates of actual investment [columns (2), (3), (4)] are presented "in current prices". Plan data, column (1), are as in plans.
[b]Actually CSO and CSO-related sources, as referenced above (see p. 87, footnotes 1-3).

Sources: Column (1) *First Plan*, pp. 70, 71; *Second Plan*, pp. 56, 57; *Third Plan*, p. 28; *Fourth Plan*, 1966 draft, p. 42; *MFB; Perspective of Development*. Column (2) As reported in *MFB*, pp. 117-18. Earlier official documents also give "current price" figures (post-plan) for the first and second plans as Rs 3100 crores and Rs 6750 crores respectively. Column (3) CF-63, CF-68. Column (4) Lal, CF-69.

actual investment. Moreover, some aspects of the current investment estimates continue to suggest greater differences between actual and planned investment than are shown in Table 10. Real capital formation may well have exceeded planned levels; its sectoral composition differed significantly. The critical points concern depreciation allowances, actual capital replacement, direct investment in physical assets, and the separation between fixed and working capital. The following observations are not conclusive, but they do show the need for further empirical investigation before we accept the CSO evidence that actual net investment corresponded to the levels planned.

The basic CSO estimation yields *gross* capital formation; corresponding net figures are derived by subtracting estimated depreciation. Gross investment by plan periods in current prices by broad industrial category are shown in Table 11. Table 12 presents the net estimates by years in constant (1960/61) prices and in current prices for public and private sectors separately. According to the CSO, the economic content of its net investment figure is of limited significance relative to the economic content of gross investment. Thus its depreciation measure tends to be an accounting allowance rather than a measure of actual replacement of capital. Since the former measure is "likely to be on the higher side," the residual figure will be lower than the true net capital formation correspond-

TABLE 11.   Gross Capital Formation—Three Plans*

	(1) Construction			(2) Machinery and Equipment			(3) Fixed Capital Formation			(4) Change in Stocks			(5) Gross Capital Formation —Total		
	Public a	Private b	Total c	Public a	Private b	Total c	Public a	Private b	Total c	Public a	Private b	Total c	Public a	Private b	Total c
1950/51 (one year only)	176	424	600	42	214	256	218	638	856	n.a.	n.a.	96	n.a.	n.a.	952
First Plan 1951-56	1434	1636	3070	397	1256	1653	1831	2892	4723	n.a.	n.a.	392	n.a.	n.a.	5115
Second Plan 1956-61	2853	2396	5249	1389	1696	3085	4242	4092	8334	370	716	1086	4612	4808	9420
Third Plan 1961-66	5476	3522	8998	2404	4270	6674	7880	7792	15672	586	507	1093	8466	8299	16765

*In Rs crores, current prices. CSO-related estimates, as in column (4), Table 10.

Sources: Lal, p. 3, and Appendix tables; CF-69, pp. 12-13.

ing to the actual gross investment. This understatement is compounded by the fact that "actual replacement adds technically superior assets . . . Productive capacity . . . increases because of technical change caused by superior assets."[6] Gross investment can be more precisely related to increments in output than can net investment.

There are no ready rules on the "appropriate" rates for a nation's capital replacement. Certainly the ratios used in the CSO computations (40 percent of gross investment and somewhat more than 5 percent of gross domestic product) are not high when compared with rates in a developed land like the U.S. On the other hand, the CSO ratios might be high for a nation that is stepping up its rate

TABLE 12. Net Capital Formation:
Three Plans*

	Current Prices			Constant Prices (1960/61)
	(1)	(2)	(3)	(4)
	Public	*Private*	*Total*	*Total*
1950/51	191	484	675	885
1951/52	247	460	707	856
1952/53	272	196	468	553
1953/54	291	222	513	623
1954/55	355	261	616	761
1955/56	495	466	961	1187
Total First Plan	1660	1605	3265	3980
1956/57	603	675	1278	1484
1957/58	865	240	1105	1229
1958/59	745	340	1085	1160
1959/60	900	322	1222	1181
1960/61	1028	637	1665	1665
Total Second Plan	4141	2214	6355	6719
1961/62	1014	675	1689	1624
1962/63	1285	636	1920	1794
1963/64	1509	844	2353	2120
1964/65	1739	942	2681	2286
1965/66	2034	1022	3056	2442
Total Third Plan	7581	4118	11699	10266

*In Rs crores. CSO-related estimates, as in column (4), Table 10.

Sources: Lal, pp. 3-5.

---

[6]Lal, p. 10.

of capital formation rapidly, thus lowering the average age of installed capital. The main burden of any underreporting of new
investment as a result of high capital replacement allowances falls
upon the private sector, where the vast bulk of India's fixed capital
has long been centered. On the whole, private capital was in greater
need of replacement at the beginning of the planned development program. Where data permit direct comparison, and certainly
for the decade from 1956 to 1965, more than 50 percent of gross
private capital formation is allocated to capital consumption,
as against only 10 percent of gross public investment. The CSO
observes that it is difficult to measure consumption of fixed assets
in most public services. This may also mean an overstated allocation to capital consumption on private account.[7] In the third plan
years, 82.5 percent of all depreciation charges are attributed to
private sector capital. About half of all gross capital formation and
more than 65 percent of all net capital formation occurred in the
public sector during 1956-65.[8] Such an investment pattern serves to
narrow the difference between total levels of public and private
fixed investment.

In any case the CSO figures for net investment in the private
corporate sector do appear to be low as compared to alternative
estimates by the Reserve Bank of India.[9] Similar observations can
be made for the CSO estimates of private rural investment. While
capital replacement is especially hard to isolate in investment
which always includes extensive repair and maintenance outlays,
often in non-monetized form, we argue that the CSO figures seem
to underestimate net investment by the household sector in physical assets. Indeed these data alone suggest a persistent vitality in
the private sector. Both private corporate enterprise and rural
households continue to be major sources of national savings; their
relative contributions have been expanding in recent years. They
are the dominant sectors of direct saving-investment flows.[10] Moreover, their gross investment remains very high and plays an important role in subsequent output flows in the economy, particularly
in the private sector.

---

[7]CF-69, p. 3.

[8]Computed from Tables 11 and 12.

[9]RBI *Bulletin*, "Finances of Joint Stock Companies." Summary reports for
the three plan periods are in Vol. 11, September, 1957, pp. 839-99; Vol. 16,
June, 1962, pp. 840-70; and Vol. 21, December, 1967, pp. 1530-1614. All provide investment data by years.

[10]See Saving, pp. 4-20, and especially pp. 13, 16, and 19.

Our point is that current CSO figures on net investment appear to have overstated depreciation and thus underestimate the scale of net investment in India. In contrast to our initial observations on the comparable levels of planned and actual net capital formation (as in Table 10), a more appropriate view is that total new investment actually exceeded plan goals over the first three plans. This also implies that current CSO data tend to overstate the relative importance of investment in public sector activities. Private investment is probably higher absolutely and as a percentage of total investment than the CSO indicates.

Net investment has been separated into public and private categories in the CSO data (Table 12). Available information does not permit the extensive sectoral categorization given in the plans: comparisons are simply not possible. Plan investment is not articulated in a form that allows appraisal of investment performance. Even the public-private division is uncertain. Thus Table 12 indicates that net capital formation in the public sector has grown rapidly as a ratio of the national total. From 28.3 percent in 1950/51, it exceeded 50 percent for the first plan years and reached an average of 65 percent over the 1956–65 decade. This level is actually *above* the ratios projected in the original plan perspective. In Chapter 3 we noted how these plan expectations were modified because the public investment targets could not be attained.[11] And now overperformance! But enough has already been said on the possibility of CSO underestimation of the level of net capital formation in the private sector. Wide year-to-year fluctuations in the public investment ratios of the data in Table 12 — 47.2 percent, 78.3 percent, and 68.7 percent for the years 1956/57, 1957/58, and 1958/59, for example — are attributable to the limited methods available for measuring direct investment in rural areas. Both level and annual variations in private net capital formation remain uncertain figures.

This variation is most pronounced where subsistence economics persists. Investment figures here are to a large extent "estimates of construction not covered by the commodity-flow approach", that

---

[11]For further evidence on public investment lags see pp. 165-75. Also, as noted in footnote 4, p. 88, the Third Plan reported *very* different (opposite) results for public-private investment patterns in 1956–61, precisely when the CSO data stress private investment shortfalls and public investment overfulfillment. Finally, the Fourth Plan itself (p. 14) expresses the hope that net investment in the public sector will reach 60 percent of the total in the 1969-74 period. This again suggests that past CSO records overstate public investment.

is, estimates primarily of non-monetized building activities. These constituted 28 percent of the total value of construction of residential and non-residential buildings in the rural areas during 1961–66. "Other construction and works . . . both in the urban and rural sectors of the economy . . . include reclamation of land, bunding, and other land improvements, digging of (some) wells . . . afforestation . . . and laying of new orchards and plantations . . . Estimated value of all these items excepting a part of the construction of wells . . . all form part of investment in construction unaccounted in the commodity-flow approach."[12] Estimates of these less commercial transactions depend upon survey and sample data; they were, in fact, obtained for 1961/62 from the All-India Rural Debt and Investment Survey of that year. For other years they were extrapolated with the help of a combined index of growth in gross agricultural income and population with equal weight. On this basis the CSO projected increases of almost 40 percent in these types of gross investment transactions over the third plan years alone. However approximate, these changes again illustrate clearly the vitality and scale of investment in kind in housing and in agriculture proper—after more than 15 years of economic development and modernization.[13] Internal evidence of the CSO data indicates the continuing importance of this type of investment. It cannot be adequately measured by the proportions from single sample surveys. Given the importance and vigor of this activity in the Indian economy, regular sampling would seem to be an essential element in the important task of measuring the actual level and course of capital formation in India.

The preceding observations mean that the Indian economy probably created more real (*net*) capital than the plans anticipated in the years 1950/51–1965/66. Note should also be made of differences in investment composition. Thus, most of the capital formation in rural private construction — described above, and an important component of column (1b) Table 11 — is excluded from the investment figures of the plans which are explicitly concerned with monetized transactions only. Whatever the correspondence in total estimates of plan and actual investment, components must differ significantly. This is also illustrated by the division between fixed and working capital in the two sets of figures. In current CSO

---

[12]CF-69, pp. 5-6.
[13]For other evidence on the persistence of traditional types of activity, see above, pp. 27-28, 35-37.

estimates, changes in inventories and working stocks comprise 10 to 15 percent of net investment (Tables 11 and 12) in contrast to plan ratios below 10 percent.[14] Actual economic activity in India required larger investment in working capital than was planned, with important needs in manufacturing and trade as well as in crops and livestock, and in public as much as in private business activity. The composition of plan investment had therefore to be altered.

In the sectoral categorization now available for actual gross investment, we have noted that construction comprised 70 percent of gross fixed capital formation in 1950/51;[15] despite the tremendous diversification in India's investment under the stimulus of the development plans, it was not until the third-plan years that construction began to fall below 60 percent of fixed capital formation. This indicates slow change in the investment pattern. It also tells us that a large share of the products in total investment in India consists of steel and cement, wood and straw, as well as the pipes and fittings of structures. In most of these components India's domestic goods and services are predominant. Machinery and equipment were 30 percent or so of gross fixed capital formation in 1950/51 [column (2), Table 11]; they were 42.5 percent for the third-plan years together. It is in the area of equipment — still the smaller part of the total — where investment in India involves significant amounts of imported products. While exchange shortages

---

[14]The actual amounts in the official documents and their ratio of total investment are:

	Rs crores	
First Plan	n. a.	
Second Plan	500	(8.1%)
Third Plan	600*	(5.8%)
Fourth Plan (1966)	1900	(8.9%)
Fourth Plan (1969)	1760	(7.9%)

*In the Fourth Plan, 1969 draft, this figure (for 1961-66) was augmented by Rs 200 crores for inventories in the public sector. (The new ratio is 7.7%.)

We also note here that the downward adjustment in CSO investment estimates [columns (3) and (4), Table 10] was largely the result of revisions in working stock data. The new and lower levels are not consistent with the data of the Reserve Bank's on-going enquiries of joint stock companies in the private sector. (See footnote 9, p. 92.) Higher inventory and working stock levels are also indicated in a recent analysis. See K. Krishnamurthy and D. U. Sastry, *Inventories in Indian Manufacturing* (New Delhi: Academic Books Limited, 1970) pp. 10–21, 130–47. If current CSO data understate working stocks, there is a larger distortion in the composition of actual and planned investment.

[15]See Table 11, columns 1c and 3c, p. 90.

are functions of a nation's total foreign transactions, it is important to recall how indigenous are investment inputs even in a major modernization program like India's.

We emerge from this consideration of the level and composition of India's investment experience over three plans with the impression of limited correspondence between the investment program and actual capital inputs, in fact, less correspondence than is implied in the comparisons of Table 10. There still is little knowledge about the totality of saving–investment flows in a poor land like India. True, government controls and allocations were meant to guide new capital formation, but market forces remained decisive for modern enterprise while patterns of the past continued to prevail for most traditional enterprise. Wide flexibility was provided through inventory adjustments and depreciation policy, and through the persistent importance of construction activities and of non-monetized economic transactions. In Chapter 3 we stressed the limited basis on which rested the statistical framework for the plans' private investment estimates. Departures from the plans may thus simply constitute an index of how little is officially known about actual the potential investment in India. What happened is relevant, and the continuing CSO studies are beginning to provide answers. But *plan* investment in the past may have had only limited relevance to actual investment.

These are striking observations for a nation that sets so much store on its investment program in the pursuit of its growth objectives. The scrupulous care with which the investment program was articulated over the years and the priority commanded by investment in India's development plans stand in contrast to the flexibility inherent in a scheme with uncertain conceptual and actual dimensions. Of course the possibility that investment could and did actually exceed the levels planned scarcely means that capital was abundant (or redundant). Rather the plans may simply have understated the amount of investment needed for the output achieved, to say naught of the output planned.[16]

International Investment in India

Any changes in estimates of domestic investment imply changes in estimated domestic savings, since the revisions in the capital formation magnitudes would not ordinarily bring changes in the level of the net resource flow from abroad. Earlier we discussed the

---

[16]In this context, there are again questions about the capital–output ratios used in India's programs for development. See below, pp. 137-39.

scale of foreign assistance and of net international transfers in the five-year plans.[17] In Table 13, column (1) provides this plan information, the official expectation of India's deficit on current international account in each of the programs. Authorized aid, column (2), was below the planned deficit in 1951–56, a difference more than compensated in the following plan period. On the whole, aid authorization tended to correspond with the actual deficits that India had to meet — whether on current or capital account.[18] While precise comparisons of plan and performance on foreign aid are difficult, authorizations over this period seem to have more than matched the planned deficits. Indeed this last would tend to be true even if authorizations were converted to a net basis, by deducting debt service requirements from the gross amounts.[19] We might

TABLE 13.   Foreign Aid: Authorized and Used[a]

| | Plan | Actual | | |
| | Deficits on current account[b] | Foreign aid authorized | Deficits on total account | Foreign aid utilized | Changes in official reserves[c] |
	(1)	(2)	(3)	(4)	(5)
First Plan	800	381.7	241.0	201.7	− 39.3
Second Plan	1200	2538.8	2144.1	1430.3	− 713.8
Third Plan	2500	2898.3	3033.3	2867.7	− 165.6
1966-69 (3 yrs.)	(3800)	3080.2	2903.5	3097.7	+ 194.2

[a]Rs crores, current prices: Rs 4.76 = $1.00 (to June 4, 1966); thereafter Rs 7.59 = $1.00
[b]Prices of individual plans; 1966-69 figure is 60 percent of fourth plan (1966 draft) deficit. All data based on Table 2, p. 59.
[c]Residual: column (3) minus column (4). Correspondence with officially reported changes (*including* net IMF drawings) is approximate.

Sources: Column (1) Based on Table 2, p. 59. Column (2), (4) G.O.I., *Economic Survey 1969-70*, pp. 117-38. Column (3), R.B.I., *Bulletin, passim.*

[17]Above, pp. 50-52; Table 2, rows (1) and (7); Table 8.

[18]For which, in other words, provision could be made only through public foreign credits and grants or through changes in foreign reserves, as in columns (4) and (5).

[19]The repayment burden has been increasing; during the third plan, 19 percent of aid utilized [column (4), Table 13] went for amortization and interest payments. For the years 1966–69 this ratio was 31.5 percent. The absolute level of debt service will increase fairly steadily over the next 10 to 15 years even with no further aid on a loan basis. Actually loans constituted about 80 percent of all assistance during the third plan years; that ratio was maintained in the interplan period, 1966-69, and there is no clear indication of a future reduction in this ratio. In India's 1969 draft fourth plan, foreign aid requests were formulated on a net basis. See below, p. 189.

also note in Table 13 that in the first plan period India used significantly less foreign assistance than had been planned, and less than what was actually authorized by foreign lands. Actually, as we see below, India's domestic product advanced much more rapidly in those years than the plan anticipated.

Apart from its implications for actual aid levels relative to use, Table 13 is interesting on matters that warrant at least passing reference. India's foreign reseīve position declined rapidly over the early plan periods, from more than $2,000,000,000 in 1951 to some $600,000,000 in 1965 and 1966. India was also making regular use of its drawings privileges from the International Monetary Fund. By the end of the third plan India's reserves were near their operational minimum level; they could no longer serve as a source of "external" finance [column (5), Table 13]. India had to plan new measures to generate more foreign earnings — or obtain further loans and grants from abroad.[20] A second point is the narrowing gap revealed between columns (2) and (4), aid authorized and utilized. Involved here are many factors—from project commitment before India was prepared to utilize the capital to a long-time tendency on the part of important donor nations to tie aid to specific projects. The higher degree of utilization in the 1960's reflects in large part an expansion in so-called non-project assistance, although relative inflexibility of foreign aid continues to aggravate India's debt repayment burden. And finally, the record of aid reflects the wide-scale world involvement in India's development effort, a point made in the opening pages of this study. Many lands of different political persuasions provide assistance — alone or in cooperation — to aid India's economic growth (Table 14). The World Bank Group and its Aid India Consortium have predominated, with almost 90 percent of total authorizations and a larger ratio of total utilizations; but the USSR has been the second largest donor among nations after the USA. The rate of growth of foreign assistance authorizations slackened during the third plan, but moved ahead again in the interplan years — a time of economic crisis when India needed maintenance-type imports relative to new capital installations. Communist lands were less important in providing this type of assistance. Indeed, the wider gap between authorization and use

---

[20]In fact, with the end of the third plan, the government of India embarked on a conscious program to expand the level of its foreign exchange reserves (up to one billion dollars in mid-1970). This effort, of course, reduced the supply of exchange India actually used for international transactions in the recent past. This development is also discussed below on pp. 224-25.

TABLE 14.   External Assistance to India, Authorized and Utilized[a]

Source	Authorizations				Utilizations			
	Through First Plan	During Second Plan	During Third Plan	Interplan 1966-69	Through First Plan	During Second Plan	During Third Plan	Interplan 1966-69
1. Aid India Consortium:								
Total	303.5	2152.4	2694.7	2707.0	195.5	1342.0	2606.6	2857.7
Austria			8.5	8.6			4.7	9.8
Belgium			11.4	12.4			4.9	3.5
Canada	32.3	72.8	117.9	231.5	19.7	76.0	65.9	218.2
Denmark			2.2	8.9			0.6	7.0
France			72.0	67.5			21.0	54.4
West Germany		135.2	307.3	147.1		120.5	221.7	192.9
Italy			80.9	27.4			11.7	56.0
Japan		35.8	130.5	87.5		16.4	88.3	122.3
Netherlands			22.8	23.4			9.5	19.3
Sweden			6.0	16.4			3.5	7.2
United Kingdom	.4	123.1	238.0	188.4	142.0	122.3	171.2	229.0
USA	213.6	1525.0	1285.7	1524.5	33.8	784.0	1679.6	1524.4
World Bank Group	57.2	260.5	411.5	364.6		222.8	324.0	413.7
2. Communist Nations:								
Total	64.7	374.1	171.4	349.6	—	76.1	245.0	198.8
Bulgaria				11.3				
Czechoslovakia		21.1	40.4	25.0			13.0	36.1
Hungary								
Poland		14.7	21.4				11.3	4.1
USSR	64.7	320.3	109.6	253.3		76.1	211.0	138.6
Yugoslavia		18.0		60.0			9.7	20.0
3. Other Nations:								
Total	13.5	12.3	32.2	26.6	6.2	12.2	16.1	41.2
Australia	11.1	2.2	12.4	19.6	5.2	7.4	7.0	26.9
New Zealand	1.7	1.7	0.9	0.2	0.3	2.9	0.5	0.3
Norway	0.7	1.9	2.6	3.8	0.7	1.9	2.6	1.7
Switzerland		6.5	16.3				6.0	12.3
TOTAL ASSISTANCE	381.7	2538.8	2898.3	3083.2	201.7	1430.3	2867.7	3097.7

[a] In Rs crores, current prices. With relatively small exception, pre-devaluation rupees through third plan; current rates thereafter.
Source: G.O.I., *Economic Survey 1969-70*, 1970, pp. 134-42.

of their assistance does reflect their preference for providing aid in heavy industry with its longer lag between plan and plant.

Domestic Savings

The higher levels of total investment over the plans were not achieved through higher levels of external assistance alone. Domestic savings seem also to have exceeded plan expectations. The data in Table 15 provide some support for this view, although they bear upon it but partially. We have argued above that the recent CSO estimates tend to underestimate actual investment over the plan years, and particularly in the private sector. But alternative numbers are not available. "Actual" in Table 15 is therefore taken from the CSO series in Table 12. It offers but a point of departure for judging domestic savings performance. Nonetheless, with the exception of the second plan years, the savings calculations in row 5.0, Table 15, are above the plan levels. As a ratio of the actual

TABLE 15.   Investment and Savings[a]

| | First Plan | | Second Plan | | Third Plan | |
| | 1a | 1b | 2a | 2b | 3a | 3b |
	Plan	Actual	Plan	Actual	Plan	Actual
Domestic Investment (Net)						
1.0 Total	3500	3265	6200	6355	10,400	11,699
2.0 Public Sector	1850	1660	3800	4141	6100	7584
2.1 Ratio	53%	33%	61%	65%	59%	65%
Net Import Surplus[b] (Current Account)						
3.0 Total	900	150	1400	1915	2500	2574
4.0 Public Sector	800	170	1200	1715	2300	2374
Domestic Savings						
5.0 Total	2600	3115	4800	4440	7900	9125
6.0 Used in Public Sector	1050	1490	2600	2426	3800	5210
6.1 Average Ratio	40%	48%	54%	55%	49%	57%
6.2 Marginal Ratio	9%	41%	70%	70%	42%	60%

[a]In Rs crores, current prices.
[b]Components of net import surpluses are shown in Table 25, p. 184 below.

Sources: Plan data: *First Plan; Second Plan; Third Plan; Fourth Plan,*
1966 draft. Estimates where data are not fully available. See Table
9, p. 80. Actual data: Lal, pp. 3–5; R.B.I. *Bulletin, passim.*

national product,[21] these domestic savings did increase over the three-plan periods:

1951–56:   6.2%
1956–61:   7.2%
1961–66:   10.5%

If total capital formation was actually higher than Table 15 reports, the evidence on above-plan domestic savings becomes stronger.

We note the consistency with which the CSO–based data show growth in the public sector's ratios of use of domestic savings (row 6.1, Table 15), which regularly exceeded plan expectations. This is a surprising result, given the evidence presented earlier that plan financing arrangements were modified precisely because of the difficulties of expanding public savings directly and of attracting private sector savings for use in public investment.[22] Again these ratios will be significantly reduced with higher estimates for private and total investment. An important element in this revision is the scale of resources that the public sector finds difficult to attract — those flowing directly from private savings into private investment.

Capital inputs over the past plans probably exceeded plan targets, and they were financed by higher levels of foreign assistance and of domestic savings. Both theory and policy prompt greater reliance on domestic resources in future development activity. And, as we see below, India's new plans seem to push vigorously in this direction. A much greater expansion in domestic savings levels and ratios is expected to accompany India's lower foreign aid targets of the (1969 draft) fourth plan. Specifically, "28 percent of the increase in national income (. . . will be diverted to . . .) savings throughout the next 12 years (to 1980–81)." This would double India's savings ratio over this period "from about 8 percent in 1967/68 to . . . 18 percent by 1980/81." Households were the source of almost 75 percent of domestic savings in 1967/68. By 1980/81, households are expected to increase savings by 45 percent and private corporations by 27 percent; government savings are to multiply almost eight-fold. The relative importance of the household contribution to savings would decline to 54 percent.[23] These devel-

---

[21]Except for the first plan years, India's total product has been *below* what the plans visualized. (Chapter 5, pp. 133–37.)

[22]See pp. 75–78.

[23]*Fourth Plan*, 1969 draft, p. 42.

opments would mean even higher ratios of domestic savings used in the public sector than were shown in Table 15.

While past performance does indicate higher savings, this "expansion" reflects persistently higher levels more than rapidly expanding levels. This is supported by our figures on average savings for three plans (see p. 101); it is strengthened by any interpretation of pre-plan experience with a 7 percent rather than a 5 percent average savings rate.[24] Clearly India's plans anticipate acceleration, and in two directions where past experience is relevant: growth of public savings proper and diversion of private savings to public sector use. We have already had occasion to note the record on public savings.[25] The early plans envisaged that these surpluses on current account will provide some 15 percent of total domestic savings at existing tax rates. Consistently, surpluses were, in fact, generated through new tax provisions at rates beyond plan expectations. As we noted earlier, current account expenditures grew more rapidly than originally planned, especially relative to growth of domestic product. For the 1961–66 period, for example, the plans anticipated a surplus on current account of Rs 550 crores at 1960/61 tax rates. Instead there was a deficit of Rs 419 crores. Public enterprises proper began to show surpluses by the end of the third plan; they were well below plan expectations for the five years as a whole. It was the additional sources of taxation and of other revenues—beyond those envisaged in 1960/61—that were decisive.[26] India's tax record is one of buoyancy: as income expanded, new types of taxes and changes in rates of existing taxation have brought proportionately more revenue. For the most part the increases are not a consequence of built-in elasticity that automatically provided growing shares of larger incomes. Greater reliance was put on sales levies and other transaction-types of revenue measures. The over-all system has thus become more regressive; it poses increasing burdens on major components of the urban population. From recent levels somewhat below 13 percent of national income, tax revenues will need to reach 15 percent by the end of the current plan (and 18.5

---

[24]See Chapter 3. The official position places more emphasis on growth in the rate of domestic savings. In particular Saving (pp. 19–20) indicates expansion by one-third in the average rate from 1960/61 to 1965/66, a marginal savings rate of about 15 percent over the third plan years.

[25]See pp. 78–82.

[26]Instead of providing Rs 1710 crores (some 23 percent of planned public development outlay) these additional sources yielded Rs 2892 crores (34 percent of the significantly larger outlays). For official plan and performance in public sector financing over these years, see *Fourth Plan*, 1969 draft, p. 78.

percent by 1980/81), if the official savings program, oriented to the public sector, is to be achieved.

Apart from the question of tax burdens proper, the outlook for national savings depends also on the influence of taxes on the scale and flow of private voluntary savings. There is limited knowledge of actual tax incidence or of income changes under growth. The public sector competes for mobile private savings through many borrowing programs, ranging from provident funds, postal savings and other small savings schemes to market loans. The plan estimates of these borrowings seem actually to have been achieved over each of the past three plans, in total if not by specific type of transaction.[27] In addition, and in growing volume over the years, borrowings through net Reserve Bank credits to the government have provided a facile form of what could be private-to-public transfer of resources. Deficit financing exceeded original plans by a significant margin, and increasingly so from 1961 through 1969 as Table 16 indicates.

TABLE 16.   Deficit Financing: Annual Averages[a]

	Plan	*Actual*	
First Plan	58	69	
Second Plan	220	191	
Third Plan	110	227	
Fourth Plan (1966 draft)	0	(—)	
1966–68	14	242	
1968/69	307	320[b]	
Fourth Plan (1969 draft)	170	520[b]	(1969/70 only)

[a]In Rs crores, current prices.
[b]Revised estimate (1968/69); Budget estimate (1969/70)

Sources: *MFB*, pp. 116–18; *Fourth Plan*, 1969 draft, pp. 78–83; G.O.I. *Economic Survey*, 1969–70, 1970, p. 89.

The new fourth plan anticipated some deceleration in deficit financing; but, especially since the early 1960's, this type of borrowing has played a significant role in India's attempt to expand domestic savings and to increase the flow of private savings into public investment. As the data for the first year of the fourth plan (Table 16) suggest, it may continue to be important.

There remains the direct savings–investment component of household surpluses; we have seen that this is a main unknown area

---

[27]Thus see Table 8 above (p. 77) and *Fourth Plan*, 1969 draft, p. 78.

both for capital creation and for financing. These savings are not readily converted to more mobile forms; past experience with non-monetization rates makes this clear. As more precise measures of total capital formation become available, programs for influencing the scale and pattern of these direct flows will need to be given higher priority. In any event our examination of past savings behavior does suggest that programs which concentrate predominantly on public sector savings will require modification. They are part of a development emphasis which underrates the significance of the private sector, and particularly the significance of agriculture and the more traditional and subsistence parts of the economy in the growth prospectus of a nation like India.[28]

In sum, what were held to be the main thrusts of India's development effort over more than three plans—the level of new investment and the allocation of a large part of it to the public sector—seem to have been achieved. Indeed capital also may have gone into private investment beyond what the plans anticipated. While the pattern of public investment is known to differ some from the plans, greater departures have probably occurred in the private sector. On the whole, detailed facts are not known. For however important the role of capital creation in the official scheme for growth, there has not been commensurate official concern with measurement of actual investment activity. Concepts of capital creation in the plans were not conducive to straightforward observation. This is true with respect to the use of net as against gross investment concepts, the limited consideration of investment in working stocks, and the fact that plan investment data did not deal with construction separately. Finally, without a consistent and persistent position on non-monetized transactions, India's official data aggravate the task of assessing performance. More fundamentally perhaps, this last has turned administrative and professional interest away from this source of savings and investment. Here is an important dimension of what seems to be a relative neglect of agriculture's role in India's growth effort.

Investment was the major device for structural change in the economy. It turned out to be available in the amounts called for in the plans. One might then conclude that the investment input has not been a deterrent to planned structural change. Also relevant to this process is the record of labor inputs in growth, primarily the human side of the development picture, which we appraise in the

---

[28]See below, pp. 216–22.

following section of this chapter. But first we note again that the past record of capital availability scarcely assures the adequacy of future supplies. This is obvious with respect to foreign assistance. On the domestic side, the past record does not assure future savings that will grow more rapidly than in earlier plan periods. Unless new approaches to rural households become part of the official mobilization effort, only limited shares of domestic savings — perhaps not more than 50 percent — are likely to find their way to public investment. Resort to deficit financing is not a costless process, especially if other forces exert price pressures in the economy. Were India to continue to draw net credits from the Reserve Bank on the scale of recent years, the agricultural sector would need to provide a rapid expansion in food and raw materials as well as in purchasing power for most Indians. Improvement in agriculture will thus continue to claim its central position in change in the entire economy. And this improvement in turn demands a greater concern about non-monetized transactions in rural savings and investment; these are integral to the dynamics of India's rural economy.

The Use of Labor

Labor is the other major input in a program for expansion of an economy. This fact leads to quantitative economic propositions on incremental capital–labor proportions in productive activities and on the relationship between maximum increments in output and maximum use of the nation's capital and labor endowments. However modern and sophisticated such analyses and prescriptions, they run the danger of missing important aspects of labor's role in moving an economy from persistent stagnation to persistent progress. Since the development process involves a human as well as a structural transformation, a plan for growth needs to approach the *use* of labor with a concern for technical skills, for administrative and entrepreneurial talents, and indeed for the achievement motivation integral to a process of continuous expansion. Finally, decisions on labor use are intimately related to what happens to demand for output in the economy. In Chapter 1 we referred to this Keynesian reality; an important consideration in the choices among production processes in Indian agriculture, we argued, is their alternative effects on total demand.

In addition to the danger of an approach to labor use that passes over some of these basic considerations, planning in India also confronts the familiar scarcity of facts about labor supply and use. In a poor and traditional economy most labor is self-employed; the labor force is not rigorously defined; the percentage of workers on the organized labor market is very small. In these conditions data on occupation and employment are not systematically available. It is hard to measure actual gains in total net employment from new development activity, to say naught of the gains for different categories of workers.[29] Basically, in a country like India only the decennial census can provide comprehensive labor data. This source is fundamental, but in itself it does not yield enough short-period information for continuous planning purposes.

In India's past development efforts three components of official policy on labor use can be distinguished.[30] For most of the work force by far, policy reflected no immediate concern: labor in India would best be served by an official preoccupation with tasks of capital use. The goal of maximum increases in output over a period of plans could be achieved even though labor continued to be unemployed and underemployed. Fuller use of labor would come as a by-product of very rapid growth in total output. A nation with India's relative endowments of labor and capital could look forward *only eventually* to full use of its labor supply. This primary policy approach—that volume and quality of employment are best considered an "indirect rather than a direct consequence of planning" —explains why the plans continued to project growing *overt* unemployment over the years of development.[31]

---

[29]The (1969 draft) fourth plan states: "In previous plans, estimates used to be presented of the backlog of unemployment at the beginning of the plan period, of the estimated increase in the work force during the period, and of additional employment likely to be secured through implementation of the plan as formulated. . . . There were inherent difficulties in estimating the employment potential of the vast range of projects and programmes planned during a period. These were accentuated by the uncertainties relating to implementation. An estimate of the total employment created during a plan period was thus in the nature of a guess. . . . The estimates (of unemployment) carried over from plan to plan appeared less and less firmly based. . . . The Planning Commission set up in August 1968 a committee of experts to enquire into the estimates of unemployment worked out for previous plans. . . . The report of the committee is awaited. No attempt is made in this document to present data on the lines followed in previous plans." *Fourth Plan,* 1969 draft, pp. 341–42.

[30]See above, pp. 71–74.

[31]Indeed it was only in the 1966 draft fourth plan (quoted in this text sentence) that there appeared the qualification that "the ability to absorb at least the net addition to the labor force into productive and gainful employment is a test which a plan of development should endeavor to meet at the very stage of formulation" *Ibid.,* p. 106.

However intellectually satisfying, politically such propositions were unpalatable. There thus emerged, we have seen, a second component of policy: selected direct-employment activities, especially in rural and small industry projects, and relief-type programs for workers whose gains from the main policy emphasis would be long delayed. This reflected greater awareness that India's factor endowments and India's economic position did require a direct employment concern as an important element in the goal of maximizing output. But this component never took on real momentum, partly perhaps because such an effort demanded a leadership commitment that India was not prepared to make on the employment side of the development picture.[32]

The third element of policy concerned education and the supply of the technological, managerial, and entrepreneurial skills of a modernizing economy. Here major training programs are now in progress. Such programs proceed best in an economic environment where the growing supplies of skills are, in fact, being demanded. It may well be that India's basic factor-proportion approach—the main component of policy—actually retarded this demand aspect of the labor-input effort. It is particularly difficult to measure achievement on this quality side of labor use.

The information available on labor force and unemployment does not permit ready appraisal of these policies and programs for use of labor in the development effort. India's Ministry of Labour, the National Sample Survey (under the Central Statistical Organization) and the Planning Commission are all involved in study and presentation of relevant data; the Planning Commission itself seems to have been a primary source for national estimates of unemployment.[33] At least such was the situation up until the time when the 1969 draft plan officially scored the statistical inadequacies of India's position on this important matter.[34]

With respect to extent of labor use, the 1961 census reported that 1.04 percent of the urban population and 0.162 percent of the rural were unemployed, a total of 1,400,000 persons—830,000 urban and 570,000 rural. Essentially for the same period, however, the National Sample Survey (sixteenth round) provided estimates of 0.82 percent of the urban and 1.62 percent of the rural popula-

---

[32]See Chapter 3, p. 75.
[33]Also involved is the Home Ministry with its Directorate of Manpower under which comes the Institute of Manpower Planning.
[34]See p. 106, footnote 29.

tion; these yield a total unemployed of 6,470,000—640,000 urban and 5,830,000 rural. But the second plan had reported unemployment as of April, 1956, at about 5,000,000—2,240,000 urban and 2,800,000 rural. The urban estimate was based on a sample survey of September, 1953[35]; the rural was derived from data on the agricultural labor force.[36] This Planning Commission figure for 1956 then permitted still another calculation for 1961, the end of the second plan.[37] Thereafter figures in the seven to nine million persons range have come to represent the national unemployment position for that date. The specific estimate of eight million [column (2), Table 17] is 1.8 percent of India's total population or 4.8 percent of the work force. Most of these unemployed are taken to be in rural areas; that is, the 5,830,000 reported in the sample survey's sixteenth round. The 2,170,000 urban unemployed falls between other estimates that range from 1,500,000 to 3,000,000 or more. Support for these figures may also be found in the live registers of India's employment exchanges. These urban and rural estimates mean that nearly three of every four unemployed workers in 1961 were in rural areas. They constituted 1.6 percent of the rural population and 4.2 percent of its work force. Corresponding ratios for urban India were 2.7 percent and 7.9 percent. Proportionally, unemployment was significantly higher in urban areas. (At least this is what is contained in the 1961 estimate of Table 17.)

That table provides a consistent series of total unemployment estimates on this 1961 base, more or less as in the official plans. Before we appraise this "record" of the actual extent of labor use, some observations are in order with respect to concepts measured and to their magnitude. In this regard, we note that the numbers in column (2), Table 17, are presented on the assumption that they refer to *persons accepted as members of the labor force*; they are persons who actually seek remunerated work of a more or less full–time nature, and whose present employment—if any—regularly absorbs not more than one-fourth the time they want to work.

The National Sample Survey provides estimates of urban unemployment for six or seven of the years from 1953/54 to 1967/68. Rural surveys were undertaken for 1958/59 and 1960/61 only (N.S.S. rounds 14 and 16). Together these indicate that the rural unemployment *rate* is higher than the urban unemployment rate.

---

[35]N.S.S., No. 8, *Report on Preliminary Survey of Urban Unemployment, September, 1953*, 1956, pp. 45–46.

[36]G.O.I., *Agricultural Labour*, 1954, pp. 12-14.

[37]See note c, Table 17, p. 109.

This is an unrealistic enough result to raise questions about the concepts measured in these surveys. For a much larger percentage of the rural work force is associated with relatively small, family-oriented enterprises than is true for the urban work force. A large part of the labor force is self-employed. While these factors tend to reduce the extent of real unemployment, the seasonality and the underemployment in rural enterprise may serve simultaneously to understate actual employment and thus to exaggerate unemployment. And this may result in high unemployment records for a situation which should show low ones. A further point made in most surveys is that the ranks of the unemployed include a large per-

TABLE 17. Unemployment in India: G.O.I. Planning Commission Estimates

Year[a]	*Labor Force*[b] millions (1)	*Unemployed*[c] millions (2)	% *of labor force* (3)
1951	145	2.5	1.7
1956	154	5.0	3.2
1961	166	8.0	4.8
1966	183	11.5	6.3
1971	206	15.5[d]	7.5

[a]As of April 1, beginning date for each plan (1971 was terminal year of fourth plan in original development perspective).

[b]Constructed series on the basis of the "conventional estimate" of labor force in 1961. (See G.O.I. *Brochure on Revised Series of National Product for 1960-61 to 1964-65,* August, 1967, p. 5.) All other figures derived on the assumption that the following additions (million persons) occurred in the labor force: 9, 12, 17, 23 (see Table 2, p. 59) over the successive five-year periods. These are the increments presented in the plans — before 1969. It should be noted that the 1961 Census itself provided a labor force of 187,000,000 million, 12.5 percent higher than the conventional estimate *(Ibid.).* This larger total is used in the CSO national product calculation for 1961 and after, but it does not appear explicitly in later plan documents.

[c]More or less as presented in plan documents. The basic device is the difference between increments in the labor force and in the full-time jobs actually generated by the plans. The specific figures in column (2) use 8,000,000 for 1961: the *Third Plan* (p. 156) suggests 9,000,000; the *Fourth Plan,* 1966 draft, 7,000,000 (p. 106). The type of calculation used should yield a more rapidly expanding unemployment ratio. The number of new jobs created in the 1960's may also be overstated, as the text indicates; hence unemployment could be higher.

[d]"Conservative" according to *Fourth Plan,* 1966 draft (p. 108).

Sources: Five-Year Plans, especially *Second Plan,* pp. 109–19; *Third Plan,* pp. 154–61, 750–58; and *Fourth Plan,* 1966 draft, pp. 106–9. See also *Fourth Plan,* 1969 draft, pp. 341–42.

centage of new workers. Over any period of years, at least 80 percent of new workers begin in rural areas, while the plans seek to create most of the new jobs (75 to 80 percent) *outside* of agriculture. And it is outside of agriculture where the major shortfalls in new employment occur. If, in fact, the bulk of India's unemployed were in the rural areas (73 percent of the 1961 figure cited in Table 17), then most new workers must remain back on the farm when non-agricultural job opportunities are limited. This has not been the experience of poor lands.[38]

Rural unemployment might thus have been overstated in some surveys by the inclusion in this category of employed persons in off-seasons and of employed persons with very low levels of productivity. On the other side, the 1961 census itself probably contributed to some underestimate of urban unemployment. It did yield a high total labor force because it included as *employed workers* all those in trade, professions, services, business, or commerce who worked during any *one* of the 15 days preceding the enumeration.[39] This would probably understate unemployment as conceived in Table 17. The expectation of higher urban unemployment levels and ratios finds support in other source materials. Job applicants registering at employment exchanges increased from 1,800,000 in 1961 to 2,600,000 in 1966, or 45 percent in the period of the third plan; and this rate of growth seems to have been maintained in the interplan years. There are obvious qualifications to the unemployment significance of these figures. They certainly are affected by the increasing spread of the exchange facilities themselves. There were 312 exchanges on April 1, 1961, and 444 by January 1, 1969; their increasing availability in more of India's urban and industrial centers makes registration easier. Also, while listing is not compulsory, and thus not inclusive, the lists are available for those already employed (even full-time) who seek better jobs. The live registers do not conform to our definition of unemployed.

Last, we note new employment statistics now available on a current basis. These are essentially the only measures presented in the 1969 draft plan after the document stressed the inadequacy of earlier unemployment estimates. The new statistics reveal marked

[38]See, for example, W. Baer and M.E.A. Hervé, "Employment and Industrialization in Developing Countries," *The Quarterly Journal of Economics* (*QJE*), February, 1966, pp. 88–107. Also, M.P. Todaro, "A Model of Labor Migration and Urban Unemployment in Less Developed Countries," *AER* Vol. 59, No. 1 (March, 1969), pp. 138–48.

[39]See note b, Table 17, p. 109.

growth of employment over the years of the third plan—by more than 5 percent each year, far above total population and labor force (up 2.5 percent) or real national product (also up 2.5 percent). For the interplan 1966–69 period, however, employment grew no more than 1 percent each year. And the service industries are reported as the single most important contributor to new employment over the 1960's. Far beyond its relative size, this service sector provided half the total of new jobs in those years.[40] While the new data's comparability over time may provide insights on important structural aspects of changes in employment—as in the case of the services—coverage is too limited to yield valid overall measurements of labor use. Thus the estimates do not encompass agriculture, or household establishments and the self-employed; that is, they pertain to less than 15 percent of the total labor force. It would be incorrect to infer unemployment developments from the employment data reported, even in urban areas. Still we should note here that the national sample surveys referred to earlier did suggest declines in unemployment ratios—both for urban workers in the 1960's and for rural workers in the late 1950's. While these N.S.S. measures posed definitional problems, they do correspond somewhat with the urban employment growth reported in the 1969 draft plan. But such a pattern is not consistent with the persistent growth in overt unemployment traced in Indian plan documents and in reports of plan progress. There are no systematic wage data to offer evidence of a narrowing gap between labor supply and demand on a national basis.

New data collection and analysis are needed, preferably through sample surveys at relatively short intervals (quarterly perhaps). In addition to measures by functional categories, data might also be assembled by states or regions.[41] Such results will also ease the task of interpreting the past. Pending new materials, there is no alternative to a record like that of Table 17 as an over-all summary

---

[40]During 1966–69 the services more than absorbed employment reductions elsewhere. These employment characteristics are important for appraising service output (see pp. 140–41 below). The data cited are from the *Fourth Plan*, 1969 draft, pp. 342–43 and *Economic Survey, 1969–70*, pp. 94–95. See also R.B.I. *Bulletin*, August, 1970, pp. 1357-64.

[41]See p. 106, footnote 29. A recent article by P. C. Mathew, formerly a senior official of India's Ministry of Labour, summarizes available unemployment data, with more or less the same conclusion as in the text above, and offers specific suggestions for remedying the measurement problem. See his "Special Article" on unemployment in *Indian Labour Journal*, Vol. 10, No. 7 (July, 1969), pp. 863–72.

interpretation of the balance between growth of labor supply and of the Indian economy's capacity to make effective use of it.

In Table 17, Column (1) minus column (2) provides some measure of the growth of employment. At best this concept cannot be precise in a nation where at least 70 percent of the work force is not remunerated regularly on a wage payment basis. Labor rewards are often at least partially in kind. For small enterprises, including those in agriculture, returns to labor are not separable from entrepreneurial profits. This measure of employment grew about 1 percent each year over the first decade of planning, 1951–61. The rate for the second decade shown in Table 17 increased to some degree, but this last increase encompasses employment expectations of the 1966 draft plan with its very optimistic projections of growth. On the whole, employment seems to have grown at a rate well below that which was assumed for the first three plans. The unemployment ratios of Table 17 [column (3)] evidence a gap in labor utilization that has widened over the past plans, although the rate may be diminishing. If Table 17 does portray the general trends of the past — and the evidence seems to provide no better alternative — the forces for balance between national supply and demand for labor are not strong. India's prime policy for labor use — derived demand associated with the relationship between the supply of capital and of labor — may need to be further supplemented with additional employment programs.

The employment measured in the difference between column (1) and column (2) of Table 17 also encompasses underemployment. This may not be readily distinguishable from employment in those important sectors where output productivity of entire family units is low. In this situation some workers contribute less to total product than they consume. Some might even be able to leave the family enterprise without any appreciable effect on its total product. Among the underemployed are those who actually want to undertake additional work; but many, perhaps most, are not aware that their product is appreciably below other workers' in the enterprise. From such characterizations, varied definitions have been ventured for this concept in an attempt to make it measurable. However elusive, the phenomenon is real, and its existence may be important in the national development effort. In India's official documents, underemployment has been taken to be more extensive in rural areas than the overt unemployment we discussed earlier. Thus the third plan suggests it might have been "of the order of fifteen to eighteen million" in 1961.[42] And the direct employment efforts of all the plans, we indicated in Chapter 3, were as much concerned with additional use of this part of the work force as with new employment as such.

No comprehensive record is available on the employment directly created by India's action in this area. Direct employment activity was a limited policy at best. Statements have often been made about its potential and its importance, not least of all in the plan documents themselves, as we noted earlier. But actual results on any broad basis were always disappointing and the explanation invariably points to the absence of appropriate determination and leadership.[43] The scope for such direct additional employment in rural India might well be of the order of two to three million persons per year, apart from the new employment created under the main program efforts above. Targets in excess of the unemployment totals of column (2), Table 17 may be appropriate, for these programs seek also to reduce the extent of underemployment, which is not reflected in that column. There are many "successful" rural programs which demonstrate the potential of direct employment policies. In a program relevant to the present context, six villages in Raipur District (Madhya Pradesh) achieved very large expansions in total output on small farms over a five-year period. Labor use increased three-fold apart from the additional man-hours of the small landowners themselves. Wage rates more than doubled. Non-labor inputs in these villages parallel their availabilities in hundreds of nearby villages. Organization and will were the essential elements in the actual accomplishment.[44]

Finally, with regard to the programs directed at up-grading quality of labor, there has been notable achievement in expanding edu-

---

[42]See also *Fourth Plan*, 1966 draft, p. 110. For two surveys that show underemployment at least at the 10 percent level, see J.P. Bhattachargeè, "Unemployment among Indian Farmers: An Analysis of its Nature and Extent Based on Data for Bihar," *Artha Vijnana*, September, 1961, pp. 246–79; and S. Mehra, "Surplus Labour in Indian Agriculture," *The Indian Economic Review*, April, 1966, pp. 111–29. See also below, pp. 153–54.

[43]Above, pp. 72–73 and 106–7. For a broad appraisal of the potential for such use of labor, see V.M. Dandekar, "Utilization of Rural Manpower," *The Economic Weekly*, Vol. 14 (February, 1962), pp. 267–76.

[44]Martin E. Abel, "Agriculture in India in the 1970's," *E.P.W.*, Vol. 5, No. 13 (March 28, 1970), pp. A-5–A-14. See also B.D. Shastry, "Quickening the Pace in Village Improvement," Intensive Agricultural District Programme, Ministry of Food, Agriculture, Community Development, and Cooperation, New Delhi, July, 1969.

cation and skills, less in assuring their use. Description and analysis of the programs are available in official documents.[45] The Constitution of India called for free and compulsory education for all children through age fourteen within a decade. This was optimistic; however, in some two decades (by 1968/69), 63 percent of children in that age category were actually enrolled; and this is an impressive expansion. Children's education made more progress in urban than in rural areas, particularly among males. There have been the familiar lags among disadvantaged classes and in such states as Bihar and Rajasthan where educational facilities were long backward. India's university and college enrollments increased by 200,000 during each of the first two plans and by 500,000 during the third; almost 1,000,000 students are to be added in the new fourth plan. From a current ratio of 2.5 percent of all those in the 17-23 age group, enrollment may exceed 3.5 percent over the next five years. University enrollments have increasingly been in science subjects — from about 20 percent of the total in the 1950's to almost 40 percent in 1968/69. Important too is the pronounced growth in technical training facilities: for craftsmen through practical and systematic experience in industry, for laboratory technicians in school-and-work programs, for management in special institutions that expose students to the actual problems of enterprises in a modernizing society.

Even with this new applied emphasis in preparing people for the tasks of economic development, India today still experiences serious unemployment among the educated. This problem was pointed up in early surveys; it continues to be acute.[46] The results of the fourteenth round of the National Sample Survey are shown in Table 18. The pattern is generally that of the earlier date, but intensified. And recent official statements again attest to the persistence of this problem: most of the unemployed have education "ranging from the middle courses in schools to the first or second year at college."[47] Are the educated unemployed improperly educated, without enough practical experience to cope with productive activities of a modern

---

[45]G.O.I., *Report of Education Commission 1964–66*, 1966, and *Fourth Plan*, 1969 draft, pp. 278–300.

[46]A summary statement is available in Wilfred Malenbaum, "Urban Unemployment in India," *Pacific Affairs*, Vol. 30, No. 2 (June, 1957), pp. 138–50. "In the very large cities (in the early 1950's) 27.9 percent of the *unemployed* are matriculates or more . . . (the) more educated have been longer unemployed . . ." *Ibid.*, pp. 145–46.

[47]See *Third Plan*, pp. 165–66.

TABLE 18.   Educational Status of India's Labor Force, 1958/59

Educational Status	Gainfully Employed (%)	Unemployed (%)
Illiterate	42.58	57.88
Literate below matric	45.59	23.74
Matric and higher	11.65	18.38
	100.00[a]	100.00

[a]Figures do not add to exactly 100.00 because some of the gainfully employed would not provide status data.

Source: G.O.I. National Sample Survey, No. 14, 1960.

economy, or was the growth in demand for their services more limited than expected?

Perhaps many of India's educated, so predominantly arts majors, are still inadequately prepared for the skilled tasks of the modern technologically-oriented world. But there has also been limited employment demand in India for trained engineers, scientists, and even skilled craftsmen. Recently fewer people have sought training in the large programs for agricultural and veterinary specialties, and for engineering too. The economic reversals of the 1966-69 interplan years have taken a high toll in employment opportunities; they have discouraged new trainees.[48] Yet there can be no doubt that basic technical skills for the modernization effort are in short supply. Temporary imbalances may be inevitable in the demand and supply of new special skills in a developing nation. But official policy toward the role of labor in India's development has aggravated these possibilities. The assumption has been that additional employment of labor in India is contingent upon additional capital creation: labor's is a derived demand.

This is not so in a land where more output can be obtained through additional labor plus imaginative and committed leadership, through skilled labor convinced of the importance of its role in the developing nation and society. Such sparks are ignited only when government is convinced that larger labor inputs can of themselves contribute to expansion in some sectors of the economy, that skilled and educated workers can accelerate the speed with which dynamic change replaces stagnant traditionalism in these sectors.

---

[48]The relevant interplan experience is discussed in the *Fourth Plan,* 1969 draft, pp. 341–44.

This is precisely what some of the plans did envisage, although their programs were not in very specific terms.[49] Government cannot be too explicit about its determination that opportunities for advancement of workers in these sectors, and especially for educated workers the expectations and aspiartions of a modernizing world.[51] intensive tasks in the total development effort.[50] Such a presentation of labor's key role is not found in the plans. Special programs notwithstanding, the demand for labor continues to be judged relative to the installation of new capital. This is true even in the official programs for improvement of labor quality through education and skill development. Somehow these fall short of imparting to Indian workers the expectations and aspirations of a modernizing world.[51]

In sum, India's preoccupation with capital *and* labor as physically-balanced inputs of the growth process has been costly. The nation suffered deficiencies of demand, especially marked in the past four to five years. Where there were drive and enthusiasm among workers (e.g., the Raipur illustration), there were large gains in output. This could have happened broadly — more output, more investment and more consumption as well as more employment. Indeed, persistent underuse of labor and persistent unemployment in a nation like India always have adverse influence on total output. India needs effective demand from its millions of workers and their families. Employment policy in the past did not serve these objectives well.

Planning in India has become increasingly concerned with impediments to plan implementation. There is growing awareness of the absence of adequate regulating mechanisms for the tasks of growth. Decision-making centers are needed over a wide range of public and private activities. And there must be some arrangement for efficient cumulation of these decisions into the total program. The regulating problem is visualized at the institutional level (ministries, corporations, cooperatives, panchayats) and at the individual level (plant managers in public enterprise, big entrepreneurs in private enterprise, small businessmen, farmers). While the plans have begun to discuss these tasks of regulation and implementation, both in their private and their public dimensions, they have yet to offer a comprehensive program for efficient and imaginative use of

---

[49]*Third Plan*, pp. 163–67, 174–77.

[50]For a systematic analysis of such needs and possibilities see Wilfred Malenbaum, "Government, Entrepreneurship, and Economic Growth in Poor Lands," *World Politics*, Vol. 19 (October, 1966), pp. 52–68.

[51]See John Vaizey *et. al., The Economics of Educational Costing (I)*, (Lisbon: Center of Economics and Finance, Gulbenkian Institute of Science, 1968), pp. 63–82.

the labor force. Again, labor is considered an input dependent upon, and mostly *technically* related to, capital inputs. It is not viewed as a key element of the regulating mechanisms that govern capital and other inputs.

Factor Inputs and National Growth

Economists no longer expect that analysis of the changes in the classic economic inputs — capital and labor — can provide a more or less complete understanding of the changes in national output over a period of years. What is variously termed "the unexplained residual," the "area of ignorance," or the "productivity factor" has in the past decade or so become an integral element of growth doctrine. This new factor does measure changes in productivity of capital and labor inputs, but its very status as a residual means that its statistical relationship to growth in the supply of capital and labor is *not* straightforward. It is not an index of *technological progress* alone; it also encompasses changes in *entrepreneurial and motivational* attributes of the work force and in the *organizational efficiency* with which resources are combined in the productive activities of the economy.

The emergence of this new factor is thus a striking manifestation of the importance of human transformation along with structural transformation in the development process. Moreover the new factor is responsible for the important proposition that underutilized resources and persistent imbalances in an economy are major deterrents to its forward progress.

Most of the relevant empirical work is based on analysis of data from the developed lands. Primarily these are the sources for "unexplained residuals" of 50 percent and more of the total change in economic output.[52] Data preclude comprehensive analysis in developing lands. Still, the limited evidence yet available suggests different results. For periods a decade and longer, total productivity gains encounter difficulties in effective resource use.[53] Despite progress in modernization of equipment and skills, problems of entrepre-

---

[52]R.R. Nelson provides an excellent summary of the current doctrine, the orders of magnitude in the context of U.S. growth experience, and the pioneer contributions of scholars (notably Abramowitz, Arrow, Denison, and Solow). See his "Aggregate Production Functions," *AER*, Vol. 54, No. 5 (September, 1964), pp. 577–90.

[53]Two pertinent references here are H.J. Bruton, "Productivity Growth in Latin America," *AER*, Vol. 57, No. 5, (December, 1967), pp. 1099–1116; and J.G. Williamson, "Dimensions of Postwar Philippine Economic Progress," *QJE*, Vol. 83, No. 1 (February, 1969), pp. 93–109.

neurship, motivation, and organization tend to offset the important productivity benefits. Changes in supply of capital and labor alone more nearly account for changes in output. Technical progress is impeded; its gains are in some measure lost.

How might all this bear upon output expansion from India's growth in capital and labor inputs, coupled with persistent modernization of the capital stock and with greater skills and sophistication of the work force? We have not been able to present systematic accounts for capital or labor, despite the importance attached to these inputs — and particularly to capital — in official development schemes. The following discussion is therefore very general by necessity.

Over the 15 years of the first three plans, India's capital plant more than doubled; net capital stock thus grew at an average rate of about 5 percent per year. Comparable figures for labor supply are 26 percent and 1.6 percent respectively. If we divide capital and labor shares in Indian national income in the ratio of 40:60, our basic factor inputs alone can be considered the source of a national product growth of 3 percent per year. Since actual output growth averaged 4 percent per year, total factor productivity must have expanded at an annual rate of 1 percent.[54] This "unexplained residual" thus amounts to 25 percent of total change — a factor productivity gain about half as important relatively as that in advanced lands. And this low level of performance reflects the importance of problems of economic motivation and integration. Relatively high levels of capital growth were not accompanied by the human capacity to use the new material inputs fully. Moreover, the time patterns of input and output growth suggest a declining level of total factor productivity in the 1960's as compared with the earlier decade. Where the residual factors grow on the average by 1.2 percent per year (28.5 percent of total product growth) in the first two plans, the corresponding measures for 1961–66 are 0.65 percent per year and 16.5 percent of total product growth. These results are parallelled in the developments recently analyzed in the Philippines and a number of Latin American lands.[55]

As we indicate in our analysis of the output record, actual growth of India's total product turned out to be below what was planned.

[54]These computations use net capital data and labor force data from Tables 12 and 17 above. For output data, see Table 19. An estimate of capital stock in 1950/51 at 1.7 times the level of the national product in that year was also used. For derivation of results, see R.R. Nelson, *op. cit.*
[55]J. G. Williamson, *op. cit.*; H. J. Bruton, *op. cit.*

Indeed the first three plans seem to show progressively less expansion in output relative to inputs and relative to official expectations for growth in output. Moreover our analysis suggests larger increments in capital stock than were anticipated in these plans, and probably smaller additions to employment. Incremental capital-labor ratios in India's economy would therefore have exceeded what the plans envisaged. Plan arguments would thus anticipate *larger* output gains from the more capital-intensive effort as well as some tendency for the employment lag to decline more rapidly than in the plans. Neither of these is yet manifest. The record of inputs in the Indian economy, over the first three plans at least, thus testifies to a shortage in those factors of production beyond capital supply and labor supply.

We have noted the growing attention given this problem in the recent plans. But new human dimensions are neither readily planned nor achieved. Education and training are inevitably involved, as are public policies to identify the people of a poor land with programs and processes that promise greater individual well-being. Social scientists search for more predictable means for achieving such human transformations. We have mentioned scientific endeavors to generate achievement motivation ("n-Ach"). There are some suggestive, preliminary results on the significance of health programs in poor areas for easing the transitional path, for making the typical poor-nation self-employed worker aware of his own role in the economic status of himself and his dependents.[56] Such programs may well offer promise.

The initial five-year plan counted heavily upon India's release from colonialism as a force for implanting in the individual a sense of responsibility for his own and the new nation's accomplishments. However thrilling this expectation of release for man's innate aspirations, it made few demands upon national program or effort: Indians were simply to respond to their new opportunity. But the Planning Commission was more prosaic in the second plan. "Generally speaking the people are willing to shoulder greater burdens if they feel assured that the resources raised by the Government will be utilized with economy and efficiency, and there will be no wastage."[57] This proposition assumes considerable popular sophistica-

---

[56]Thus see Wilfred Malenbaum, "Health and Productivity in Poor Areas," in H.E. Klarman with H.H. Jaszi, eds., *Empirical Studies in Health Economics,* (Baltimore: Johns Hopkins University Press, 1970), pp. 31–54.

[57]*Second Plan,* p. 132.

tion. Unhappily, this transference to public sector behavior of the responsibility for integration of human and physical change could scarcely solve the problem of popular incentives. This was acknowledged in the third plan. The public sector would scarcely document its own inefficiency; but it did recognize ". . . that the possibility of full involvement of the people in the process of change and growth are not being realized to a sufficient degree."[58] For, ". . . in the last analysis the Plan rests on the belief that the requisite effort will be forthcoming and that, at each level in the national life within the limits of human endeavor, an attempt will be made to implement it with the utmost efficiency. Of the many assumptions on which a Five-Year Plan is based, this is not only the most important but also the most difficult."[59]

These are strong words, for there is little basis for assuming that private actions will be directed to the type of objective and program embodied in the plan. Moreover, even if there was motivation to common objectives, there is no assurance that the operational units would know how to achieve "utmost efficiency." The plans do not assess the alternative opportunities that beckon the leaders of large-scale private enterprise: the opportunities to meet consumption requirements for high-income groups, to use the foreign exchange and the capital allocation mechanisms for private gain rather than for national economic advancement. Business leaders could operate with "utmost efficiency" but not necessarily toward plan objectives. On the other side are the millions of small entrepreneurs with lesser managerial skills. Their productive activities are often highly subsistence-oriented and their ties to national goals not readily delineated. The plans present little program substance as to how the talents for optimizing can be instilled and how the people can be oriented to plan achievement.[60]

To date, therefore, the plans have not come up with a specific action program that offers promise for requisite human transformation along some predictable lines. However, they now place greater

---

[58]*Third Plan*, p. 291.

[59]*Ibid.*, p. 276.

[60]The 1966 draft of the fourth plan was explicit that "attitudes and behaviour patterns have to change for meeting the needs of our developing economy . . . the changes have to be such as to maximise work efficiency, savings, and resource mobilization. They must motivate and move the people in the direction of economic development." *Fourth Plan*, 1966 draft, p. 30. The plan calls for specific measures in terms of policies, machinery, and communication to attain these objectives. But these programs are not explicit in the draft, and that version of the fourth plan was not implemented. See also below, pp. 221-23.

emphasis on *public* action for effective national economic operation. Clearly ". . . administrative machinery and procedures as well as managerial functions at all levels have to be geared to the basic economic and social tasks" confronting India today.[61] Professor D.R. Gadgil, operating head of the restructured Planning Commission from 1967 through early 1971, has long attributed India's difficulties in plan implementation to its neglect of the regulating mechanism that would bring actual goal achievement from a plan of labor and capital inputs. The 1969 fourth plan addresses this need from its first pages: ". . . the Centre and States . . . must have greater command over the economic resources of the country."[62] More broadly, "all strategic economic decisions are (to be) made by agencies informed with social purpose."[63] While these statements seem to imply a shift toward expanded governmental control of economic activity, the plan does rationalize a decentralized decision system involving cooperative and private profit-making enterprises as well as public administration and enterprise. We shall say more on this later; here we need but observe that the planners did feel strongly that a technologically-balanced array of inputs and outputs is but one phase of the plan effort. A new input is required: the human machinery to make decisions on actual use of other inputs.

Articulation of input-output tables or of a comprehensive system of material balances does of course provide the structure of interdependence for all enterprise, both private and public.[64] These show total output and its use for the entire range of final and intermediate purposes. But the data (even for past years) are approximations, since requisite detail is not available for many parts of the economy. In some measure, the figures are derived from the more complete information for the same types of enterprise in developed lands — the United States, for instance. And the patterns, for future years especially, are closer to being "right" in an engineering and technological sense. They provide only a partial guide to what each sector, including its public enterprise components, will in fact do under the actual circumstances of the plan years.

How can these flows of goods and services actually be achieved?

---

[61]*Fourth Plan*, 1966 draft, p. 21.
[62]*Fourth Plan*, 1969 draft, p. 9.
[63]*Ibid.*, p. 25.
[64]As indicated in the previous chapter, such devices are implicit in recent plans; they are explicit in *MFB*, pp. 39-80 and (appendix) Charts for 1964/65, 1970/71, and 1975/76. These tables were part of the underpinnings of the 1966 draft fourth plan.

Government might attempt to make them happen through a comprehensive system of controls on private individual actions (allocation, rationing) plus major direct participation by government itself as purchaser, provider, seller. Some such characteristics may describe what has been taking place in Mainland China, or Cuba, or to a degree, the USSR. At the other extreme is a market mechanism. In today's poor countries the latter probably could not achieve stipulated plan goals; at the least, government would need to take special action to assure supplies of foreign exchange or of such key products as foodgrains, steel, cement, and fuel. Perhaps no poor country now permits an essentially free market economy. More usual, as in the case of India — a nation that eschews totalitarian controls — the public sector produces and disposes of certain goods and services (some transportation, power, and steel, to cite a few; and even these may need to compete with comparable private output). Most of the economy lives with market decisions, although there are some central restrictions on use of capital, perhaps, or of foreign exchange. Neither doctrine on controls nor actual experience can yet prescribe those specific combinations of private and public actions that most nearly assure plan achievement.

The answer requires analysis of the experience of the economy; particularly it requires some careful research investigation of India's (and other nations') actual development experience. It will take study of the supply elasticities of public, private, and joint ventures in many fields. Such analysis needs to encompass systematic examination of supply behavior of small agriculturists who still dominate supply and who operate with a high subsistence orientation and a high ratio of non-monetized transactions. The objective must always be greater understanding of the forces that influence the actual decisions on what to produce in many sectors of the nation. Without a larger body of applied knowledge on the economics of enterprise, the right regulating mechanism will be impossible to create.

We have a record of familiar inputs in this chapter and of outputs in the next; we see the persistent and growing official concern about the tasks of plan implementation.[65] Both are testimony to the lim-

---

[65]Through 1968/69, official plan "investment targets in the private sectors were broadly achieved or even exceeded, but the investment pattern varied greatly from Plan priorities. While larger capacities than needed were set up in certain industries, there were sizeable shortfalls in important basic industries like fertilizers, aluminum, cement, and agricultural tractors." This statement was put before an industry advisory group in New Delhi in late September, 1969, when the Planning Commission was presenting its current views (as above, pp. 116–17) on the need for regulating mechanisms in India's plans.

ited state of India's knowledge about additional input factors of the growth process — those that convert paper plans into actual development. In particular the official approach to labor inputs needs to recognize labor as the carrier of new attitudes for dynamic change, rather than the handmaiden of additional capital inputs. There is an urgent need for major research and analysis on how the present economic output system reaches decisions on production and use.

After two decades of modern planning, of large capital investment and foreign assistance, India's development record points to better labor use and improved economic research as basic determinants of India's future economic expansion. Modern growth is featured by high "productivity factors," large "unexplained residuals." India has yet to benefit from these fundamental relationships.

Twenty Years of Development Experience: Agriculture, Total Output **5**

Decades of Achievement

In the year preceding April 1, 1969, the last year before the beginning of India's fourth plan, national product was Rs 28585 crores, 80 percent and more above the comparable product of 1950/51, before India's development plans. At this level per capita income before the fourth plan was roughly one-third higher than in 1950/51. Perhaps the record of output can be more systematically presented if we consider the achievement through 1965/66, the final year of the last completed five-year plan, without the three inter-plan years preceding the present program. In 1965/66 the Indian economy generated a national product in real terms more than 60 percent above that of 1950/51. In that interval total population increased by over 135,000,000 persons. Yet, for this larger population, real income in 1965/66 was about 30 percent more per person than it was for the smaller population in 1950/51. Persistent expansion by 1.75 percent each year in per capita terms is impressive — and especially so for the beginning years of organized development activity in a country which has long been very poor. Indeed this rate of progress compares well with long-term growth records of the past in today's rich lands.[1]

India's growth record as a nation stands in marked contrast to the record of India during the two decades before independence. From 1925 more or less to the establishment of a sovereign state in 1947, output and population tended to grow together: there was no real progress in average income. The first quarter of the century, however, does seem to show evidence of steady growth in per capita product, although at a rate well below the average of the plan years.[2] In other words, spurts of progress over a decade or two in the past scarcely meant that India had embarked upon a course of continuous expansion. As we noted in Chapter 2, the long-period record for the century up to independence averages insignificant gains in annual per capita income, and this while India's population was growing at a relatively slow rate.

In truth the trend in output over the plan years is in itself not a decisive one. Growth through the end of the third plan was dominated by performance in the decade of the 1950's. Thereafter, real product per capita in 1965/66 was not significantly different from that in 1960/61. National product in 1965/66 did suffer the largest setback of any single year since independence, a real decline of almost 6 percent (more than 8 percent in per capita terms) from the record levels of 1964/65. The years of interim plans, 1966/67 through 1968/69, do show a recovery, as noted above. In 1967/68 real output exceeded the previous peak in 1964/65, and there have been further increases since then, but in per capita terms the level of 1964/65 still remains a peak. Growth in the 1960's is thus very much the achievement of years of record harvests, notably 1964/65 and 1967/68. This accounting scarcely provides a picture of continuous and reinforcing growth over the period of the past plans.

Perhaps we are too close to the changing scene to read long-term growth significance into the output record of a nation seeking development anew in an economy dominated by agriculture and by the vicissitudes of weather. The growth position will become more clear as the fourth and later plan years pass. On the other hand, the sequence of plans forms a perspective that has shown continuing, and

---

[1]On the whole these countries showed growth rates which averaged between 13 and 19 percent per decade for 70 or more years. In most cases there was some tendency for decade growth rates per capita to expand from the early years of development. See Simon Kuznets, *Modern Economic Growth* (New Haven, Conn.: Yale University Press, 1965), pp. 63–72.

[2]The observations on the pre-independence record are from M. Mukherjee, "National Income," in V.B. Singh, *op. cit.* Recent statistics are primarily from the G.O.I., *Economic Survey 1969-70,* March, 1970.

even accelerating, rates of output growth. Behind this perspective were input patterns for change, carefully created within the economy to achieve such growth. Development actions were directed toward altering the structure of the economy in terms of its capital plant and its human skills, as well as in terms of its actual product. The programs sought to increase internal interdependence in the economy and to expand output relative to inputs. An appraisal of performance at this stage of Indian development must be concerned with internal changes in structure and in efficiency as well as with the level and pattern of output. Consideration has already been given to some of these in the preceding chapter, where we discussed actual new investment and employment over the first three plans. Before we turn to the relationship of these inputs to the major components of India's product, we summarize some main and familiar evidences of India's progress. These all come from official publications; the plan documents present most of this material in much fuller detail.

We would expect from the 30 percent expansion in per capita product that average living levels have improved.[3] Thus average caloric intake in recent years exceeded 2000 calories per day, as against some 1750 in 1950/51.[4] This average level of food consumption seems to have withstood the agricultural setbacks of recent years, thanks to public effort in food distribution and of course to heavy imports of foodgrains. More food and expanded health programs have been important factors in extending life expectancy at birth to 52 years, which is probably 50 percent greater than it was at independence. Greater school enrollment and adult education activities have reduced illiteracy to approximately 80 percent from 90 percent two decades back. Then 40,000,000 persons could read or write in some language; today, perhaps 100,000,000 may be able to do so. No simple generalization is possible with respect to housing and associated water and sanitation, but the evidence is that new

---

[3]When account is taken of higher domestic savings ratios and expansion in current public expenditures not directly related to individual consumption (*e.g.*, for military purposes), perhaps two-thirds (about 20 percent) of the increase in product per capita reflects the growth in real consumption. This is consistent with the findings of the G.O.I., *Report of the Committee on Distribution of Income and Levels of Living* (the "Mahalanobis Report"), Part I, February, 1964, pp. 4–7. See also M. Mukherjee and G.S. Chatterjee, "Deflation of Private Consumption Expenditure," *EPW*, September 7, 1968, pp. 1373–80.

[4]The 12 to 13 percent increase in caloric intake and a 20 percent increase in real consumption expenditure (both private and by government) provide a plausible index for the income elasticity of foodstuffs, about 0.63.

installations have not kept abreast of population and family growth. Measures of space per capita in urban housing indicate a decline of at least 20 percent between 1951 and 1966.[5] Housing expenditures average some 3 percent of total consumer expenditures per year in India so that the decline here has limited effect on the over-all improvement in the average level of living. However, deterioration characterizes the housing situation in rural India and in the growing slum areas of the large cities.

It is here, where we deal with the average improvement in the well-being of India's five hundred and more millions of people, that some observations are needed on the distributional aspects of income growth. Two facts are clear. India's national averages encompass significant regional differences — real differences in all probability. Also, any regional figure, as the figure for the nation, is a composite of wide differences at the personal and family income level. For states, firm data are only now becoming available from current research. Among India's 17 states (excluding Delhi and other Union Territories) per capita incomes in 1955/56 showed a range of more than 2:1, with West Bengal and Bihar at the top and bottom extremes respectively. All the states together showed roughly a 20 percent average deviation about the national per capita figure, and this degree of variation seems to have persisted at least through 1960/61.[6] On the other hand there are also data which suggest some *narrowing* of the spread among regions with respect to average value of output per acre[7] and with respect to per capita use of industrial power.[8] These results are essentially for the decade of the 1950's. Together these facts tell us that we have much to learn about trends in state income distributions. Yet, the fact of regional differences has been accepted by the government of India; the new fourth plan actually makes provision for allocating a share (10 percent) of central assistance to state development plans on the basis of "their per capita income if below the national average."[9] We can anticipate increasing refinement in the measures of state income.

---

[5]Shanti S. Tangri, "Urban Growth, Housing, and Economic Development: The Case of India," *Asian Survey*, Vol. 8, No. 7 (July, 1968), pp. 519–38.

[6]These observations on state incomes are from Mahinder D. Choudry, *Regional Income Accounting in an Underdeveloped Economy: A Case Study of India* (Calcutta: 1966), pp. 45–53. The estimates are most tentative and preliminary.

[7]A.W. Heston, *op. cit.*, pp. 174–87.

[8]P.N. Dhar and D.U. Sastry, "Inter-State Variations in Industry; 1951–61," *EPW*, March 22, 1969, pp. 535–38.

[9]For the draft (1969) plan, this 10 percent involves Rs 350 crores, and this of course provides pressure for additional research on the levels of state incomes. See *Fourth Plan,* 1969 draft, especially pp. 54–59.

There is more definitive information for the distribution of income and expenditures among families and individuals. The low income 40 percent of all consumers is responsible for only 20 percent of total consumption; the high income 20 percent for 40 percent of total consumption.[10] With mean monthly per capita consumption in rural India at Rs 22, the bottom decile averaged but 35 percent of that figure. Comparable urban data are Rs 33 and 28 percent.[11] There is no clear evidence of a narrowing of this distribution, despite national planning goals to that end. The Mahalanobis Report in 1964 was categoric on this conclusion; it was less certain of the proposition that consumption differences were not widening.[12] Even in 1969 greater income equality in India could not be reported by the Planning Commission.[13]

The weight of evidence suggests growing inequality among persons and families. Thus rural hunger may have increased in the third plan as compared with earlier years. In any event there is some evidence that the percentage of the rural population with actual food consumption levels at least 25 percent below a stipulated standard level has been growing, from less than 35 percent at the end of the second plan to more than 40 percent in the early 1960's.[14] India has made efforts to assure at least minimum food supplies to all. In recent years a rationing system encompassed nearly 240,000,000 of India's 510,000,000 persons; it included a network of about 140,000 fair price or ration shops. Consumer subsidies were well in excess of one billion rupees annually. With respect to inequalities we also note that India's industrial production of high income consumer goods (passenger cars, refrigerators, air conditioners) grew much more rapidly during the plans than did output of goods for use by the middle income class (bicycles, electric fans, sewing machines) or of mass consumption

---

[10]Data from N.S.S. Round No. 22, July, 1967–June, 1968, as reported in the *Fourth Plan*, 1969 draft, p. 33.

[11]Prices are higher in the urban areas. Data are from the N.S.S. Round No. 18, February, 1963–January, 1964.

[12]The Mahalanobis Report, pp. 4–7.

[13]*Fourth Plan*, 1969 draft, p. 8. Persistent inequality has not brought gains to the economy through an expanding rate of domestic savings. Indeed we noted an estimated rate of 8 percent of national income in 1967/68 as against 10 percent in the early 1960's. See Chapter 4, p. 101.

[14]The percentage of hungry declined in the record crop year 1964/65 but presumably expanded thereafter. See S.S. Madalgi, "Hunger in Rural India," *EPW*, Annual Number, 1968, pp. 61–68. The intensity of rural hunger seems to have been greater in Andhra Pradesh, Bihar, Kerala, and Uttar Pradesh than elsewhere. These states ranged well below the average in the regional distribution of per capita incomes.

goods (soap, kerosene, cotton piece goods).[15] Finally the number of individuals assessed for income tax more than doubled between 1956/57, and 1963/64, again suggesting a differential growth in personal income on the part of those who already had high incomes.[16]

This digression on distribution of income is meant to be suggestive rather than definitive. Only new research results can throw clear light on the complex and diffuse situation. In total there is little support for the proposition that inequalities are narrowing in India; the opposite possibility, that the personal income distribution is widening, finds stronger support. Still, there has been no unequivocal identification of any specific low-income group (of significant size) where average real consumption declined over the sequence of plans.[17]

The gains in the average well-being of the Indian people is a measurable consequence of many major developmental activities. Thus the number of children in schools more than tripled between 1950/51 (23,500,000) and 1967/68 (70,100,000). Currently over 80 percent of all children aged 6 to 11 are registered in primary grades, although this ratio differs significantly among states. There has been a dramatic growth in the numbers of schools and teachers; greater quantity is now of less concern than is progress in the quality of teaching and teaching facilities. Still more rapid growth has taken place in technical training — especially for engineers, where numbers now exceed four times their level in the pre-plan years. In the health area, hospitals, beds, doctors, and the facilities for medical training have more than doubled. Doctors actually in medical practice have kept abreast of population growth: today's ratio of

---

[15]G.O.I., *Statistical Abstract of the Indian Union*, 1967, pp. 118–34. Broadly, mass consumption goods increased by less than 50 percent from the first plan years to the third plan years; middle-income and high-income consumption goods, by about 100 percent and more, respectively.

[16]James Cutt, *Taxation and Economic Development in India*, (New York: Frederick A. Praeger, 1969), p. 90. However, the expansion is probably less significant than the limited proportion of the total population subject to (individual) personal income tax (less than 1 percent of household heads in 1963/64).

[17]For a careful assessment of the forces for "gains and losses" in rural and urban India, see George Rosen, *Democracy and Economic Change in India*, (Berkeley: University of California Press, 1966), pp. 154–96.

A more recently published study explores the record from 1960/61 through 1967/68 and concludes that inequality has definitely increased over the years. See V.M. Dandekar and Nilakantha Rath, "Poverty in India," *EPW*, Vol. 6, No. 1 (January 2, 1971), pp. 25–48, and Vol. 6, No. 2 (January 9, 1971), pp. 106–46. This study was made by the Indian School of Political Economy, Poona, under contract from the Ford Foundation.

one for almost 6000 persons is essentially the same as in 1950/51, although the doctor shortage in most rural areas seems to have been aggravated. Numbers of students in medical schools have increased at a growing rate. There are about four times as many doctors in training as in the pre-plan years — and the promise is for a more favorable doctor-population ratio in the future.

Since independence India's agriculture has benefitted from a wide range of programs aimed at expanded output and particularly at higher productivity. While more and improved irrigation, fertilizers, and seeds have constituted the major physical inputs of these efforts, the national objective is steady improvement in the conduct of farm enterprise. We look at actual development in agriculture later in this chapter. Here we mention the rapid growth in use of some major physical inputs. By 1968/69 there were actually about 45,000,000 acres in large schemes for storage and distribution of surface water for agriculture, as against 24,000,000 in 1950/51. Minor irrigation schemes, involving primary tubewells and pump-sets for groundwater, also added some 20,000,000 acres to an original 27,000,000 over the same time interval. The number of tubewells, usually privately owned, increased more than ten times. More than one million pumpsets may now be in operation, as against 150,000 in 1960/61. More and more of India's irrigation sets are electrically controlled; because of limited rural electrification, there were less than 20,000 electrically controlled sets in 1950/51. Today almost one-fifth of India's villages have electricity. Production and use of improved seed varieties became important in national policy during the second plan years, and seed farms multiplied. Hybridization techniques were introduced in 1960 and took hold during the third plan. Mexican wheat and exotic paddy seeds are responding well to improved cultivation, assured water, and adequate fertilizer. They hold the key to India's new agriculture. More than half the *additional* output in the new plan is expected from the relatively small percentage of total grain area under the "miracle" varieties.

The achievement of agriculture in food and raw material production is dwarfed by the expansion and diversification of modern industry. The index of industrial production, predominantly "big industry" production, was, in 1966, 160 percent above its 1951 level. It increased by an average of more than 7 percent annually over the decade through 1966. And the composition of output changed markedly. The major industries during the colonial period, textiles and food processing, have in recent decades lost relative importance to steel, chemicals, engineering, and electrical goods — basic non-consumer goods industries growing at a much more rapid rate. As measured by value added, their output has caught up to the consumer industries. Today India produces a wide variety of modern industrial products for Indian consumers, for Indian industries, and for India's export markets. The ratio of modern industrial production entering export trade is a multiple of its (very low) level in the beginning of the plan period. Industrial output encompasses complicated machine tools, heavy electrical equipment, and power transmission lines which now are sold throughout the world; in some measure it also reflects expansion in output of sewing machines and bicycles — testimony to the vigor of India's modern small-scale industry. Special mention might be made of the growth of manufactured products like locomotives for India's railways, power transformers for India's multipurposes projects, and power-driven pumps for tubewells, and the rapid expansion of the production of the chemicals needed in Indian agriculture. Thus from limited output of nitrogenous fertilizer (9000 tons, N) in 1950/51, production has increased more than 25 times to some 230,000 tons in 1965/66. Comparable figures for sulphuric acid are 100,000 and 660,000 tons respectively. In industry, new production serves the entire range of India's modernization.

Finally, there has been marked expansion in the overhead sector of the economy. This is reflected in railway freight tonnage that more than doubled since 1950. There are more than 300,000 trucks and commercial vehicles now, almost three times as many as in 1950/51. The relatively long lag in the use of highways for goods movement seems to be disappearing: the volume of goods moved over India's expanded highway network in 1965/66 is six times the volume moved in 1950/51. Internal communication was eased through a great increase in telephones in service — more than a fourfold expansion, with roughly parallel increases in all telecommunications and cable facilities. In energy, installed capacity of 2,300,000 k w of electric power in 1950/51 grew to more than 10,000,000 k w in 1965/66. Today there is electricity in about 20 percent of India's villages and towns, in contrast to less than 1 percent in the pre-planning years.

These continuing achievements have brought a new face to the Indian economy. Where modern, large-scale manufacturing enterprises (including power and mining) provided about 6 percent of India's domestic product in 1950/51, their relative importance is now at least 50 percent higher, or almost 10 percent of domestic product. Agriculture and associated activities, formerly responsible for more than half the national output (55 percent in 1950/51) did decline somewhat in relative importance. This is true both for the favorable agricultural years 1964/65 and 1967/68 (some 47 percent) and for the adverse years 1965/66 and 1966/67 (43 percent).[18] Early official projections for 1970/71 indicated accelerated reductions in the relative share of this broad sector — to almost 40 percent.[19] Increasingly the total national effort has become more advanced technologically and more large-scale. New (net) investment in some recent years may have reached 14 percent of national product, about twice the pre-plan ratio. Almost 40 percent of this capital formation was in large modern industry, with perhaps 20 percent more in other modern enterprises.

Taken together the record of the first 20 years of planned development shows a real surge in output, with important shifts in the pattern of the economy's product. Per capita income did grow more than 30 percent on the average, but there has been no evidence of a narrowing of income inequalities. The contrary appears more true. Despite overall growth, actual gains in national product have declined progressively relative to official projections. Thus actual increments of total product as a ratio of planned increments are:

1951-56	1.48
1956-61	0.86
1961-66	0.40

Moreover, as we shall see, the pattern of output differed from expectation; the national output does not evidence increasing efficiency in factor use.

This is not a record of close correspondence with plans. Nonetheless, during the middle 1960's the government still projected persistent progress in essentially the old perspective for growth. Shortly after the end of the third plan in 1966, it released a comprehensive statistical tableau of an expanding economy from 1964/65, the last year for which data were available, through 1975/76, the final year in the original five-plan perspective. The growth rates

---

[18]These ratios are computed from Table 19, columns (2) and (3), p. 135 below. They are in 1960/61 prices. More relevant to the argument of the text are the ratios in *current* prices, reflecting the actual relative positions that prevailed in each year. Those ratios have departed little from 50 percent, in good or bad crop years. (See G.O.I., *Estimates of National Product*, October, 1967, p. 5, and subsequent national income releases.)

[19]In some contrast to the 50 percent now projected for 1973/74 (and 45 percent in 1980/81) in the *Fourth Plan*, 1969 draft, p. 36 (in 1967/68 prices).

would accelerate; investment ratios would expand; output per unit of factor input would grow.[20] These expectations from the perspective were in sharp contrast to what was happening under the original programs. The contrast is even greater with the decision a year or so later to proceed no further with formal conduct of the original fourth plan. It was by then apparent that past programs no longer had a meaningful relation to India's human and material resource position; for they were not eliciting appropriate economic responses from the economy. The twenty-year development effort was thus interrupted—temporarily at least—for new insights and new directions.

The Record of Total Growth

Statistics on actual growth of India's national product and of three major components are given in Table 19. The data from 1960/61 alone are available officially on a consistent and revised basis. All other data have been approximated from earlier official estimates prepared on another "constant-price" basis, and mostly in the older "conventional" form.[21] Despite the limited time sequence for which there are fully comparable data, some broad trends can be noted. First we make explicit what has been mentioned before: output performance was below plan expectation. Increases over the three successive plan periods were 18 percent, 21 percent, and 13 percent in contrast to the projected 11.2 percent, 25 percent, and 34 percent.[22] Except for the first plan, actual growth rates were less than those programmed. And the higher levels for 1955/56 provided a base for the new plan beginning in 1956. This cumulative aspect

---

[20]Thus see *MFB*, especially pp. 135-49.

[21]The "revised" series of national products became publicly available in August, 1967. With them came the shift to a 1960/61 base year, as against the 1948/49 base which had been used in the original conventional series, and the 1958/59 base used for preliminary work on the revised series. The revisions were primarily concerned with improvement of the conceptual basis of the data, as well as with the introduction of new source material which was in turn influenced especially by improved census data on labor. The large changes occurred in the less organized part of the economy, including agriculture and especially many service activities. For basic sources, see Table 19. An official revised series from 1950/51 is in preparation. Tiwari presents series in which the official estimates from 1960/61 for gross domestic product have been carried back to 1950/51 on a comparable basis. Presumably the official data will not depart significantly from these. Textual discussion here on the basis of the adapted data of Table 19 is consistent with the Tiwari series.

[22]As in Table 2, row 4.3, p. 59 above.

TABLE 19. Net National Product: Total and Major Originating Sectors[a]

	(1)	(2) Net national product (national income)		(3) Agriculture		(4) Modern industry[d]		(5) Trade transport services	
	Population								
	Index	Total	Index	Total	Index	Total	Index	Total	Index
1950/51	100	9325	100	5150	100	610	100	2510	100
1951/52	101.7	9400	102	5250	102	640	105	2620	104
1952/53	103.5	9775	105	5410	105	660	108	2715	108
1953/54	105.4	10325	111	5875	114	685	112	2790	111
1954/55	107.4	10625	114	5925	115	735	120	2890	115
1955/56	109.5	11000	118	5960	116	825	135	3020	120
Average growth rate, first plan	(1.7%)	(3.4%)		(3.0%)		(6.2%)		(3.7%)	
1956/57	111.7	11550	124	6125	119	895	147	3190	127
1957/58	114.0	11450	123	5925	115	945	155	3300	131
1958/59	116.4	12300	132	6450	125	970	159	3460	138
1959/60	118.7	12475	134	6375	124	1040	171	3640	145
1960/61	121.5	13294	143	6857	133	1215	199	3870	154
Average growth rate, second plan	(2.1%)	(3.9%)		(2.8%)		(8.1%)		(5.1%)	
1961/62	124.1	13763	148	6925	135	1320	216	4070	162
1962/63	127.2	14045	151	6747	131	1463	240	4280	170
1963/64	130.3	14845	159	6940	135	1610	264	4570	182
1964/65	133.5	15917	171	7558	147	1723	283	4880	194
1965/66	136.9	15021	161	6520	127	1777	291	5130	205
Average growth rate, third plan	(2.2%)	(2.2%)		(-0.9%)		(7.9%)		(5.8%)	
1966/67	140.0	15123	162	6442	125	1794	294	5265	210
1967/68[b]	143.5	16586	178	7629	148	1799	295	5453	218
1968/69[b]	147.0	16943	182	7558	147	1899	312	5700	228
Average growth rate, interplan years	(2.5%)	(4.1%)		(5.0%)		(2.2%)		(3.6%)	

[a]Rs crores, 1960/61 prices; index numbers, 1950/51 base
[b]Preliminary data
[c]Includes animal husbandry, forestry, and fishing
[d]Large scale manufacturing, electricity, gas and water plants.

Sources: Data from 1960/61 are *revised series* from CSO reports (G.O.I., *Estimates of National Product*, October, 1967; and August, 1970; comparable data released subsequently in G.O.I. *Economic Survey 1969/70*, 1970, pp. 62–64.) Data to 1960/61 are based primarily on official conventional estimates (1948/49 base) shifted to 1960/61 price level.

CHART 1.   National Income: Plan Projections
and Actuals (1960/61 Prices)

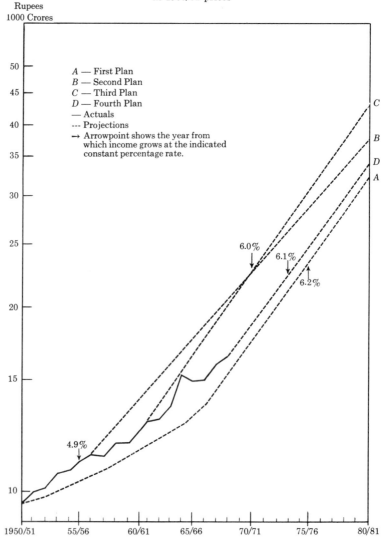

Plan Projections and Actuals
at 1960/61 prices

Source: *Fourth Plan*, 1969 draft, opposite p. 29.

emerges in the accompanying chart, presented by the Planning Commission in the 1969 draft fourth plan. Within each plan growth rates were to accelerate, at least over three or four five-year periods. The new fourth plan now uses a growth rate close to that of the

TABLE 20.   Projected National Income in 1970/71

	Rs crores[a]
First Plan	18190
Second Plan	23370
Third Plan	23540
Fourth Plan (1966 draft)	23900
Fourth Plan (1969 draft)	19200

[a]1960/61 prices

Source: *Fourth Plan*, 1969 draft, p. 46; *Fourth Plan*, 1966 draft, p. 61.

original plan perspective (D and A respectively, Chart 1). It is at a lower level than the second and third plans (B and C) and at a slower rate than the third. The effects of actual output developments may be measured in the alternative estimates of national income for 1970/71. As these are shown in Table 20, fourth plan projections are almost 20 percent below the 1970/71 output targets of earlier plans.[23]

The national output data can also be related to the actual investment statistics of the preceding chapter. For present purposes the simple relationships of new investment and of actual output change, all in 1960/61 prices, are compared to corresponding measures in each plan. Table 21 reveals the striking contrast between the plans' low (and possibly declining) ratios of average new capital per unit of new output [column (2)] and the increasing ratios of actual experience [column (1)]. On the whole more new investment has been associated with increases in output than the plan anticipated. Still, the data of column (1), Table 21, may well overstate what lies ahead with respect to the capital needs for growth in the Indian economy. They testify to the high costs of expansion in a situation where underutilization of resources persists because it does not in itself generate corrective adjustments toward higher degrees of capital utilization. This is certainly an area where remedial action is desirable. If programs to that end are undertaken, capital coeffici-

[23]In 1960/61 prices, actual net income in 1970/71 did not reach the Rs 19200 crores of Table 20. The gap is therefore a wider one.

TABLE 21.   Incremental Capital Output-
Relationships

	Actual[a] (1)	Plan (2)
First Plan	2.4	3.1
Second Plan	2.9	2.3
Third Plan	5.9	2.4
Fourth Plan (1966 draft)	b	2.7[c]

[a]All these ratios would be higher if, as argued above (pp. 90–96), the net investment data of Table 12 understate new capital formation. With respect to level and change see comparable computations in Lal, pp. 11, 12.
[b]Investment data for 1966–69 not available, but the ratio would be lower than the 5.9 of the third plan years. See text.
[c]The current Fourth Plan (and its 1969 draft) projects 2.5 for this relationship.

Sources: *First Plan, Second Plan, Third Plan,* and *Fourth Plan,* 1966 draft; and *Estimates of National Product,* October, 1967, and *Economic Survey, 1969–70,* 1970.

ents appropriate to the Indian situation may well lie in the 2.5–3.0 range—over the next decade in any event.[24]

When the actual incremental capital-output ratio for 1966-69 can be computed, it may itself show a decline from the third plan computation. The growth rate of investment did slacken while output growth increased above recent levels [column (2), Table 19], but these were rather special developments. The change in investment activity reflected both a planning establishment in some disarray and the nation's recessionary economic position. Output, on the other hand, was more nearly the consequence of the record agricultural crops of 1967–1969 than of new capital formation. In 1968/69, and during 1968 especially, there was a greater degree of use of capital plant, as we shall see in Chapter 6. The data for 1966–69 will not in themselves indicate a new and more relevant level for the capital coefficient; only conscious policy and action by government can achieve this desirable relationship over the next few plans.

The record in agriculture and in other important components of national product is shown separately in columns (3), (4), and (5), Table 19. These offer important comparisons with plan. While there are some problems of consistency in the individual series the following statements reflect differences over time that are probably inde-

[24]See pp. 225–26.

pendent of definitional adjustments. We again note the tendency for agriculture to retain its importance as a source of domestic product, in contrast to the perspective view that showed marked declines as testimony to a dynamic expansion of modern industrial activity in a developing economy. Persistent reductions were to provide a ratio of 42 percent in 1965/66 and 40 percent in 1970/71.[25] Indeed even the data of Table 19 exaggerate the decline that has occurred. The relevant comparison is in *actual* prices and this reveals limited downward movement. It is not clear that a ratio *below* 50 percent will pertain while India is still in process of establishing a basis for its long-term growth.

Much of the present chapter is concerned with actual agricultural development in the context of India's over-all growth. While it is obvious that different sectors of the economy do grow at different rates, agriculture in a traditional, labor-intensive economy like India's permeates other sectors. Product of these sectors will tend to vary sympathetically with product in agriculture. It is unusual for adverse agricultural conditions to be offset by marked advances elsewhere. On the other side, favorable agricultural development stimulates more rapid growth in the rest of the economy. On the whole, therefore, we find agriculture's course of real growth more or less mirrored in the total economy. Agriculture's product ratio thus declines more slowly than would be true if other sectors were less dependent upon the pattern of agriculture's development. India's current emphasis on agriculture recognizes the role of this sector in creating the framework for persistent growth in India. During this development phase — and it will persist for another decade at least — the ratio of agriculture to total product cannot change significantly.

The experience and promise in agriculture are of basic significance to continuous growth in the economy and in its modern industry component particularly.[26] Expansion in this industry category [column (4), Table 19] has been rapid over the years 1950/51–1965/66, but again not to the extent visualized in the plans (for reasons already suggested). It did, of course, grow relative to total national output—indeed more than twice as fast, as shown in Table 19. Growth rates in modern industry tended to increase over the plans until the setbacks of recent years. The entire record poses fundamental questions about what actually determines industrial ex-

---

[25]*MFB*, p. 9.
[26]See pp. 172–75 and 218–23.

pansion in a nation seeking modernization from a broad-based agricultural, primarily traditional, structure. We discuss these questions
in the following chapter.[27]

The record of Table 19 indicates relatively rapid growth of output in the service category as a whole. The difference in growth rate
between services [column (5)] and total product [column (2)] has
actually been widening over the three plans. We note that the service estimate is less homogeneous than are the series for agriculture
and modern industry, with respect both to the variety of its components and the methods for their measurement.[28] Given the weight
of this sector in total output (currently one-third the total) uncertainties arising from conceptual or measurement problems reflect
importantly on the total output picture of column (2). If the actual
contribution of services is exaggerated in column (5) — if the product grew only as fast as the rest of India's output, say — then total
national product in 1965/66 would have been 145 percent of its
1950/51 level rather than the 16 percent shown in the table. Progress in per capita terms would have proceeded at a very low rate
over the course of India's development effort; much of the exciting
progress in the nation might thus be attributed to this differential
growth in the services. The output of services actually increased
more rapidly than did the goods production of agriculture and industry together. This is a rich-nation growth phenomenon, a point
noted years ago by Indian observers. But roughly similar changes
have also been observed in other poor lands. It has even been suggested that this pattern is a core element of an efficient process of
national expansion from persistent poverty. On the other side, there
is evidence in India that some growth in the service sectors reflects
ease of entry for workers unable to find preferred employment; the
product thus generated does not reflect preferred national demand.[29]

---

[27]See Chapter 6, pp. 163–75.

[28]See G.O.I., CSO, *Brochure on Revised Series of National Product for
1960–61 to 1964–65*, August, 1967, pp. 45–76.

[29]Thus see Walter Galenson, "Economic Development and the Sectoral Expansion of Employment," *International Labour Review*, Vol. 88 (June, 1963),
pp. 506–10. This optimistic view has been questioned by Baer and Hervé (*op.
cit.*, pp. 104–7) who show that such a "beneficial" service expansion depends
upon the existence of higher service multipliers from capital-intensive as
against more labor-intensive industrial production. But this has not been dem-
onstrated either theoretically or empirically.

In the Indian context see V.K.R.V. Rao, "Changes in India's National Income: A Static Economy in Progress," *Capital: Annual Review*, December,
1954, pp. 15–17.

Finally, on pp. 110–11 we have already noted the atypical behavior of service
employment.

Be all this as it may it is certain that India's planning authorities did not pursue a shift from goods to services as the type of structural change in productive potential that would assist India's economic progress. This is amply clear within the five-plan perspective. As we observed in earlier chapters, there was some deliberate shift away from service investment after the first two plans. For the third, for example, it was expected that planned investment would achieve a 6 percent annual expansion in total product, but agriculture would increase 5 percent annually, production from factory establishments more than 15 percent, and all service output somewhat less than total product. Similar ideas are found in the second plan documents. And the new fourth plan also seeks to lower the role that the service industries as a group play in generating growth in national product. The record here, as in the case of agricultural output and of modern industry mentioned earlier, reveals performance different from what was planned. National product was lower in 1965/66 than had been anticipated; it also had a different composition.

Departures from a programmed result may be inevitable, and especially so for an economy where weather fluctuations influence such important components of total product. They should not simply be attributed to random factors. In any event, gaps between India's plans and performance are important enough to warrant an attempt at systematic explanation. The fundamental questions concern the adequacy of the basic output relationships with capital, labor, and decision inputs. It is true that India's planning was becoming increasingly scientific and objective with reference both to input/output relationships and to intersectoral and interproduct dependencies. The fundamental aim was to use factor inputs to achieve a maximum flow of a combination of final goods, where consumption and investment would best meet India's development goals. Inputs and outputs within industries and among sectors were planned in appropriate technical balance. Implementing such an effort encounters at least two major problems in a poor nation like India. There is simply not enough knowledge of these relationships and interdependencies. Secondly, particularly in a mixed economy like India's, such a technically balanced goal must have an obverse in economic forces that impel the system to the desired, *and required*, sets of inputs and outputs.

The differences in total level of actual final product and its different sectoral mix mean that in some measure India's programs for change were not tied together by such economic forces. Factor prices did not induce productive resource growth and use to meet the plan targets. The mechanism — motivational, organizational, economic—could not convert technological relationships and possibilities into what the planners saw as realities.

Sectoral Product: Agriculture

Within agriculture, more disaggregated analysis can provide further insights into the problems and possibilities revealed by India's actual development record. Value added in this sector did expand about 35 percent in the years since 1950/51,[30] essentially as much as the growth of India's population (columns (1) and (3), Table 19). From one point of view, agriculture's output was inadequate: domestic contributions to food and raw materials were below what was expected and needed. Thus trends in foodgrains output coupled with expanding rates of population growth and higher levels of per capita food consumption set the pattern for India's food deficits. Foodgrains imports in the last year of each of the three plans were 1,400,000 tons or 2.3 percent of total consumption in 1955/56; 3,500,000 tons or 4.6 percent in 1960/61; and 10,300,000 tons or 14.4 percent in 1965/66. Imports in 1966/67 and 1967/68 remained close to this last level. The dramatic increases in agricultural output in 1967/68 (a level essentially maintained in 1968/69) permitted grain imports to decline, but they were still of the order of 6,000,000 tons in 1968. Shortages of domestic raw materials in recent years also aggravated India's industrial activities.

From another point of view India remained more agricultural than the planners anticipated. We have noted that the ratio of agricultural to total income persisted at high levels in contrast to the expectations of important reductions in line with familiar growth doctrine. The actual growth in this dominant sector—with most of India's income, workers, and people — was insufficient to spark rapid growth rates in the rest of an economy so dependent upon agriculture. There is a broad spectrum of views on the degree of achievement in the nation's agriculture over the first three

---

[30]Actually from 1950/51 to an average for 1964/65–1968/69, years of great diversity in crop output. Value added in recent favorable crop years (especially 1967/68) showed significantly higher increases above the 1950/51 level. The text comparison may also underrate the significance of the upward trend in agricultural output revealed by the data after 1966/67. We return to this below, pp. 158–62.

plans.[31] There can, however, be no question that output was somehow too low, and that actual progress in this sector provided little assurance of future success.

The record in agriculture prompted major policy shifts; these became increasingly apparent as the new fourth plan took final shape in the late 1960's. Agriculture has been given higher priority: its rate of expansion was planned well above past performance. But in fact the changes go beyond recognition of agriculture's importance to India's development programs. The changes are inseparable from new development objectives. In brief, the original plans — from independence until very recently — saw growth in agricultural output along with growing *equality* among farmers and regions of the nation. In today's new agriculture greater *inequality* seems built into the very process of expansion. The social and political consequences of this change will also be affected by the different economic development prospects under the two policies. For, as indicated earlier, national development goals are better assured in a land like India if economic change spreads broadly through the traditional sectors of the economy and society. This promise did exist in the original policy, however small was the actual attainment. Such diffusion is much less likely with the new agriculture. Output targets can be reached in agriculture, but they need not be accompanied by achievement in other parts of the economy. Inadequate economic performance would aggravate the social and political consequences of growing rural inequalities.

These possibilities are considered in our concluding chapter. Here we trace the main lines of actual agricultural performance over the first three plans; we seek insights for the potential of the new policy. Table 22 shows the official agricultural (crop) output indexes for final plan years, with annual data from 1964/65. The record over the first three plans is familiar from our preceding dis-

---

[31]Foreign observers, from the United States especially, have on the whole tended to reflect disappointment in the record of past years, in the 1956–65 decade in particular. Among Indian experts, Professor V.M. Dandekar of the Gokhale Institute and Professor M.L. Dantwala of the University of Bombay are outspoken in their different interpretations. The issues emerge clearly in the former's critical analysis: "Agricultural Price Policy: A Critique of Dantwala," and the latter's "Reply," both in *EPW*, March 16, 1968, pp. 454–59, 459–61 respectively. The original Dantwala article, "Incentives and Disincentives in Indian Agriculture," appeared in the *Indian Journal of Agricultural Economics*, April-June 1967, pp. 1–25. On the whole this emphasized strengths in the Indian record.

cussion and Table 19. The production series for all commodities tended to grow at a declining rate over the successive plans, with only the 1951–56 performance up to plan goals.[32] Whether mea-

TABLE 22.   Index Numbers of Agricultural
Production (1949/50 = 100)

	All Commodities	Foodgrains	Non-foodgrains
1950/51	95.6	90.5	105.9
1955/56	116.8	115.3	119.9
1960/61	142.2	137.1	152.6
1964/65	159.4	150.8	176.7
1965/66	132.1	120.9	154.8
1966/67	131.6	123.8	147.4
1967/68	161.0	159.0	165.1
1968/69	158.7	157.5	161.0

Source: G.O.I. *Economic Survey 1969–70,* 1970, p. 66. (Agricultural year
begins July 1.)

sured from 1949/50 (a better base year for agriculture) or from 1950/51, there has been significantly greater progress through the third plan in crops other than foodgrains. Thus the 1965/66 indexes were 120.9 and 154.8 respectively. For the period 1949/50–1964/65 compound growth rates were 3.2 percent for all commodities, 2.8 percent for foodgrains and 3.9 percent for other crops. On the whole, commercial output tended to decline less in such adverse weather years as 1965/66 and 1966/67 (relative to 1960/61, say). Superior performance reflects greater exposure of these crops to market forces. There are, of course, wide variations in the output record of individual commodities. With new miracle seeds in the past five or six years and with better farming methods, foodgrains showed the differential gains manifest by peak output levels in 1967/68 and after (Table 22). In particular, wheat production had a spectacular growth of some 35 percent between the record years 1964/65 and 1967/68. A further 10 percent increase occurred in 1968/69.

National averages for crop output cover a wide variety of regional agricultural development performance over the plan years. This is

---

[32]Here the textual discussion is confined to crop agriculture and excludes the animal husbandry, forestry, and fishing component of column (3), Table 19. Crop agriculture constituted 80 to 85 percent of the total over the period considered here, with animal husbandry the main part of the residual. Output variations are primarily due to crops.

highlighted by the broad range of rates of growth in total crop output among states.[33] Between 1951–54 and 1958–61, total output in Gujarat expanded by 56 percent (6.54 percent annual rate) and in West Bengal by 1.5 percent (0.21 percent each year). Nine states grew more rapidly than did the nation as a whole; eight less rapidly. States with above-average growth rates accounted for some 50 percent of the total expansion in agricultural output over the first decade of planning, as against their 35 percent share of output in the pre-plan period. There is a striking regional pattern in these developments. Rapid expansion was manifest from Kerala to the Punjab, from Gujarat to Madhya Pradesh — broadly the states of the west and north. Slow growth characterized agriculture in the states of eastern and northeastern India. Where growth was rapid *both* acreage and yields per acre tended to expand more than for the nation as a whole.

More marked internal differences are revealed below the state level. Thus 25 percent of the districts of India, with 24 percent of total crop area, increased output by at least 7.5 percent or more each year over that decade. An additional 18 percent of the districts (19 percent of crop area) had an average growth rate between 5 percent and 7.5 percent. In only one-third of the districts (and crop area of India) did output grow at less than 2.5 percent over these years, and of course in some it actually fell. The fast growing districts are distributed widely in India, but disproportionately in Gujarat, Mysore, and Maharashtra. Obviously there are regions in India that have been able in recent years to attain rates of growth of agricultural output above those in nations widely recognized for their agricultural development achievement, such as Taiwan and Israel — nations with less total population than many of these districts in India. Both this capacity to expand and the regional concentration are stressed here.

In addition to such significant regional variations, total agricultural growth in India was neither steady nor consistently upward. It was much more rapid in the early years, until late in the second plan, than it was for five or ten years thereafter. Even the record harvests of 1964/65 and 1967–69 did not raise the growth rate over the past ten years (an average of about 2.0 percent annually) to

[33]See B.S. Minhas and A. Vaidyanathan, "The Growth of Agricultural Output in India, 1951–54 to 1958–61," *Journal of the Indian Society of Agricultural Statistics*, December, 1965, pp. 230–52. The *Fourth Plan*, 1969 draft, p. 111, also provides data on a state basis, but for the period 1952/53–1964/65. The pattern corresponds roughly, at least for years prior to the "new" agriculture.

the 1950/51–1958/59 level (an average of 3.3 percent).[34] An important element in these two trends is the role played by acreage expansion as against increase in productivity per acre, including the effects of a shift in acreage to higher yielding crops. For all agriculture and over the entire series of plan years, more than half the increase in output can be associated with increases in gross acreage, including the double cropping made possible by expanded irrigation. And less than half the increase in output was due to increases in yields per acre as defined above.[35] But these two sources of expansion were not equally strong over the entire period. In the early years of more rapid rates of growth in output, expansion was dominated by acreage increases. When productivity gains became more important, output growth for the nation slowed down. Increases in acreage were associated with more than 70 percent of total agricultural growth in the first plan years; they provided about 25 percent of the growth in output in subsequent years.

This pattern is understandable. In India as a whole the supply of new lands, even of recoverable wilderness, forests, or wastelands, is very limited. Increasingly such extensions of area will be the result of new irrigation facilities.[36] Double cropping "adds" land; systematic control of water benefits output per acre, although the gains may well be due to fertilizer and improved cultural practices that are feasible only after water is available. While the acreage route is considered a more straightforward path to expansion, the extensive margin merges with the intensive. Both are now costly routes.[37]

For foodgrains particularly, output growth will need to depend primarily upon productivity increases. In any event gains in yield per acre have characterized recent expansion to a greater degree than is the case for more commercial crops. There actually has been some loss of acreage from foodgrains production on a national basis. In the record crop year 1967/68, for example, foodgrains output grew essentially from increases in productivity.[38] Of course it is in

---

[34]Against this record, note that the new fourth plan calls for increases in agricultural output at an average rate of 5 percent in 1969–1974. See *Fourth Plan*, pp. 35, 120.

[35]For a comparison by years from 1950/51, see G.O.I., *Economic Survey 1969–70*, 1970, p. 65.

[36]See, for example, the comprehensive statement on such possibilities in the *Fourth Plan*, 1969 draft, 1969, pp. 182–200.

[37]Thus, see Ester Boserup, *The Conditions of Agricultural Growth* (Chicago: Aldine Publishing Company, 1965, pp. 56–69.

[38]For all crops in 1967/68, acreage was 124.6, relative to the pre-plan period; the corresponding yield per acre was 123.5. But within these totals the non-foodgrains ratios were 153.6 for acreage and 107.9 for productivity.

the foodgrains where the prospect now is most promising for a green revolution with its yield-per-acre gains. Still, the closer one looks at the complex pattern of agricultural change in India over the recent past, the less reliance one can place on broad general statements to the effect that future output gains will be very difficult because they depend on gains in productivity. While past output gains for the nation as a whole were principally due to acreage expansion, the regional data highlight *diversity* in this regard. By state, and by district particularly, the record also shows persistent improvement in yields per acre in some parts of the land (Gujarat, Tamil Nadu, Mysore, Madhya Pradesh) as well as marked shifts to higher-yielding crops and varieties (again Gujarat in particular).[29] A study of 28 crops during the 1952/53–1961/62 period attributes to acreage expansion 41 percent of total output growth in all India. This ratio was much lower in Gujarat, Tamil Nadu, and probably in Mysore also; productivity increases were correspondingly greater. In recent decades in India, reliance has been put on *both* the acreage and the yield routes to output growth. The limited scope for acreage expansion need not confront India with new and unfamiliar problems. Growth in land under crops may be much less important in future years, but the tasks of productivity growth have long been practiced in important producing regions.[40]

Finally we turn to internal differences that reflect the most significant characteristics of the record in Indian agriculture. One such pattern is that statistics at district and state levels reveal an *inverse* relationship between initial levels of yield per acre and growth rates of output. In the high growth districts to which we referred earlier average yields per acre were some 80 percent of the all-India average yield; in the low growth districts, initial yields were 105 to 115 percent of that average. As agricultural output has grown, there has been some narrowing of internal differences in per acre yields.[41] Some such "catching up" effect is a fundamental component of the growth process, and we have earlier observed the limited scope such spread effects had in India's past. In this regard, the states of India's west and northwest — broadly census zones 1

[39]B.S. Minhas and A. Vaidyanathan, *op. cit.*

[40]See A.W. Heston, *op. cit.*, pp. 174–83; also G.O.I. Ministry of Food and Agriculture, *Growth Rate in Agriculture, 1949–50 to 1964–65*, 1966.

[41]A.W. Heston, *op. cit.* The Symposium of which Heston's work was part (with Malenbaum, Behrman, and Gotsch) deals with the subject of internal differences in productivity. Thus in addition to India (Heston), analyses of Pakistan (Gotsch) and Thailand (Behrman) also reveal that higher rates of growth have been more characteristic of initially low productivity than of high productivity agricultural areas.

and 2 — always tended to be low-yield regions.[42] And these are the areas where we found that output expansions, through acreage and yield advances, were most marked.

Another basic pattern associates agricultural output and scale of enterprise. From sample surveys we have a clear picture of the size distribution of operational holdings in 1959/60 (Table 23). While there are no comprehensive data for changes over time, there are some regional patterns for the 1959/60 distribution. There is also

TABLE 23.   Distribution of Operational
Holdings, 1959/60

Size category (acres)	Number of households (%)	Area operated (%)
0– 4.99	63.0	18.9
0 – .49	10.9	.4
.5 – .99	8.5	.9
1.0 –2.49	21.3	5.4
2.5 –4.99	22.3	12.2
5– 9.99	18.8	19.9
10–29.99	14.8	36.0
30–	3.4	25.2
	100.0	100.0

Sources: G.O.I., The Cabinet Secretariat; N.S.S. No. 113, Sixteenth Round, July 1960–June 1961, "Tables with Notes on Agricultural Holdings in Rural India," Table (4), p. 21.

information on factor use and output by size of holdings. Together these permit strong inferences as to what happened over the plan years.

For India as a whole, Table 23 tells us that 63 percent of farm households cultivated 19 percent of all farm land. Another 19 percent of households operated an additional 20 percent of the land. Thus more than 60 percent of the land in farms was worked by well under 20 percent of India's farm households. Thanks to rainfall differences primarily, the historical evolution of tenurial arrangements assured reasonably distinct regional patterns that are concealed in the national distribution of land holdings in Table 23. One pattern is provided by the states of census zones 1 and 2 (mostly India's north and west), another by census zones 4 and 5 (essentially the northeast and north center). The southern and south central states

---

[42]On past yield differences by regions see pp. 36–42.

(zone 3) form an in-between pattern of holdings which may conform more nearly to that of zones 4 and 5. In any case we refer to two categories: the west and north—Mysore, Maharashtra, Bombay, Gujarat, Rajasthan, Madyha Pradesh, Harvana, and Punjab; and the south and east — Kerala, Tamil Nadu, Andhra Pradesh, Orissa, Bihar, West Bengal, Uttar Pradesh, and Assam.

In the first group (primarily zones 1 and 2) holdings and operational units tend to be in excess of 10 acres. In these zones 70 to 80 percent of the land is operated by 25 to 30 percent of all farm households, on operational units that are at least 10 acres in size. In other groups (zones 3, 4, and 5 essentially) only 25 to 35 percent of the land is in such large holdings. There, most land, by far, and more than 90 percent of the households are on holdings below 10 acres in size. Average farm size is well below 5 acres, as against an average above 10 acres in the first group of states.

With few exceptions, the first group of states—those where farms tended to be of larger size—are those where rates of output growth in agriculture have been *above* the national average growth rate in this decade. Our second group — states where smaller farm units were more predominant — tended to have *below* average growth rates. Large-farm areas were areas with lower yields per acre. The catching-up that we observed must thus have been primarily on the part of operators of the larger farms. It was the small (and generally poor) farmer that had higher yields per acre of land; the large (generally rich) farmer was narrowing this yield difference in the early years of India's planned development.

The 1959/60 sample survey is in itself revealing on intensity of agricultural operations by different size categories. *Per acre of farm land* smaller farms used more chemical fertilizers, more attached farm workers, and more irrigated area. In the case of all three inputs, the ratios (*i.e.*, input per acre) decline steadily after 2.5 acres; as farm size increases these ratios fall to one-third to one-fourth of the levels on small farms.[43] The agricultural land in larger holdings was simply used much less intensively. By and large, the landlords and owners were not driven to maximum output; it is not even clear that they sought to maximize net returns. Zones 1 and 2 in India are much more nearly characterized by larger-scale farm operations than are the other zones. The sample data reveal a basic pattern: larger farm units have higher incomes and lower productivity. Less output per acre is more than offset by numbers of acres.

---

[43]N.S.S. Number 113, *op. cit.*, Tables 20-24, pp. 65–73.

In zones 1 and 2 average incomes per rural household (and average incomes from agriculture) are well above levels in other parts of the country.[44]

These regional and scale data are also consistent with the relationship discovered in farm management surveys in India during the years 1954/55–1956/57.[45] These comprehensive collections of statistics and analysis provide clear evidence of the *inverse* relationship between size of farm and crop output per acre. All the samples show more intensive use of inputs in smaller farms. While gross output per acre declines steadily with size, some measure of net returns per acre (value of output minus cost outlays to others than to the owner or to the landlord and his family, for example) tends to remain fairly steady or even to increase. Per farm, of course, such profits mount rapidly with the growth in farm size.[46] In India the larger and richer farms — heavily, but not exclusively, in the west and north — had obvious potential for expansion in output and in output per acre. The districts and the states in which larger farms

---

[44]We recall Professor A.R. Beals' account of farm operations by a large scale and rich farmer of Gopalpur in Mysore State. See above, p. 40.

Zonal average income per household in 1960/61 shows the following relationships to the all-India rural average:

Zone 1	128.5
2	110.0
3	83.4
4	97.7
5	98.5

In this connection, see following text, especially footnote 45, this page.

[45]See Chapter 2, pp. 41–42 above. These surveys were made for farm samples in the states of Bombay, Madhya Pradesh, Tamil Madu, Punjab, Uttar Pradesh and West Bengal (the Madhya Pradesh study begins in 1955/56). The results were published by the G.O.I. Ministry of Food and Agriculture in 17 volumes, over the period 1957–62. They appear as *Studies in the Economics of Farm Management,* by state and year. For a readily accessible discussion and analysis, see Morton Paglin, " 'Surplus' Agricultural Labor and Development," *AER,* Vol. 55, No. 4, (September, 1965), pp. 815–34. Few empirical observations from the recent agricultural scene in India have been so discussed as this relationship between farm size and output per acre. For extensive bibliographical material and appraisals and for critical discussions, see J.N. Bhagwati and S. Chakravarty, "Contributions to Indian Economic Analysis," *AER,* Vol. 59, No. 4, Part 2 (September, 1969), pp. 38–48.

[46]Thus, for Uttar Pradesh, as an example, compare size groups under 5 acres and over 20 acres:

	large/small
Gross output/acre	0.75
Costs/acre	0.55
Profits/acre	2.10
Total profits	20.00 (at least)

(Data are derived from Paglin, *op. cit.,* p. 817.)

were predominant were the regions where output growth was most impressive. In any event, growth in output on India's larger farms was responsible for a disproportionate share of the total growth in agriculture over the early plans.[47] Even before the green revolution of recent years, India's agricultural development seems to have brought greater benefits to the larger and richer farmers.

What mechanism induced this differentiated pattern of growth rates? What attributes of the Indian scene or of the total effort in agriculture resulted in special incentives and greater accomplishment on farms and areas with lower productivity that seem long to have coexisted with farmers and regions with high output per acre? The complex facts and relationships of the Indian agricultural scene make answers difficult.[48] We might note the major lines of official policy through most of the first three plans. First was the provision of social and economic overhead investment: here was promise of greater productivity from the farmer's own inputs of capital, labor, skill, and aspiration. Direct inputs also became more available under the plans. The combination of better transport, more water, more seeds, more fertilizer and equipment, and more technical knowledge did create a situation in which progress could occur. The question was whether the opportunities would be taken, and by whom. Presumably richer farmers were better able to do this, as they were more aware of the opportunities. On the other hand, we did observe in Chapter 2 that the history of India's agricultural development, over a hundred years or so, revealed opportunity and facilities for growth. These did not engender widespread expansion.

Earlier we outlined the development of irrigation facilities in India and indicated its potential relevance for growth in crop acreage and in productivity per acre. These possibilities were especially great for India's larger farm holdings which may have been relatively less well off in this regard in the early years of independence. Considerable detail now available on the regional distribution of irrigation over the plans indicates differential expansion in the

---

[47]See above, pp. 147–48.

[48]After some years of intimate association with problems of rural change in India, Professor Charles Lindblom observed that "no one knows just how the expansion in agricultural output through 1964/65 has been achieved"; he gives credit to "powerful, persuasive, local and 'spontaneous' forces within the Indian peasant." These expansionary forces might continue to be captured by realistic public programs. Lindblom's provocative analysis of some years back still warrants reading: "Has India an Economic Future?", *Foreign Affairs,* Vol. 44, January, 1966, pp. 239-52.

states of the west and north.[49] More irrigation facilities offer benefits to agriculture other than water alone. The 1959/60 sample
survey showed only 5 iron ploughs per 100 households.[50] There was
a very rapid acceleration in use of such ploughs in the 1960's: "universal adoption" today exaggerates the actual situation, but perhaps not by much. Steel points, improved seeds, and the application
of chemical fertilizers are agricultural improvements that have become widespread in India over the past ten years. Again these gains
tend to bunch with new availability of water: together all these
seem to support the observed differential gains in product, generally
by scale of enterprise and by region.

Benefits from the spread and variety of government's extension
efforts are not readily documented beyond what might be made explicit from the summary observations immediately above. In regard
to modernization, important needs of farmers remain unfilled —
improved hand tools, including hand-operated dusters and spray-
ers and seed-plus-fertilizer drills, to name a few. The sequence—
from establishing the merit of a tool, to farmer demand for it, to
production and availability — is not complete for such farm tools.
In part, the failure reflects lack of sufficient interest of research in-
stitutes and manufacturers.[51] On the other side is evidence that
useful tools actually developed for conditions in Indian agriculture
and produced in India find too few takers, at least domestically.[52]

Rural institutions that might automatically help in these interrelated farm problems are still in their early formation stage. It
will be remembered that these evolved through a sequence that included community development and extension, cooperatives and
panchayati raj: institutions that emphasize democratic participation in rural affairs. "Lukewarm interest shown by the people,
casteism and communalism, poor leadership, unwillingness of panchayats to impose taxes, lack of self-confidence . . . bickerings and

---

[49]*Fourth Plan*, 1969 draft, pp. 182–200, especially Annexure II, p. 197.
[50]As against 3 plows per 100 households in the 1953/54 sample. N.S.S. No. 116, *op. cit.,* p. 13.
[51]This was the conclusion of an official Committee on Plan Projects with re-spect to Improved Agricultural Implements (Planning Commission, June, 1966).
[52]Ninety percent of the current production of a water-lifting device with a "technological capacity to improve . . . the wretchedly inefficient agriculture in the Kanpur region" was being exported to Africa, the Middle East, and Northeast Asia, while inadequate marketing, credit, demonstration, and trans-portation facilities made it almost impossible to sell in the Kanpur locality where it was produced. E.A.J. Johnson, *The Organization of Space in De-veloping Countries* (Cambridge, Mass.: Harvard University Press, 1970).

factionalism, corruption and manipulation of accounts. . . ." is a characterization by interested Indians; but such problems are in process of solution. The local institutions are gradually helping rural development, as they are contributing new political consciousness to the average farmer in India.[53]

Policies for more assured water supplies and for institutional facilities for mutual improvement in rural areas provided the major externalities in India's agricultural efforts since independence. Within them many specfic programs were made available to the individual producer. The range was comprehensive: better credit facilities, dissemination of scientific and economic research pertinent to agricultural output, technical assistance, access to improved seed and fertilizer, and others. But these had to be used by the farmer. Individuals must both want them and must be able to take advantage of them. To want them, the farmer needs to appreciate the opportunities for gain through efficient production and marketing; to be able to use them he must have resources not already fully committed to current consumption and production needs. The fact is that in India most of the smaller, poorer farmers — already exploiting their resources more fully than other farmers — had limited additional facilities. The larger, richer farmers — mostly underutilizing their land and equipment — were more able and willing to take advantage of the new opportunities. They were already more market-oriented. Gains from the programs tended to be localized and differentiated in favor of the larger producing units.

The question of scale of enterprise has always been at the center of India's policies for rural change. Yet the complex of programs — land ceilings, consolidations, cooperative farming — did not combine into a clear guide for changes in the average size of holding or of actual farm operation. Indeed policy was itself equivocal. "Land for the tiller" would broaden ownership and probably reduce (certainly not expand) the size of operational units. On the other side was the objective of greater efficiency through larger-sized operations through cooperatives rather than private agglomerations. Official policy stressed equality; it hoped this would also be accompanied by increased productivity. On the whole these classic policy lines certainly underrate the reality of the need that compelled small holdings to generate large volume of output per acre. They

---

[53]The quotation (from the Fourth National Convention of the All-India Panchayati Raj, Bangalore, 1964) and the conclusions are given by John W. Mellor, *et al*, *Developing Rural India*, (Ithaca, N.Y.: Cornell University Press, 1968), pp. 75–79. See also Chapter 7 below, pp. 210–13.

failed to recognize the need for incentive toward greater output per acre on the part of the richer farmer.

Neither policy nor actual achievement is clear on trends in scale in agriculture. Farm land per person certainly did decline over the years from 1950/51. Rural population in agriculture increased more than did acreage under cultivation. Land reform did convert some tenant operators to laborers. Village industries did lose out to modern urban enterprise, thus reducing the availability of non-farm rural job opportunities. The usual figure of 20 percent for those landless in the rural labor force may have expanded over the early development years,[54] but the net effect on size of operational unit is less certain. It may well have declined on the average, but not uniformly through the land. There is some reason to believe that a trend to even smaller farm units has characterized the areas of smaller holdings, predominantly in the eastern parts of India. And the size of operational holdings may have tended up in the west and north. But with the technical knowledge already in hand both such movements could be consistent with further expansion in output. Narrowing of the range in output per acre can continue to occur. Even in the early 1960's differences in output per acre were such that there remained capacity on India's larger farms for further expansion in production through greater per acre application of fertilizer, irrigation, *and labor*. And increasingly into the late 1960's it became clear that the new agriculture could expand productivity even on the small holdings where yields per acre had long been above India's average level.

The tools for transmitting new opportunities encompassed extension and other forms of education and training, but the basic appeal of policy to farmers was the promise of profitability in improved methods. A core concern is thus the relative prices for outputs and inputs. Was price policy a conscious tool for implementing the agricultural development effort over the past plans? Much has been written and said at official and expert levels about price policy for agriculture during the 1950/51-1965/66 years. Here we confine ourselves to two considerations. First, a price policy di-

---

[54]Some underlying numbers are straightforward. Total population increased about as much as did agricultural output. The percentage of farm population was maintained. Gross acreage increased about half as much as did agricultural output. Between 1950/51 and 1965/66 acreage expansion of the order of 20 percent was accompanied by rural population expansion closer to 40 percent. With respect to tenancy, National Sample Surveys (sixteenth as against eighth round) show 12 percent of all agricultural land under lease in 1959/60 as against 20 percent in 1953/54 (N.S.S. No. 113, *op. cit.*, page 12).

rected to more rapid agricultural growth would have been hard to formulate and implement at that time. Even today relatively little is known about agricultural supply and demand elasticities, whether on the economic or technological side. In this situation, the right policy is a controversial matter at best. Second, it is scarcely clear that government was interested in pursuing a price policy that favored agriculture relative to other sectors of the economy.

On the first point, the planners did feel that at least the more commercial producers seek out the market opportunities in a growing economy and society. Such producers would therefore respond readily to the profit prospects inherent in extension and other farm-oriented public programs. For most farmers on the other hand, government viewed the production process as traditional and subsistence-oriented. Prices and the market would have limited influence although the government did expect market orientation to increase gradually. If this combination of responses did not meet plan needs, government was prepared to deal with specific inadequacies — as when short crops impede intrastate flows of product, or when there are local famines. These special policies need not be directed to the producer or consumer, but to the trader, who provides a convenient and, at times, justifiable focus of criticism. In any event, far from seeking a broadscale price policy to assure the right supply and demand for agricultural products, government apparently preferred to apply limited policies on agricultural procurement, importing, rationing, fair-pricing, and the like.

Indeed it would be very difficult for price policy in a nation like India to play decisive roles in agricultural change and in the agricultural-industrial realignments of the development process. Despite an impressive and growing body of empirical studies, it is not yet possible to indicate how familiar economic factors are apt to influence product adjustments in agriculture. A recent survey of Indian economic analysis reviewed the contributions by "Indian or India-based" economists on such subjects as economic rationality in agriculture, behavior of marketed surplus and of production, efficient resource use under different tenure arrangements. On the whole, the conclusion is that the need exists for continued and expanded research investigations if a basis is to be found for reasonably reliable statistical relationships.[55]

---

[55]Bhagwati and Chakravarty, *op. cit.*, especially pp. 29–60. Consideration is given to the work on these subjects by many specialists, including V.M. Dandekar, C.H. Hanumantha Rao, A.M. Khusro, Raj Krishna, T.N. Krishnan, P.N. Mathur, B.S. Minhas, D. Narain, A.P. Rao, and K.N. Raj.

Relative price changes apparently do influence acreage shifts among crops, clearly among cash crops and perhaps also among cereals. Yet acreage-response is scarcely a production-response relationship; note the importance of changes in output per acre, during the past decade particularly. It is again relevant that subsistence production is dominant in the nation as a whole — over 80 percent of crop output has been in foodgrains; only some 25 percent of foodgrains output normally leaves the rural area. Urban and industrial activities thus exert local and slow influence on agricultural output and productivity. Non-money transactions were estimated at 43.1 percent of total rural consumption expenditures in 1951; they were unchanged at 42.7 percent in 1957/58.[56] Subsequent data are not available, but the (smaller) ratio of foodgrains production that left the rural areas may not have increased. It was 27 percent in 1953/54 and 26.1 percent in 1961/62.[57] Middlemen played a buffer role for much of the foodgrains output that did leave the rural area. All in all the market system did not seem to reflect the real value of foodgrains to the producer. In years when the national development program suffered from slow growth in foodgrains output and when increasing quantities of grains came from abroad, "market" forces were driving acreage out of foodgrains production.

As regards inputs into agriculture, net value added in all agricultural activities (commercial, as well as subsistence) was only 20 percent below the gross value added. Of this difference — about Rs 1500 crores on the average during the 1950's — inputs from industry provided less than 4 percent.[58] Such purchases of industrial products seldom involved as much as 1 percent of agriculture's net value added. These inputs have been expanding in the past few years as fertilizers and fuel oil become more important in farm operations. But there could be little stimulus to agriculture through industrial inputs from modern industry over most of the plan years, and this was true for a very large part of the agricultural establish-

---

[56]Basic data are from the N.S.S., No. 18 and No. 71. In the latter there are also state-wide data which indicate the widespread nature of the phenomenon of non-money transactions. Also see M. Mukherjee, "The Role of Transactions in Kind in Developing Economies," *The Review of Income and Wealth*, Number 4 (December, 1967) pp. 335–51.

[57]Estimated by Prof. Pranab K. Bardhan, in his "Chinese and Indian Agriculture: A Broad Comparison of Recent Policy and Performance," *The Journal of Asian Studies*, Vol. 29, No. 3 (May, 1970) especially pp. 533–35.

[58]These data are from G.O.I. National Income Committee, *Proposals, op. cit.*, pp. 45–63; and *MFB*, pp. 1–13.

ment. With respect to these two major types of economic forces — relative prices and forward-backward linkages — agriculture was but a limited respondent at best. We conclude that the structure and state of Indian agriculture in the past development years probably meant that even a comprehensive price policy could have played only a limited role in achieving India's over-all agricultural production targets along with the more equitable income distributions that was plan policy. But the market may have been one force for greater activity on the part of larger and richer farmers, who earlier had apparently not been motivated to high productivity levels.

Our other point on the role of price policy in India's past agricultural programs is that, even with the best knowledge about agricultural responses, a price policy to help agriculture would have required explicit differential treatment for agriculture as against industry and other sectors of the economy that used agriculture's products. This would have meant a preferred status for agriculture in national development. Actually modern industry had this dominant role. In the official view, agriculture would gain from the nation's focus on industrial expansion. This would provide an outlet for excess rural labor and population. A vigorous industrial sector hastens monetization, commercialization, and agricultural progress. Indeed *lower* food and other agricultural prices in a growing market best serve urban food costs and the supply of urban labor. Such industrial gains would sooner or later spread greater efficiency through agriculture. During most of the first three plans, government was scarcely seeking price policies to discriminate in favor of agriculturists.

The index of agricultural prices did remain more or less in balance with that of industrial prices in the years through the early 1960's. While the ratio of agricultural to industrial prices fluctuated from 88 to 113, most by far of the annual ratios were in the 95 to 105 range. Given the diversity within India these measures may not be relevant throughout the land. Yet the absence of any direction of movement suggests that there were no special price advantages for agriculture as a whole. Indeed given the marked restructuring (and increasing productivity?) in modern industry over those years, an unchanging ratio may well have been more favorable to industry. In any event it was dramatic setbacks in agriculture, not official policy, that brought a dramatic spur to food and agricultural raw material prices. In the last three years of the third plan rates of increase in prices of these two commodity groups were more than twice as great as in prices of manufactured products.[59] But these price advantages for agriculture were reflections of agriculture's weakness and not its well-being. They did not help most farmers nor did beneficial influences spread to other parts of the economy. But these price developments did provide an additional impetus for the formulation of a new official policy toward agriculture and toward the role it played in India's future development.

While modern industry did grow in relative importance over the plans, its growth was impeded by agriculture's uncertain development. It is ironic that the very sectors where official plan and policy expected stimulation for agriculture were themselves impeded by agriculture's performance.[60] Anticipated balances among sectors were not attained. Equilibrating mechanisms did not serve to rectify persistent imbalances. Below target agricultural output meant record import levels of food and other crops, and these may in turn have served as a deterrent to agriculture's expansion. Large-scale PL 480 assistance tended to reduce the availability of other forms of foreign aid. By the last years of the third plan Indian officials were ready for new directions in India's agriculture.

Experience with an intensive agricultural district program, IADP, initiated in April, 1960 (with some stimulus and assistance from the Ford Foundation), suggested the joint strategies of concentration of effort in small regions and of package programs that assured producers the ingredients demanded by science and modern technology. In marked contrast to the earlier programs, where new rural institutions, new social and economic overhead were to motivate farmers to new processes and new inputs, India's new program involved the application of a stipulated package of practices. This scarcely meant universal adoption. They were limited to areas with assured water supply; the package is in effect also confined to farmers able to afford investment in increased working capital. Where the earlier efforts turned out in the end to provide differential opportunities and benefits to wealthier farmers, the new efforts did so from the very start.

The intensive district program was adopted gradually, first in three districts in 1961, and thereafter in one in each state over the next three or four years. By 1964 plan authorities had become convinced that the strategy of integrated activity in selected regions

---

[59]G.O.I. *Economic Survey 1969-70*, 1970, pp. 103–5.

[60]These observations on industry and trade are discussed further in Chapter 6 below.

was essential for India's agricultural improvement. In a modified form the program was launched (October, 1965) in 114 of India's 325 districts. This was the IAAP, Intensive Agricultural Area Program; it focused more on particular crops and made more limited demands on skilled extension personnel. It was shortage of staff that constantly impeded the early spread of IADP. Output responses from the new inputs were for a while not dramatic enough; early disappointments dampened popular enthusiasm for greater participation.[61]

This situation improved with the formal initiation in 1966 of the High Yielding Varieties Program, HYVP, now a key component of India's new agriculture. In the past year or two there was also added a new multi-crop emphasis seeking to capitalize on the prolonged growing season made possible by short-duration varieties of paddy, maize, jowar, and bajra.

Already there is an extensive literature on the experience of the new agriculture. The record harvest of 1967/68 benefitted from the program as it did from favorable growing conditions. On the other side, 1968/69 was not a very favorable weather year, yet output was at a high level (Table 22). Agricultural output expanded in 1969/70, and in 1970/71. There are, of course, many accounts of local setbacks (rice in Burdwan District, 1967/68) as there are of phenomenal achievements (wheat in Ludhiana District, 1967/68 and again in 1970/71). There is concern about the gap between fertilizer and pesticide technology for paddy varieties especially, about the shortages of adequately trained field workers who are the links between laboratory and the farmer. Similarly, will fertilizers be in large enough supply if they are, in fact, demanded? There is the new and very important problem of local storage facilities, not for seed and fertilizer only but increasingly for the record grain supplies. And the tasks of local-state-central administration with their overlapping lines of authority seem always to become more rather than less difficult as a program expands. HYVP and its associated activities in the new agriculture remain a solution still being tested. Their scientific, technological, and economic aspects are not yet fully in hand. One may still ask whether national and local policy is sufficiently committed to the new effort to assure resources and leadership for coping with inevitable problems. Yet

----

[61]See G.O.I. Ministry of Food, Agriculture, Community Development, and Cooperation, Expert Committee on Assessment and Evaluation, *Third Report on the Intensive Agricultural District Program*, September, 1967.

the new agriculture persists and grows. It provides an entirely new dimension of hope for achievement of the high output India needs.

The new agriculture has led to optimistic expectations. The present plan (for 1973/74) visualizes 60,000,000 acres in high-yielding varieties by that date. This is almost three times the 21,000,000 sown for 1968/69. In 1968 a target of 15,000,000 for that year (1968/69) was considered unrealistically optimistic; the target for 1973/74 can not be discounted. On these 40,000,000 additional acres (some 20 percent of the acreage under foodgrains) officials expect an output increment that is two-thirds of the total expansion in foodgrains planned for in the fourth five-year plan period.[62] Even critical evaluations of recent agricultural production and policy provide support for concentration in this type of effort.[63]

If the program does more or less achieve the output and growth goals of present plans, will this bring with it success for agriculture? Will agriculture spark the total development process? These questions refer to our earlier concern about the significance to the rest of the economy of demand on the part of the agricultural population.[64] Past programs in agriculture seem to have brought differential gains to the larger and richer farmers; it is not at all certain that the IADP and HYVP emphasis will, in the near future, go much beyond the rich farmer.[65]

Within the first years of the developing IADP and HYVP program, an early official report indicated that, with a few exceptions, the district average holdings of participating farmers tend to be above 10 acres (Table 24). In most districts they were of the order of at least twice the size of the operating units not participating. On the whole the package arrangements presuppose a resource availability as a condition for entering into the new agriculture. No contrary tendency has become manifest in the past two or three years, nor indeed is any to be expected under present policies. In essence, the agricultural program that offers hope for achieving output targets promises to aggravate rural inequalities. Insofar as it passes over a large share of the farmers, it may well pass over the mainspring of agriculture's potential in a newly dynamic econ-

---

[62]*Fourth Plan*, 1969 draft, p. 125.

[63]See, for example, the G.O.I. Ministry of Food, Agriculture, Community Development and Cooperation, *Report on the Intensive Agricultural District Program* (1960–68), Vol. 1, 1969, p. 4.

[64]See Chapter 1, pp. 8–11.

[65]For an early and insightful appraisal of the new programs with particular regard to this matter, see J.R. Desai, "Reliance on Rich Farmers for Development: Its Implications," *Economic Weekly*, No. 38, September 18, 1965.

TABLE 24.   HYVP Districts, 1966/67: Size of
Operational Holdings (acres)

District	Participants	Non-participants
Kolaba	3.18	1.70
Cuttack	5.96	3.12
Ernakulum	8.59	3.39
Thanjavur	9.76	4.74
Mehsana	10.99	6.61
Aligarh	12.59	10.41
Krishna	23.59	12.86
Karnal	41.48	11.56
Average, 8 districts	12.01	6.41

Source: G.O.I. *Report of the High-Yielding Varieties Programme: Studies in Eight Districts, Kharif 1966-67*, 1967, p. 31 (as quoted in H. B. Shivamaggi, "Crucial Aspects of Agricultural Development," *EPW*, September 1969, p. A-135).

omy: agriculture's demand influence on the rest of the nation. The technological achievement of the new agriculture could thus stand apart from over-all development achievement.[66]

Even within agriculture itself the changing pattern of interpersonal relationships — among farmer, tenant, farm laborer — has high costs. These will offset at least part of the gains from rapidly expanding output. Accelerated agricultural growth has already precipitated severe clashes between landlords and landless workers.[67] There is evidence of a growing cleavage in rural areas — between tenants and large farmers offering less and less land for rent; indeed between the large-scale farmers in the new agriculture and the smaller farmer left out. These aggravated social and political cleavages impair the nation's well-being. In particular they render more difficult the determined governmental action that is a precondition for effective national development programs.

Difficulties raised by growing internal inequalities are becoming familiar in India today, and solutions are being proposed. The 1969 draft plan actually projected special programs for "the small farmers (who) have not benefitted in proportion either to their numbers or their needs from the various programs of rural develop-

---

[66]See also Chapter 7, pp. 218–20.

[67]An outstanding illustration is the bitter conflict and killings in Thanjavur District of Tamil Nadu of December 25, 1968. For an account of the progress of the green revolution in Thanjavur and in other original IADP districts, see Francine R. Frankel, *India's Green Revolution: Economic Gains and Political Costs* (Princeton, N. J.: Princeton University Press, 1971), especially Chapter III.

ment." A Small Farmer Development Agency was to reach 1,500,000 farmers within the plan years, mostly to provide credit and irrigation — basic requirements for the new agriculture — and to permit small farmers to "participate in development and share its benefits."[68] The record of Indian agriculture, including the new directions of recent years, continues to pose the need for policies that offer the promise of change throughout India's agricultural structure and not primarily change for the richer and larger farmers.[69]

Before turning to a consideration of India's modern industrial development experience, we might summarize the main aspects of the past record in agriculture on which, we have argued, modern industry and indeed the total Indian economy are so dependent. The first five-year plan apart, output targets for the agricultural sector were not attained. Slackening growth rates in agriculture did not provide an obvious promise of future achievement on the scale necessary for successful development in India. Yet some regional performances in Indian agriculture were truly impressive, even when compared on a per capita basis with growth experience in other lands that the world hails as outstanding. The encroaching ceiling on national acreage expansion does not constitute a decisive deterrent: yields per acre have long been increasing in parts of India. There is evidence of some narrowing of yield difference among regions. The catching-up process itself offers scope for expanded future levels of national agricultural output, apart from productivity gains that can occur in the already higher-yielding regions.

Still, the record has disquieting aspects, for an important part of past expansion took place on the large farms of India's richer farmers. This aggravates internal income inequalities even before the advent of the "new agriculture" with its promise of special (further) gains to the larger farmer. India's agriculture over the first three plans did not fulfill its role in total national development. It needed a faster rate of output, with gains more equitably distributed through the land. So new tasks remain for the future. Output growth in agriculture seems more assured. But its regional and scale aspects continue to pose a threat for the total national development India seeks.

---

[68]*Fourth Plan*, 1969 draft, p. 115.
[69]See Chapter 7, pp. 217–24 below for some further outlook.

Development Experience: Industry and Trade

6

India's Modern Industry

The record in modern industry over the past two decades is easier to portray than is the record in India's agriculture. Despite the complexity, diversity, and dynamism of India's new manufacturing activities, the major forces that have influenced them are reasonably straightforward. This is again in contrast to what we found in agriculture: that sector so permeates the entire life of India that its behavior patterns are not easily discerned. It is ironic that familiar agriculture poses the very difficult and central problems of India's modern development. Deterrents to the growth of new and unfamiliar industry are relatively routine; for the most part they are overcome by broad-based growth in agriculture. This interpretation does not correspond to India's official approach: major efforts were to be directed to the new tasks of modern industry; gains in industry would then provide important assistance to agriculture's progress.

In past plans, and with the second plan explicitly, the keynote of the programs for national growth was the expansion of modern industry. Problems of effective demand for industrial product were not considered significant, especially relative to the problems of

163

supply expansion. While demands for agricultural products were held to be inelastic in a more developed India and even in an expanding world, there were virtually unlimited horizons for demand for industrial products. Industry held the promise of jobs for a growing labor force, particularly for workers not effectively utilized in agriculture. In addition there was always the possibility of continuous improvement in productivity per worker with its promise for gains in the well-being of labor. For India's planners, industry also constituted the prime sector of import substitution and of export stimulation. Through its potential for diverse production and its promise for productivity, modern industry could make India essentially self-sufficient in machinery production. Growing industrialization permitted India's planners to foresee a time when domestic output would replace reliance on foreign sources for capital goods. In all these possibilities lay assurance that there would be adequate levels of effective demand for industrial output. And finally, the complexity of industrial structures, with their high inter-industry and intersectoral relationships, put a premium on sophisticated technical knowledge. Unless planned expansion in one area, steel for example, is coordinated with balanced expansion in others, such as coking coal, coal-washing facilities, and specialized transport; and unless the steel expansion corresponds with growth in industries that use the steel, economic growth may start but not spread and persist. Planning for modern industry demands the articulation of input-output matrices and the derivation of dynamic capital coefficients. It was India's modern industry programs that from the very start attracted India's outstanding statisticians and economists to the staffs of the Planning Commission.

In preceding chapters we saw how planned investment in modern industry was increasingly to dominate all investment in the economy; how the importance of modern industry in India's total national output was to grow from below 6 percent in 1950/51 to some 15 percent by the end of the 1960's. More striking still was the internal shift within modern industry: 70 percent of factory output was in the consumer goods category in 1950/51; by 1965/66, value added in all modern industry had increased to near three times its pre-plan level, but the consumer goods component provided but one-third of this total.[1] There has been a dynamic ex-

---

[1] Until 1968, India's index of industrial production (base year 1956) gave a weight of almost 56 percent to the output of food processing and textile manufacturing enterprises. Changing industrial structure brought the weights in a new index (base year 1960) to about 39 percent. See R. B. I., *Bulletin*, "Index Numbers of Industrial Production — Revised Series," Vol. 22 (August, 1968), pp. 1016-19.

pansion in basic industrial products — for consumer, for industry, and for foreign trade. The actual investment data (Table 11, p. 90) reflect the relative growth in importance of new plant and equipment, and this within a total investment that may have grown even more than planned.[2]

Still, output of total industry and even the relative output of machinery and of machine-input products were actually below what the plans anticipated. Again the specific details of the record — plans and actuals — can be found in official publications of the government of India.[3] In over-all terms some 85 percent of the real industrial growth projected for 1960/61 in the first two plans may have been achieved by that date; its composition and its private-public mix also differed from plan. There were larger shortfalls in the third plan. Value added in modern industry was 47 percent higher in 1965/66 than in 1960/61; the plan called for doubling of a higher base figure. The extent of fulfillment of the industrial plan was smaller yet over the three interim annual plans; 1966/67–1968/69 were years of recession conditions. The index for all industries increased at an average rate below 2 percent over those three years. For major industries (including steel and fertilizer) that we discuss below, output in 1969/70 had not attained the target levels the third plan set for 1965/66.

These contrasts between actual and planned levels of output should differentiate shortfalls due to capacity creation and those due to degree of use of capacity in existence. For the most part the 85 percent ratio for 1951–1961 is related to the shortfall in capacity creation. There was no significant change in the degree of capacity utilization over those years. During the third plan, performance ratios reflect both factors in more or less equal measure. And in the three interim years before the new fourth plan, capacity under-utilization has certainly been most responsible for the failure to achieve anticipated growth in industrial output.

On the whole the *private* component of modern enterprise seemed more able to attain officially announced goals than was public enterprise, at least during the first three plans. But some of this may have been more apparent than real. Most private ventures were relatively small and were not articulated in great detail in the plans. Actual completion dates might be newsworthy; less so, advance plan announcement. In the public sector, on the other hand,

---

[2]As indicated earlier (p. 88) direct comparisons with plan are not readily made, either in total or in the composition of actual investment — even between public and private industrial ventures.

[3]*Monthly Statistics of the Production of Selected Industries of India.* These are available regularly in the R.B.I. *Bulletin.*

political considerations prompted publicity in some detail, often before satisfactory completion of plans and financial arrangements. These were years of mounting construction costs; there were difficulties in scheduling imported components, particularly after the 1957/58 foreign exchange crisis.[4] Publicly announced costs turned out to be too low, especially when plans encountered unexpected technical delays in construction and when foreign financing arrangements needed to be restructured. Both these problems occurred in steel, fertilizer, and heavy machinery industries, as well as in less basic public ventures. One might expect lags in capacity creation in a poor nation because of shortages of investment resources, or of unexpected imbalances in the supplies of inputs. But significant underuse of industrial capacity that was planned and actually created in such nations is not expected. There is need for modern product in a developing land; low incremental costs would encourage expanded and more efficient plant utilization. Yet the fact of both types of shortfall poses general problems about the modernization process in a poor land like India.

Some Important Industries

The record in steel is particularly relevant since India has been a modern steel producer from 1911 and has always been known to have the resource base for relatively low cost steel production. By 1951 national policy was explicit on public sector responsibility for new ventures in steel. Soon (January, 1954) government established Hindustan Steel Ltd. (HSL), a private corporation entirely owned by government, to operate the growing steel complex in the public sector. During the first plan some expansion was to take place in existing capacity in private steel enterprise, along with some output from a first mill in the public sector. While little new production was in fact achieved through 1955/56, plans were drawn up for three one-million ton public-sector steel mills as well as for the private steel expansion — mostly an essential doubling of the capacity of the Tata mill at Jamshedpur, in Bihar. These programs became core components of the second plan, which set a target of 4,300,000 tons of finished steel by 1960/61, with 2,000,000 of these in the three public-sector mills. The actual output in 1960/61 was

---

[4]This crisis seemed to have affected capital imports on public more than on private account! See, for example, Wilfred Malenbaum, "Economic Crisis in India," *The Economic Weekly*, July 6, 1957, pp. 839–43.

2,400,000 tons, with 600,000 tons from the public sector. There were understandable delays in scheduling component parts and construction, all complicated by the fact that different foreign authorities (British, German, and Russian) were integral parts of the individual projects.

The third plan target for finished steel output was 6,800,000 tons. Most of this was to come from expanded capacity of the three public mills (Durgapur in West Bengal, Rourkela in Orissa, and Bhilai in Madhya Pradesh), plus some from the very beginnings of production in the fourth mill (in Bokaro, also in Bihar). Total production in 1965/66 was actually 4,500,000 tons. The so-called "first stage" expansion of the Russian plant in Bhilai was completed; comparable expansion in the other two remain in process (as of 1971). There were delays in financing, especially at the Rourkela (German) mill where the expansion planned for 1965/66 may perhaps be farther from completion than at Durgapur (British).[5] After long international discussions on U.S. participation and funding for Bokaro, construction was begun in 1967 on the basis of an agreement with the U.S.S.R., some 5 years after the original starting date for the Bokaro project. The 1966 draft fourth plan projected total steel ingot capacity in India at nearly 15,000,000 tons (1970/71) with actual output of steel ingots at 12,000,000 and of finished steel at 8,800,000 tons. This goal involved production from second stage expansions in the three operating public mills, plus capacity output from a first stage at Bokaro. Actually, in 1969/70, the last full year of record, finished steel output was 4,700,000 tons with comparable capacity of 6,900,000. Bhilai was operating at about 70 percent of its capacity, Durgapur at less than 40 percent, and Rourkela at an even lower ratio. The private mills were producing at higher percentages of their capacity levels. These data mean that the actual fourth plan has more moderate capacity goals for 1973/74 (12,000,000 tons of ingots) than were the goals for 1970/71 in earlier versions of that plan (14,800,000 tons).

So much for what happened to output and to capacity. Growth of capacity in steel is primarily a consequence of public decision and action. Delays in fulfillment of facility construction, especially to the early 1960's, were inevitable aspects of a complicated engi-

---

[5]Both these plants have been allocated sizeable investment in the 1969 draft fourth plan for completion of the first stage of expansion. A second stage expansion (from 2,500,000 to 3,200,000 tons) is to be undertaken in the Bhilai mill during the current plan.

neering, financing, and administrative task, the dimensions of which could well have been underrated. While some of the false starts in discussions on financing were unduly expensive in time, and while improved programming of construction and of starting-up operations could have made actual plant completion somewhat more rapid, India's achievement in building one of the world's largest modern steel complexes in less than two decades is impressive. It is a tribute to what public decisions and action can do even in a poor and traditional economy. Yet the problem in steel, as in all modern industry, goes beyond capacity creation to plan content, and to the economic environment India provides for industrial growth. Though steel has increasingly become a public sector product, demand for steel in the market has always been influenced by public policy on prices and on distribution control for steel and for steel products. The level and pattern of steel output and of steel imports (and exports) have been sensitive to differentials in quality, price, and delivery dates between Indian and foreign steel products. India is an economic producer of steel, but the gradual reduction in India's net import status in steel products has been dependent upon government policy on prices and on product controls at least as much as upon expansion of presumably low-cost domestic capacity.[6]

In recent years it has taken rigorous licensing and certification of non-availability of supplies from domestic steel producers to encourage full consideration of domestic output by important users, including government agencies themselves. The product-mix of domestic output has still to be geared to domestic needs. Over-all economic policy has not assured that actual demand meets this need; this is particularly so for the requirements of public programs themselves.[7] While India will continue to require annual imports of about one million tons, mostly special steels not planned for production in India, there is broad scope for exports of pig iron and structurals. Only in the past few years has Hindustan Steel appeared to take seriously the importance of such trade to the Indian economy, and exports began to expand in late 1967. These specific developments are important, but major segments of the steel industry in India still have critical cost frontiers to pass. On the

[6]Early insights on the nature of these persistent internal balance problems in steel were provided in the G.O.I. Ministry of Steel and Heavy Industry, *Report of Steel Control*, 1963 (called the "Raj Committee Report," after its chairman, Prof. K. N. Raj of Delhi University.

[7]In 1968/69 India was still a net importer of steel of various kinds. Official estimates place domestic production at just above 90 percent of total use in that year. During 1951–1961 this ratio varied in the 60 percent to 75 percent range.

whole, the industry has been able to remain too isolated from actual market conditions.[8] After 15 years, Hindustan Steel, with more than one-third of all the investment in public industry in India, persistently incurs losses. The actual level of steel output has not increased for more than three years, despite continuing "need" for steel in public and private development activity in India and elsewhere in the developing world. In this environment, capacity creation and capacity utilization both lag.

The position of the fertilizer industry (especially nitrogenous fertilizer) underscores more dramatically yet the strength of internal pressures that can counter industrialization in a poor land. Expansion in fertilizer output has been a high priority objective throughout the entire planning period. In 1950/51, consumption of nitrogen was about 60,000 tons (N basis) with some 9000 tons produced domestically. Capacity of 300,000 tons was set for the first plan, but less than one-third of this was achieved: actual output was 80,000 tons (N) in 1955/56. Factory construction at Nangal in the Punjab, at Neiveli in Tamil Nadu, and at Rourkela, scheduled to begin in the first plan, was actually started during the second. But some expansion did occur at the government plant at Sindri in Bihar as well as at smaller private plants. The target for 1960/61 was again set at 300,000 tons, but Nangal was the only new plant in production by that date. India's actual output was 101,000 tons. Capacity in public plants was originally planned at 800,000 tons for 1965/66, with a national goal of one million tons. Growth of private capacity through new facilities and through expansion of existing facilities was also encouraged. So promising did the potential of private fertilizer production appear in the early '60's that capacity planned in public plants was scaled down to some 650,000 tons for 1965/66. By that date, however, total capacity reached 550,000 tons, essentially in the public sector. Actual output in 1965/66 was 232,000 tons. Little of this was in private plants; but three projects (Goa, a Union Territory; Kanpur, in Uttar Pradesh; and Kotah, in Rajasthan) which had been discussed over many years were actually being built. The last two did go into production in 1969. Major public installations at Madras, Durgapur, and Cochin (in Kerala) were still in construction in 1970.

This uncertain pace of growth of new capacity was accompanied by rapid growth in the level of fertilizer application — and rapid growth in foreign dependence. Under the stimulus of the new agri-

---

[8]See below, pp. 172–74. The Planning Commission attributes the low level of use of capacity to low efficiency at the steel plants, as well as to limited demand (*Fourth Plan*, 1969 draft, p. 231). There has been extreme disorganization at Durgapur and to a lesser degree at Rourkela.

culture, nitrogen consumption in 1968/69 seems to have reached
1,385,000 tons; over 60 percent of this had to be imported (at a
cost of some Rs 200 crores). Higher prices of foodstuffs and the
attendant reduction in India's high fertilizer/food price ratios seem
to have stimulated farmers' demand; this was, of course, also helped
by government's own pressures for agricultural expansion and the
green revolution. Nitrogen capacity did exceed a million tons for
1969/70, with actual output of 716,000 tons.[9] Tremendous further
growth is projected for the early 1970's, to outputs of more than
3,000,000 tons.

The record of the fertilizer industry reflects the long ambivalence
of India's policy-makers on development activity in agriculture;
public resources were committed less enthusiastically to fertilizer
than to steel, for example. When government did decide there were
to be large-scale domestic fertilizer enterprises, private interests
were not very responsive. Now, more than a decade later, uncertainty still remains as to the long-term position of this sector.
Private fertilizer investments of the recent past involved lengthy
preliminaries; government had to assure freedom from price and
distribution controls for seven years, with government retaining a
right to negotiate for 30 percent of the new plant's output.[10] The
Indian economy will probably need nitrogen supplies and domestic
production of at least the 3,000,000 tons now planned. A strong
case can be made for a major role for private activity in this type
of industry, although current programs anticipate less than one-
third of capacity in the private sector. Public ventures have not had
an easy history either of construction or operation. The high level
of industrial inputs in the production process places a premium on
efficient interindustry coordination; public nitrogen enterprises
have encountered difficulties in this regard. Thus a major explanation of the gap between nitrogen capacity and output in 1965/66
was gas unavailability and power shortages, especially for the
Rourkela plant. In 1969 the Ministry of Steel reported that the
Rourkela fertilizer plant works well below rated capacity "because

[9]Of interest are the following figures (1968/69) for phosphates (potash content) and pesticides (BHC) (in thousands of tons):

	capacity	production
P_2O_5	421	216
BHC	26.5	12

[10]These concessions of the middle 1960's are assuming a more normal status
for private enterprise now. See Chapter 6, pp. 174–75 and Chapter 7, pp.
207, 223.

of the inadequate quantity and unsatisfactory quality of coke oven gas supplied by the (Rourkela) Steel Plant."[11]

One aspect of the industry's problem is the rapidity with which domestic enterprise is approaching technological self-containment in both production and expansion. Domestic knowledge, machinery, and raw materials could within years replace imports in an industry that today still depends heavily on purchases abroad. This domestic substitution potential presents some cost and technological disadvantages to private fertilizer interests, particularly to those with foreign ties. Thus government's desire to assure maximum purchases of indigenous supplies and products caused delays in recent negotiations for an Allied Chemical-Tata Industrials project in Gujarat. With India's major commitment to machine construction, parallel uncertainties are posed in other industries.

Machines to make machines are a central cog in India's program for industry, for over-all growth, and for economic independence. In light machinery — machine tools, textile machinery, boilers, motors — domestic capacity is already large relative to India's needs. Important investments continue to be made in major heavy industrial machinery establishments, some usually with foreign assistance.[12] Some of the largest are in machine building (Ranchi in Bihar), electricals (Bhopal in Madhya Pradesh and Hardwar in Uttar Pradesh), and mining (Durgapur), in addition to machine construction intimately associated with the public steel centers. These vast industrial complexes are India's real thrust in the machine-building area. Conceived in the first decade of planning and formally initiated in the second and third plans, construction and assembly are now beginning to yield to actual production.[13] Complex machines associated with an advanced stage of industrialization are thus becoming available to replace imports, to facilitate indigenous capital formation and perhaps to provide new exports. On the other hand India's output of these heavy machines encounters competition

---

[11]G.O.I. Ministry of Steel and Heavy Engineering, *Report*, 1968–69. The 1969 draft fourth plan adds "low efficiency" as an explanation of poor output performance in fertilizers in 1968/69 (*op. cit.*, p. 231).

[12]Thus see the listings of outlays planned in the 1969 draft fourth plan on these heavy machine projects: *op. cit.*, p. 253, Annexure II (Main enterprises alone involve outlays in excess of Rs 625 crores).

[13]Output has not yet reached a meaningful ratio of capacity. Thus, some 2½ years after production "began" in the Rs 200–250 crores plant at Ranchi, output has yet to reach Rs 10 crores per year (Steel Ministry *Report, op. cit.*). Some Rs 85 crores more are to be invested there in the course of the fourth plan.

from overseas suppliers, which are already producing at much larger scales of output. This competition confronts public enterprises directly. Thus one of India's most prestigious public enterprises, Hindustan Machine Tools (HMT), sought official authorization to manufacture a tractor of Czech design in collaboration with a Czechoslovak firm, and as an alternative to the production of an Indian model, developed with the engineering establishment and the machine building facilities at Durgapur. In its application HMT argued the advantages of scale in the tested Czech model and the competitive disadvantage of an indigenous machine in an Indian market where most other tractors are produced jointly with foreign collaborators and are preferred.[14] Still, so long as demand for such machine building equipment originates in public enterprise, given present emphasis on rapid growth of public sector industry, such pressures may be contained. Sooner or later, domestic machine builders will need to compete effectively in cost and quality; and this is obviously true when India's producers of final goods seek markets abroad.[15]

On the whole, planners have been less concerned with possible shortages of demand for the output of modern industry than with difficulties on the supply side. Temporary imbalances are endemic to the growth process. Yet India's experience shows that capacity creation posed difficulties more amenable to solution than were those associated with demand for industrial products. Capacity has continued to grow in metal and engineering industries even as the problem of finding markets was becoming more acute, with plant increasingly underutilized. Licensing policy often tended to over-look the dangers of high costs, input shortages, limited demands — all in the push to expand capacity.[16]

Of course capacity underutilization has long been reported in India's modern industry, although facts on such utilization are always difficult to establish. In recent years the problem has become more acute. Over the 1950's, meaningful measures of excess capacity may have been in the 10 to 15 percent range. More precise calculations (for the large component of India's modern industry for which comparable data were available) show an increase from 17.7 percent in 1963 to 21.4 percent in 1967. The upward move-

---

[14]For an account of this case, see *EPW*, Vol. 4, No. 38 (Sept. 20, 1969), pp. 1500–1.

[15]See below, pp. 179, 190–92 (Chapter 6).

[16]For a recent analysis, with specific illustrations drawn from 163 industries (providing 75 percent of the weight of all industry in the index of industrial production, 1960 base) see R.B.I. *Bulletin*, "Excess Capacity and Production Potential in Selected Industries in India," Vol. 23, April, 1969, pp. 471–92.

ment continued in 1968 and 1969. Reasonable reductions in excess capacity would permit higher output in modern industry by 4 to 5 percent each year, even under present work shift patterns.[17] And while such a reduction would require improved programming of a wide range of inputs of the production process, the main requirement is "systematic studies regarding domestic demand . . . and the possibilities of export."[18] This modern industrial problem in India is associated with the inability of many of India's people to buy the planned level of output. And this derives mostly from what has been happening over the plan years in agriculture, the sector of the economy intimately related to the well-being of most of India's population. This relationship, manifest in India's experience over the past two decades, is readily illustrated in the developments attendant upon the agricultural reversals of 1965/66 and 1966/67.

Growth in industrial output began to slow down at the end of the third plan. Where total product of all modern industry was expanding at 8 to 10 percent annually in 1961–65, it actually fell in 1966 and 1967. Industrial consumer goods had been increasing on the average by some 5 percent annually, but at declining rates; production was significantly lower in 1967 than in 1966. Rates of increase in output of steel ingots, of structurals and pipes, and of ferro alloys fell from high levels to negative figures over the three-year period. Cement output in 1966 and 1967 grew at one-third its 1965 level. Supply was allocated up to 1965; it has become freely available on the market. At least as large were rates of decline in production of railway wagons, automobiles, electric motors, internal combustion engines — to name important capital goods.[19] India's economic expansion needs more of all these products; yet use of capacity declined rapidly over two or three important years, the cost to the development effort notwithstanding. Stocks of diesel trucks, electric motors, power-driven pumps, sulphuric acid, heavy structurals, to cite a few of many basic products, showed an increasing ratio to declining current production from early 1967 into 1969. These products were being put to use at an even slower rate than they were being made.[20]

Prices of foodstuffs and agricultural raw materials moved up dramatically in the last two years of the third plan. Prices of manufactured goods advanced 18 percent for the five years as a whole, while food prices increased 45 percent. In the single year 1966/67,

---

[17] *Ibid.*, pp. 481–2.

[18] *Ibid.*

[19] Data are from R.B.I. *Bulletin,* "Price Trends during the Three Plan Periods," Vol. 21, June, 1967, pp. 740-74.

[20] G.O.I., *Economic Survey 1969–70,* pp. 84–85.

prices of finished industrial goods increased by 7.4 percent while food articles and industrial raw materials went up by almost 20 percent. In the following year food prices increased further by more than 20 percent, and even more rapidly relative to other price movements, especially of manufactures.[21] Domestic terms of trade were moving markedly against industry. High food prices discouraged other purchases by urban consumers; they put upward pressure on wages. High agricultural prices benefitted middlemen and wealthy farmers; most agriculturists consumed their high-value grains and, like most urban consumers, were not able to buy products of industry. Disappointing tax yields and reductions in government sales of bonds deterred public investment. Where government would be expected to use its fiscal power to augment total demand, it was actually a participant in reducing the level of total output, and the rate of growth.

But the entire picture turned around with the favorable crops in 1967/68 and 1968/69. In 1968 there was a 6.4 percent rate of growth in the index of industrial production; increases also occurred in 1969 and 1970. The slowness and the uncertainty of output expansion in agriculture, and agriculture's failure to involve different regional and income groups in the process of growth were key elements in the deteriorating industrial situation from 1965 through 1968. This was also the case in past periods of unfavorable agricultural output during the years of planned development. Even now in 1971, with agricultural output at record levels, the influence on industry appears less marked; the new agriculture can achieve high output levels through the activities of a limited part of India's agricultural establishment. For industrial gains, both output level and high participation are critical. Both of these objectives must be sought in agriculture, over the next decade at least, to assure progress in India's modern industry.

The growing conviction on the part of Indian leadership that development policy needed new directions has not only brought steps toward a green revolution; it has also involved a range of actions toward less control of economic life and especially industrial activity. During 1965/66, and then increasingly with Mrs. Gandhi's government, specific steps were taken to relax the controls instituted in the Industries (Development and Regulation) Act of 1951. Simplification of licensing requirements, rupee devaluation, and some liberalization of imports over the years from 1966/67 have

---

[21]*Ibid.*, pp. 106–7.

made it easier for industries to adjust to changed market conditions and to new technological innovations. Such actions will contribute to a greater flexibility in the economy; they will be helpful in maintaining higher degrees of capacity utilization. Important as they are for India's industrialization, they remain adjuncts and never substitutes for concerted programs directed initially to widespread progress in India's agriculture.

Import Substitution

India's goal was to become essentially independent of imports of machinery by 1975/76, the scheduled end of the fifth plan; at that time India's machine industry was to generate a value added of some Rs 1650 crores, in 1960/61 prices, or about four times the 1960/61 level.[22] This meant an early focus on machinery imports to provide a base for India's own production of machines. To date perhaps Rs 4000 crores have been invested in machinery and related manufacturing by the central government alone. Close to 60 percent of this (almost Rs 2500 crores) took the form of payments for imports. And we noted that large expenditures on these plants continue, particularly for those producing heavy machines. While output of these machines has yet to reach more than a small fraction of planned capacity, India is certainly producing capital goods of a type formerly purchased abroad. It is hard to assess fully what has been gained in this substitution.

Thus the (1966) draft fourth plan stated that

". . . in machine tools we used to import 91.6 percent of the total supply in 1950/51; the figure went down to 44.6 percent in 1964/65 . . . . By the end of the Fourth Plan we would be meeting 75 percent of a much larger demand . . . . In sugar machinery the figure has gone down from 100 percent to 4.1 percent, textile machinery from 100 percent to 56.5 percent . . . . In petroleum products (other than kerosene) from 91.5 percent to 1.6 percent and in aluminum from 74.8 percent to 29.7 percent. However, in several cases the total demand has increased so much that in spite of a larger proportion being manufactured indigenously the total imports have tended to increase. In some cases there are substantial imports of components."[23]

---

[22]Thus see *MFB*, September, 1966, pp. 23–25. Items covered include transport equipment plus electrical engineering, electronics and industrial machinery.

[23]*Fourth Plan*, 1966 draft, pp. 13, 268.

Imports of products involved in domestic substitutes did in fact expand. As more "final" industrial goods were produced, more components of these machines came from abroad. Obviously the import-saving involved when the import percentage of commercial vehicles is reduced from 35.7 to 0.5 percent over the three plans[24] must be modified by the growth in foreign supplies of parts for vehicle assembly. In an earlier illustration, we saw that domestic production could not in fact assure a growth in intermediate goods output from Rs 300 to Rs 775 crores; import substitution was much less than it first seemed to be.[25] And India's total import bill has of course been characterized by a growing ratio of maintenance to new project imports, especially since 1960.[26]

Beyond this shift in import composition, it is still true that the major heavy machine substitution lies ahead. Machinery and components from abroad still constitute nearly 30 percent of annual machinery requirements (in contrast to 45 percent in 1960/61), and the substituted machines have been of the lighter varieties — in textiles and food processing. Similarly, most of India's steel alloys and almost half its fertilizers are still imported. A careful official judgment some years back was that the total impact of the import substitution program upon required imports had been relatively small.[27] In any event, total imports into India have continued to grow relative to income in most years, as we see below.

Import substitution helps industrialization because it provides domestic output for a commodity in actual demand. It promises to replace the imported with the indigenous and thus benefit the nations' foreign exchange position. But domestic industrial products do not automatically replace foreign supplies. Price and quality considerations are relevant, even when exchange controls restrict

---

[24]*Ibid.*, p. 13.

[25]See chapter 3, pp. 67–68.

[26]An interesting statistic revelant to this point is the balance of payments *deficit* of India's art-silk industry. While exports totalled Rs 35.2 crores, 1960–64, essential imports of fibres, machinery and parts over these years were Rs 112.3 crores (R.B.I. *Bulletin*, "The Balance of Payments Implications of Industrial Production: The Art Silk Textile Industry," Vol. 20, August, 1966, pp. 866–72). Further import substitution in the production of art silk textiles was not expected to reduce these deficits in large measure (*Ibid.*, pp. 71–72). Comparable results for India's cotton textile industry—India's third largest gross earner of foreign exchange and long a practitioner of import substitution for cotton fibres, dyes, chemicals and machinery—showed exports of Rs 339.6 crores and imports of Rs 429.2 crores for the years 1956–60 (*Ibid.*, Vol. 16, March, 1962, pp. 339–43.

[27]R.B.I. *Bulletin*, June, 1967, p. 748.

foreign competition. Similarly the "savings" of foreign exchange through domestic production are scarcely assured. There is the shift into intermediate products from abroad. More generally the foreign exchange gain is in fact realized only so far as domestically-utilized resources in import substitutes could not earn at least equal amounts of foreign exchange. When the domestic production is relatively expensive — the usual position, at least initially, because of the limited scale of output and because of the infancy of the enterprise — the implicit devaluation of the domestic currency may be very high. In any event new industrial output tends to be expensive in developing lands, both relative to comparable production elsewhere and relative to alternative domestic output with greater comparative advantage. The domestic market is restricted.

India's forward movement in import substitution includes many achievements, notably in machine tools and in petroleum refining, where both public and private enterprise provided new facilities and new output. By and large India's extensive developments in steel and fertilizers can be expected both to provide domestic production in place of imports, and probably to do so with economic gain to the country. This is likely despite the production difficulties encountered in recent years by these two major industries, and despite the persistence of relatively high costs. Still, the economics of the import substitution process poses complex practical problems; what appear to be straightforward cases run into major uncertainties. Recent experiences can be cited. Kirloskar Cummins Ltd. Poona, in Maharashtra, provides a good illustration — one that has already received some attention.[28]

A joint venture of two well-known engine manufacturers, one American and one Indian, Kirloskar Cummins was established in 1962 to produce diesels that were the "substantial equivalent in quality and performance" of the Cummins U.S. engines. The American firm had long exported engines to India, at an annual rate that required about a single day's production at the home plant in Columbus, Indiana. The increasing difficulty in obtaining import licenses threatened these exports; manufacture in India might thus substitute while it would also be in a favorable position to meet the growing future demand for heavy diesels in a large and developing

---

[28]This account draws upon Jack Baranson, *Manufacturing Problems in India, The Cummins Diesel Experience*, (Syracuse, N.Y.: Syracuse University Press, 1967), *passim*. For developments since 1967, use was made of the company's annual reports through September, 1970.

nation. The project was supported by the U.S. government, with AID arranging loans of $4,600,000, representing 67.5 percent of the original capital.

Production of 1500 engines was projected for 1965, and 2500 for 1967. But in 1965, the goal for 1967 was re-established at 500 engines. About half this rate of output was attained. Production costs were high, averaging some twice the landed cost of the U.S. import during the years 1963 to 1967. And the Indian engine may not have been up to the quality of its American counterpart. An underlying factor was the familiar problem of intermediate products and component parts. In Indiana the Cummins factory proper produced 40 percent of the engine; the remainder was assembled through purchases from at least 200 suppliers out of a total of some 700 always available for purchase of materials and parts. The joint venture was expected to produce 90 percent of the engine at the Poona plant; domestic suppliers could not provide all the needed components. In fact, imports of missing parts alone were costing India more foreign exchange per engine in 1967 than would an entirely imported engine. Domestic production of larger percentages of the diesel can grow slowly and at relatively high cost.

There have been important changes at the Indian plant, including especially a greater concentration of operating responsibilities on the Kirloskar side of the venture. Output has been expanding, although total production of Cummins diesels had not yet cumulated to 1200 units by October 1970; imports at the level of the 1950's have yet to be replaced. On the other side, quality may be reaching the standards of U.S. production, and the acquisition of a sales and service organization is helping assure a growing domestic market. The outlook for future production is now hopeful, although India will long continue to pay more for these domestic diesels, probably even in terms of foreign exchange outlays alone.

Import substitution demands some isolation of the domestic market. This tends to mean that producers are less concerned about production costs than they would be if competitive imports were available. Rupee devaluation in June 1966 also contributed to higher costs through its influence on prices of imported goods, although previous tariff policy had already achieved much of the same effect. While current policy adaptations in India seek to reduce the institutional and legal restrictions that have impeded producers' market adjustments, the policy continues to provide a price shelter for this expensive output. On the other side, the economic setback of the past few years — in part responsible for the new liberalization policies—has also contributed a greater awareness of cost considerations. The existence of underutilized capacity meant that the marginal costs of additional output could be lower. Recent and marked declines in the rate of growth of domestic demand have also encouraged Indian producers to take a new interest in markets abroad. There these producers meet competition from industrialists of other nations. India's manufacturing development countenanced a price structure for domestic product that was relatively high as against comparable industrial imports. Before devaluation, this difference may have meant domestic prices some 40 to 50 percent above landed costs of equivalent foreign industrial goods; domestic production did thus imply a large discount of the rupee in terms of foreign currencies.

A basic element of the program for long-term industrialization in a country like India is that "a fair proportion of India's industry will in fact (become) competitive" in world markets and thus serve, through trade gains, as a stimulant to efficient production in other goods and sectors of the economy. Recent expansion in the exports of light machinery, in 1968/69 especially, testifies to this potential, and growth in export trade is an important objective of current policy. Obviously even producers who are relatively efficient may be kept out of the foreign market because they use high-cost domestic inputs, whether raw material or intermediate product, although a system of tax rebates and subsidies can offset these excess cost items. While this may serve to discourage escalation of the adverse trade effects of high cost inputs, trade continues to suffer. There are few alternatives to the need for India's new industries constantly to press toward greater efficiency and lower costs.

Recent investigations are relevant to developments on the cost front. It seems to be true that modern industry is becoming more evenly distributed among the states of India. Distribution by states of per capita consumption of industrial power narrowed significantly between 1951 and 1961. Maharashta, West Bengal, and Bihar, the three major industrial states in 1951, with 17 percent of total population, used 45 percent of industrial power in 1961, as against 56 percent in 1951. A few states have actually multiplied their ratio of industrial power use (Orissa by six, from 1 percent to 6 percent; Punjab by four, from 2 percent to 8 percent).[29] There could be some gains for India's over-all economic growth in some

---

[29]For the data used in this argument, see P.N. Dhar and D.V. Sastry, "Inter-State Variations in Industry, 1951-61," *EPW*, Vol. 4, No. 12 (March 22, 1969), pp. 535–38.

such regional redistribution of modern industry, but these are more than offset by the fact that the recent spread also reflects politically dominated locational decisions that always yield higher unit costs than could otherwise prevail. This matter has now become critical enough to receive national attention in the basic policy guides of the new fourth plan. "In some cases industry has been inappropriately sited and some desirable adjustments in regional locations have not taken place."[30] The locational problem looms large in the Planning Commission's apparent intent that the central government (as against regional political forces), play a more decisive role in any new regulating mechanisms in the planning process. No matter what happens, Indian industry bears what could be long persistent cost disadvantages as a result of past locational decisions.

There is some more direct evidence on cost trends in modern industry over the past two decades and more. For major companies in the private sector and for most industries, available statistics *taken together* reveal that real capital per unit of product has risen over the 1946-66 period, and that output per unit of labor cost has declined.[31] Such measures are, of course, needed on an individual industry basis, and, where possible, for individual products. The study cited does not make adjustments for changes in the nature and quality of India's industrial product, now so different from what it was two decades ago. Technological change has altered the cost functions, perhaps significantly. Nonetheless, however crude, the evidence is not readily dismissed;[32] the authors of the study consider that this record places significant obstacles in the way of India's industrialization.

First, India's system of market, licensing, allocation, and price controls has served to isolate producers from competitive pressures (as we mentioned above). Second, in its allocative decisions public administration in India does not place a high priority on the objective of productive efficiency. Here we can refer to the scope provided, at least in the early plan years, to industrial location based on political considerations. We also recall our earlier discussions on the gap between the importance given investment in the development concept and the knowledge about what investment has taken

---

[30]*Fourth Plan*, 1969 draft, p. 26.

[31]Raj Krishna and S.S. Mehta, "Productivity Trends in Large-Scale Industries," *EPW*, Vol. 3, No. 43 (October 26, 1968), pp. 1655–60.

[32]Prof. Yoginder Alagh provides some support for constant (as against increasing) cost relations in a few industries. See his "Industrial Planning, Past Experience and Future Tasks," *EPW*, Vol. 3, No. 35 (August 30, 1969), pp. 107–11.

place. Finally the authors of the study claim that India's educational system is not geared to produce specialists for the important tasks of modern economic life.[33] While such broad criticisms can be overdrawn, all three of these matters have in fact been given new prominence by the new Planning Commission responsible for the new fourth plan in 1970.

Modern industry in India will encounter expansion problems unless development programs deal more directly with demand deficiencies. It will continue to suffer from pressures toward high costs in an environment where protective devices have complex, deeply planted roots. Both statements are relevant to India's export prospects. We saw earlier that India's planners had from the start visualized a gradual elimination of the nation's deficits on international account during the course of the five-plan perspective. Expanded output and higher savings ratios were the basic tools for achieving self-sustaining growth. But insofar as the nation would continue to want imported goods and services, some structural changes had to emerge over the sequence of plans in order to assure levels of Indian exports at or above the desired levels of imports. Indeed, a surplus on current account would sooner or later be needed if only to permit repayment of India's foreign debt obligations. Modern industry was to play a central role in these structural changes. High income elasticities of demand for its diverse products plus the opportunities industry offered for technical progress and efficiency meant that the planners could expect to lean heavily on manufacturing output to achieve the nation's foreign trade and exchange objectives. This is the concern of our next section.

Foreign Trade in the Plan Years[34]

The broad scheme underlying the foreign trade aspects of India's plans is familiar. Imports were to expand at a rapid rate initially, both in absolute terms and relative to national product. This growth rate would then gradually decline while exports increased relative to national product. By the end of the original five-plan perspective in 1976, and perhaps sooner, the value of exports would exceed the value of imports. It was also envisaged that imports would there-

---

[33]Krishna and Mehta, *op. cit.*, p. 1660.

[34]This section parallels my article, "Foreign Trade in India's Development," *Foreign Trade Review*, Vol. 5, No. 4, Annual Number (January-March, 1971), pp. 424–37.

after continue to grow, at least in absolute terms, in order to accommodate the so-called "noncompetitive" imports for which domestic substitutes were not to be ventured. But a net export status would both permit such imports and also provide for systematic repayment of the foreign debt accumulated during the net import years. The ratio of foreign trade to national income would probably be lower according to these plans than was the case in the early years of independence, before the initiation of formal planning. India, like Mainland China, the Soviet Union, and the United States — large nations with diverse resource bases — anticipated a greater degree of self-sufficiency as national output grew relative to population.

With respect to specific categories of products, the early programs gave priority to the import of capital goods: these were key to the rapid expansion and diversification of India's modern industry. Imports of consumer goods and probably those of intermediate products also were to be restricted. Both these areas were major centers for expanded domestic output. As domestic production (import substitution) of capital goods could expand, the ratio of imports of consumer to producer goods would rise — after the first decade or so of the development effort. Eventually, however, the import structure would focus on India's long-term requirements from abroad: for example, rock phosphate and sulphur, non-ferrous metals, crude oil, and certain specialized industrial goods. Imports of these non-competitive products would probably expand as India's own potential in industry and agriculture grew.

The plans were more explicit regarding commodity patterns on the export side. They called for marked declines in the relative importance of India's traditional exports — tea, jute, and cotton manufactures — and for rapid growth rates in "new" manufactured products, especially the diverse output of the electrical and mechanical industries. From the beginning, and notably with the second plan, export projections were said to reflect such growth and diversification, mandated by relative income elasticities of demand in world markets. With respect to the invisible account, India had long been a net earner. But the shipping and insurance services and the remittances from abroad that together used to provide the bulk of these earnings were not expected to expand rapidly. In any event, they were in fact soon dwarfed by the rapid growth in interest payments (as in amortization on the capital account) associated with the debt nature of most of the foreign assistance to India. There would thus be some growth in this deficit on invisible account over the plan years.[35] On the whole, however, the vigor of the export product expansion was to assure India's emergence as a net exporting nation on total current account — in the 1960's (according to the early plans) and sometime in the 1970's (by revised plans).

Some evidence of such an underlying scheme may be found in the plan data of Table 25. We see growth in imports over the successive plans, at least until the 1969 program; there is some indication of a lagged growth in exports; current invisibles yield a progressively smaller net surplus, until this surplus disappears and becomes negative. But the picture of a surplus on total current account is not apparent in any of the past plans. Actually this total account remains in deficit for the past three plans. This *plan* deficit increases progressively, both in money terms and relative to planned net investment and national income (Table 25: rows 5.0, 6.1, 6.2). Thus, the plan data are themselves testimony to the inability of the planning authorities to articulate a program for achieving the official scheme that relates foreign trade to the total development effort. This is reflected in the summary plan data of Table 25. The problem arises from the basic difficulty of associating output and domestic utilization with specific types and amounts of goods and services that are traded internationally. All this is true at the *plan* level. There are many additional considerations with respect to program, policy, and their implementation in the *actual* achievement of the articulated plan.

Conceptually the input-output matrices so fundamental to measuring product interdependences in an economy are not normally divisible into foreign and domestic components of the individual items. In an economy like India's, the market mechanism usually provides such divisions. At any one time these divisions may appear as deficit components (for imports) or surplus components (for exports) in some static equilibrium output level where a net resource transfer from abroad has augmented the nation's import potential. These surpluses and deficits might in fact be measured as of one point of time, but they exist subject to restraints (and costs) of foreign exchange. Indeed specific divisions exist only in a dynamic

---

[35]Interest and service payments on foreign loans increased gradually to an average level of Rs 67.6 crores in the third plan years, 1961–66. They rose to Rs 100.6 crores on the average for the three interplan years 1966–69. Comparable capital account entries for amortization payments average Rs 66.5 crores and Rs 100.9 crores respectively. (All figures are in pre-devaluation rupees.)

TABLE 25. Balance of Payments on Current Account[a]

	First Plan (1) 1951-56		Second Plan (2) 1956-61		Third Plan (3) 1961-66		Fourth Plan 1966 version (4) 1966-71	Fourth Plan 1969 version (5) 1969-74
	Plan	Actual	Plan	Actual	Plan	Actual	Plan	Plan
1.0 Exports (f.o.b.)	2800	3109	2965	3060	3700	3735	8030	8300
2.0 Imports (c.i.f.)	-3800	-3651	-4340	-5400	-6350	-6030	-13635	-9630
3.0 Trade Balance	-1000	-542	-1375	-2340	-2650	-2295	-5605	-1330
4.0 Invisibles (excluding official donations)	250	391	255	425	—	-279	-1215[c]	-920[c]
5.0 Total Current Transactions[b]	-750	-151	-1120	-1915	-2650	-2574	-6820	-2150
6.0 Total: as a ratio of								
6.1 Net Investment	21%	4%	18%	28%	25%	25%	32%	9.5%
6.2 National Income	1.6%	0.3%	1.8%	3.1%	3.2%	3.6%	6.8%	1.3%

[a] Rs crores: *First* through *Third Plans*, pre-devaluation prices; *Fourth Plan*, post-devaluation; *Actual*, current prices. See Table 2, rows 9.1 and 9.2, p. 59.
[b] Exclusive of non-monetary gold movements.
[c] Exclusive of amortization payments (combined with debt service in the plan documents).

Sources: *Plan* columns: Five year plans, *passim.*
Actual columns: Five year plans, R.B.I. *Bulletin, Economic Survey, passim.*

context. Their delineation and projection are not mechanistic in a society and economy as complex as is India's. Rather, specific foreign trade transactions are responses to dynamic forces that themselves influence the level of equilibrium output as well as its composition; they also alter national product through new price and quality differentials.

A simple illustration is provided by the changing role of intermediate products in the final domestic output that seeks to replace machines formerly imported. Expansion of domestic output of tractors, for example, requires expansion of output (perhaps new output) of components *or* new imports of these parts. What combination of these two depends on the alternative demand for these components (and for their outputs) in other products, both in India and abroad. We have already observed that import substitution of finished products has been accompanied with larger imports (or smaller exports) of intermediate goods.

Because of this situation, successive plans in India have had to raise their import levels for the same degree and level of import substitution. One might also mention that in modern parts of the economy — where such substitution tends to be focused — foreign trade is usually in the hands of sophisticated traders skilled in international exchange and in the nuances of public policy in the foreign trade area. The next plan must therefore make *ad hoc* adjustments for unexpected imports of intermediate products revealed in past import data. The difficulty in identifying the necessary imports and the probable exports is compounded during periods of important price changes. The new price levels in which successive plans are denominated are not readily translated into the specific elements to be traded in that plan. There is no question that the plan figures of Table 25, row 2.0 were meant to reveal an expansion of real imports. The large *plan* increase shown for 1961–66 imports needs to be viewed in light of the fact that the plan price level for 1961–66 was set in 1960/61 prices, and these were almost 30 percent above the 1952/53 price level used in the 1956–61 plan. In this price context, the entire upward movement of *plan* imports becomes less real.

On the export side, the plans themselves may not have called for a real growth, at least through the third plan. Here, the foreign trade aspects of early planning were subservient to an emphasis on the importance of foreign loans and grants as the means to increased imports for development. Still, within the export total, there was much talk of a shift in composition. Where tea, jute, and cotton

textiles comprised about two-thirds of the value of all exports in
pre-plan years, plans for 1970/71, for example, envisaged their importance as little more than one-third of the total, although their
absolute size was expected to increase.[36] There has been little export
performance to support this expectation (at least until the late
1960's when the entire role of foreign trade was being reassessed by
planning authorities). As noted above with respect to total current
transactions, import and export data of the plans also constitute an
uncertain guide to the trade patterns required for Indian economic
growth. Statistical and conceptual aspects of foreign trade in an
industrializing nation are not yet sufficiently precise to permit detailed planning of this sector of the economy.

Perhaps this conclusion supports the need for broad, rather than
specific, controls of industrial expansion, especially for output
changes that bear directly on foreign trade. This calls for devices
like exchange auctions, for example, that could deliver some optimum trade result within a given level of exchange availability, or
devices like entitlement schemes that could even serve to expand
exchange resources. No simple formula exists beyond the certainty
that control schemes need to be flexible, not rigid, and rational
rather than particularistic. While this is not the place to assess the
actual program, the record of action and of the action agencies in
this field is obviously one that does not conform to these broad criteria. The results of trade policy have been costly to India's development effort over the past two decades; they also help explain
recent trends toward liberalization and rationalization of the licensing machinery for regulating new capacity and output, and for
earning and using foreign exchange.

With respect to the actual trade experience, we note some parallels in plan and actual data for *total* imports. Thus the ratio of
planned to actual imports in 1961–66 (row 2.0, Table 25) is about
the same as that ratio in 1951–56. But the actual figure for 1961–66
is measured in a price level some 12 percent above that of the plan
estimate for that period. Moreover Table 25 shows that the marked
growth in imports actually took place not in the third but in the
second plan years (some of which are remembered as a period of

---

[36]The 1969 draft fourth plan projected the relative importance of traditional
exports at 28.5 percent in 1973/74 and 20.5 percent in 1980/81. "All other
manufactures"—mostly new products—provided negligible exports in 1950/51
and 1955/56 (1.5 percent of all exports). The new fourth plan optimistically
estimated exports of these new products at 26 percent (1973/74) and 38 percent (1980/81) of total exports (See pp. 43–44).

foreign exchange crisis, with great import difficulties!) Total real imports over past plans were at least 10 percent lower than plan estimates. Moreover, their composition was substantially different. Food shipments far exceeded the trade scheme's (and the plan's) expectations. Where the third plan called for 10 percent of its imports in this category, the actual ratio was close to 20 percent. Fertilizer imports were also higher than plan projections. Together food and fertilizers comprised 25 percent of imports in the last two years of the third plan, and 35 percent in the first two interplan years, 1966–68. The impact of the decline in real imports was on the industrial products so important for structural change in the economy, *i.e.*, precisely where imports would affect India's basic development strategy of substituting domestic capacity and output.

This shortfall offers a good illustration of the nature of the relationship between domestic output and foreign trade. With emphasis on the static equilibrium character of plan goals, such shifts in import needs would be expected to give rise to pressures for additional imports, or greater efforts to stimulate domestic output. In many of India's industries capacity was far from utilized. Indeed, in 1965/66 and 1966/67 especially, agricultural adversities contributed significantly to further reductions in the use of installed capacity. Shortages notwithstanding, pressures to expand supplies were neither strong nor effective. There is little indication that the system of controls adjusted to the possibilities and the needs for India's economic expansion. In this respect the favorable harvests in 1967/68 and 1968/69 offer further insights on the output-trade patterns. The crops did stimulate national product and industrial output; they provided an immediate corrective for lagging industrial imports. Here again we see *parallel* developments in output and imports more than changes in opposite directions. India's actual imports over most of the plan years (until the past two or three years in any event) appear to have been part of a pattern of investment and output different from the plans.[37] Over the entire plan sequence there has, in fact, been a slowing down in the rate of growth of the real import level, since 1960/61 especially. But this cannot be identified with the deceleration in relative import

---

[37]See pp. 183–85 above. For a summary interpretation of trade developments during the foreign exchange crisis of the second plan years see Malenbaum, "Economic Crisis in India." It is interesting to note that private imports and private sector output increased together over those years in contrast to plan intentions for lower imports in the private sector.

growth envisaged in India's basic scheme for import substitution and self-sustaining development.[38] The actual slowdown of imports was not an obverse of expansion in domestic substitute output that assured equilibrium supply. India did not have either the intermediate products or the capital goods which its development programs anticipated. It did not have sufficient amounts of fertilizers and its raw materials, of crude oil and non-ferrous metals. The slowing down of the import rate in the early 1960's reflected plan and program weakness more than achievement.

The performance record also shows low and almost unchanging export levels throughout the first decade of the plans. Indeed, due to Korean War demands for India's jute and other raw materials, 1951/52 was the highest export year until the third plan. There was a decline in India's share of world exports; there was a loss in India's share of traditional export markets. The need for a revised trade scheme for development was increasingly apparent. In the third plan document, government did indicate a new priority for export growth in the development scheme. An export goal was set significantly higher (in money terms in any event) than in earlier draft projections. For the first time the third plan stressed the importance of high agricultural production targets to assure sufficient supplies of traditional-type export commodities. It recognized the dangers of domestic competition for exportable goods. This was indeed a real concern, given high domestic costs and a system of import and export management that heavily discounted the exchange value of the rupee. In 1961–63 there was some upward movement in exports — 5 percent per year in real terms — but progress was not maintained. Export value remained at a fairly constant level (of some predevaluation Rs 800 crores) through 1967/68. The record gives little evidence of the emergence of a positive association of exports and national product, to say nothing of the more than proportionate export growth that the foreign trade scheme anticipated, particularly after 1960.

There is also no evidence of a more rapid growth in exports relative to imports. In fact, the statistics show about the same margins between these trade flows in the third and second plan years. And in 1966/67 and 1967/68 India's trade deficits were at record levels. It is true that these were years of very heavy food and fertilizer

---

[38]In Table 25, in current prices, actual imports in the second plan were almost 50 percent above those of the first; in the third plan the expansion was about 10 percent above the second. In real terms the reduction in the rate of expansion was more marked.

imports. Yet the draft fourth plan of 1966 projected foreign trade in 1966–71 with a larger imbalance on current international account than the absolute and relative deficits planned or achieved in any earlier period (Table 25, row 5.0). Only a few years back, India's Planning Commission still felt that the route to greater international balance required a large import surplus in the fourth plan years. India's development effort was still looking to net imports financed primarily through foreign grants and loans.

The shift in this position by the time the most recent fourth plan was drafted (1969) does reflect a drastic change. Suddenly new and very different directions are projected for foreign trade. Exports are to grow by 7 percent a year from the essentially constant levels reported above, while imports are to remain more or less at 1961–66 magnitudes, as against figures some 40 percent higher in the 1966 draft plan [Table 25, columns (4) and (5)]. No such trade patterns are found in the past record. The current plan's effort appears to be influenced not by this record but by a new view on what trade can and must do in a developing land. The specific focal points in the domestic efforts are a new agriculture and a new liberalization of the rules for conduct of industry and for use of foreign exchange. There are higher output targets, which call for an appreciably reduced dependence ratio on net imports.[39] In the new plans India will achieve international balance on current account much more rapidly, hoping to make systematic reductions in its debt burden. India now seeks assistance from creditor nations on a net basis rather than the earlier gross basis.[40]

So marked a shift in the scheme for self-support, and so different a view on the role of net imports, would seem to warrant fuller discussion than one finds in the new plan. It is important, therefore, to explore the new trade trends planned for the next decade or so against the background of past experience. With respect to imports we have already suggested that *favorable* domestic developments

---

[39]And though the 1969–74 years are considered to have emergency dimensions in this regard, the plan document suggests that imports will grow at a slower rate in the fifth plan (4.6 percent annually, 1974–79) than the 6.5 percent output growth rate planned. India incidentally appears still to project a lower ratio of international trade to national product than prevailed in pre-plan years.

[40]In its final form (April 1970), the fourth plan discusses the initial fulfillment of its goals for a rapid reduction in foreign dependence in terms of cutting in half the current level of aid "net of servicing" by 1973/74. It speaks of "aggregate external assistance" of Rs 1850 crores; actually this net amount assumes gross aid of Rs 4130 crores, from which payment of service charges (Rs 2280 crores) has been deducted (*Fourth Plan*, pp. 87–89).

tend to generate large (non-foodgrains) purchases abroad. Such domestic activity is usually associated with generally successful agricultural development — an annual growth rate in that sector exceeding 3.5 percent for a number of years, for example. Whenever domestic conditions were favorable in past years, India found ways to achieve high import levels, whether through more exports or through India's attractiveness for private foreign investment and for public assistance from abroad. This was true even in the face of restrictive national policies on domestic investment and output in the private modern sector, on imports generally, and indeed with a program of structural change that in itself did not encourage international flows of goods and services. In years of economic adversity an inverse relationship did exist between domestic production and the import of foodgrains. When agriculture was sluggish (an average growth that was not above 3.5 percent a year for more than one or two years), foreign assistance in the form of agricultural products tended to expand. Such upward elasticity in food assistance was associated with a shift from other forms of aid, due especially to assistance from the United States. Poor crops in India exert a depressing influence on the whole economy; they bring reduced levels of total imports — particularly non-food imports.

The past record must be interpreted as counter to an argument that import restrictions or limited total import targets serve as stimuli to growth in the domestic economy. With the (possible) exception of foodgrains production under conditions of ample PL 480 supplies, an inverse relationship between domestic output and imports cannot be expected. Even when foreign assistance is meant to initiate an acceleration in growth — when new imports are to meet some bottleneck need, for example — the domestic response has not been impressive. Use of such aid tends to lag unless other conditions are favorable for domestic expansion, for the primary direction of influence is from domestic development to imports. If the new fourth plan does essentially achieve its growth objectives, imports will also expand, probably more than output. In any case, imports for a growing Indian economy over the next five to ten years will not remain in the size range of past plans, current official views on this matter notwithstanding.[41]

On the export side, a basic requirement for the present program is again the assurance of a vigorous and competitive domestic economy that can participate in today's foreign markets. In addition, government needs to take special action to encourage larger vol-

---

[41]See Chapter 7, pp. 224–25.

umes and varieties of goods sought in foreign markets. Where such demand is expanding rapidly, as has recently been the case for exotic food products like spices or even for some modern machinery, there may for a while be a low premium on relative cost advantages. However, sooner or later alternative supply sources become available, especially for modern equipment items and usually from more developed lands. India's policies cannot persistently contribute to maintaining high cost output. Even where foreign markets offer relatively inelastic demand schedules — a situation often said to characterize the demand for India's traditional exports—deliberate action may be essential simply to maintain a relative share in such markets. In fact India's relative importance in total world exports fell from over 2 percent to less than 1 percent in 10 to 15 years after 1950. Indeed it is not the diminishing relative importance of the total market for such traditional products as tea, cotton, and even jute goods that has brought about this decline; it is the more aggressive output and sales policies of suppliers in other developing lands. Thus, Ceylon, Hong Kong, and Mainland China have pursued active sale and price programs in these markets while India has tended to underplay the true importance of its traditional exports.

Expansion of traditional exports does not generate comparable demand for imported inputs — per additional export rupee for example — as do exports of modern products. As indicated earlier, the net exchange gains from new and modern industry tended to be overstated in India's plans. Clearly, agriculture in India has direct and great relevance to the nation's export possibilities. Involved are both India's traditional products (tea, jute, and cotton textiles) and many more new items with growing external demands — oil cakes, cashew nuts, leather and its products, fish and its various by-products, tobacco, sugar and spices.[42] The past decades point up the important role of domestic supply conditions in achieving such agricultural exports. And of course agricultural progress — expansion at a rate of at least 3.5 percent annually, by methods that involve most of India's farms and of India's agricultural population — is essential to vigorous over-all economic expansion.

With respect to modern industry exports, gains can be expected through the policy shifts away from restrictive controls and toward liberalization in industrial expansion and diversification. Official

---

[42]In 1967/68 agricultural-based exports provided more than 60% of the total value of India's exports. The ratio exceeded 55% even in 1968/69 when total exports gained from the new manufactures, notably of the electrical and chemical products.

attitudes have in fact become more sympathetic to the role of market prices and competition even for achieving the goals of India's socialistic society. On the more specific trade policy front, both export encouragement and some import liberalization have received greater emphasis, at least since 1966, through rupee devaluation, selective tariff adjustment, shifts in the import entitlement scheme, and more limited licensing control, among other measures.

Actual gains from these new directions will be apparent in the current fourth plan, now in its third year. There is some evidence that the recession that began in 1965 is nearing an end. The new agriculture and the more liberal industry and trade policies have been part of this achievement. The domestic economy is moving more vigorously than in the interplan years, but it is premature to predict attainment of the fourth plan's national growth targets. With respect to total foreign trade, dependence on net foreign assistance has certainly declined, both on account of increased exports and restricted expansion of imports (measured net of grain shipments which have declined markedly). On the export side, the upward spurt in 1968/69 can be attributed in important measure to new products. Thus exports of engineering and electrical goods increased by more than twice the 1967/68 value (and some five times that of 1960/61.) Other increases in non-traditional exports include iron ore and chemical products. In some part the 1965–68 economic setback made it easier for government to encourage exports of such goods from underutilized plants. And this fact also made it easier for the nation to live with reduced ratios of imports. The key question is what will happen to exports and imports in a vibrant economy — one that actually grows more than 5 percent each year.

If we have interpreted the past record correctly, such an economy will make possible high export levels although it will not assure them. It will require and probably assure high import levels also. International account balance will occur more slowly than some current evidence suggests, even though export growth in 1969 and 1970 was maintained. India's industry continues to need capital goods imports and intermediate products at a more rapid rate than growth in industrial output itself. Consumer goods imports (non-agricultural) cannot be severely curtailed without jeopardizing the competitive efficiency of India's own domestic enterprise.

Marked import limitations fit too readily into a pattern of restrictive measures: again there is already some hesitancy in implementing the new policies of industrial and trade liberalization.

Import substitution under protection continues to exert strong political and institutional appeal. It would be regrettable if India's new trade emphasis was diverted from its key role in a more efficient economy to a primary focus on international balance, for this last is not an end in itself. India's primary task is to achieve persistent economic expansion, even if this means achievement of international balance at a somewhat slower rate than present plan goals. The Indian experience suggests that it is the state of domestic production that governs foreign trade more than vice versa. In addition there must be high priority for the production of export-oriented goods and services. Import restrictions do not in themselves spur domestic production; vigorous output does not tend to be associated with low levels of imports. India's current and capital needs remain high. Only sustained growth in the domestic economy and growing trade interdependence with other countries can assure India's self-sustaining status.

Implications of Indian Development Experience: Summary

In agriculture, in industry and in foreign trade, today's development emphasis rests on new considerations, different from those that dominated India's development efforts and experience over most of the past two decades. In an old land like India it is not likely that the post-independence experience — itself so influenced by Indian social and economic structures of a more remote past — will fail to bear intimately on achievement in the decades ahead. We therefore draw together some major aspects of India's experience with growth under planning to the late 1960's, when the effects of new directions in agriculture, industry, and foreign trade were just becoming manifest. These lessons from the past highlight the substance of our final chapter.

The record since independence has been one of progress as measured by total economic output, including product from two key sectors, agriculture and modern industry. Over the century or so for which some measures of economic progress are available, these past two decades constitute a landmark both for rate of growth and for duration of upward movement. Growth in national product exceeded a growth rate of population without parallel in past Indian history. For the five years 1966–70, average output per person was more than one-third higher than it was in 1947–51, when India's population was smaller by some 170,000,000 persons. Moreover, the changes of the past twenty years suggest that long-period declines in India's prevailing per capita income levels, like setbacks over the past century, can be judged highly unlikely for the next decades. On the other hand, the achievement under formal planning in India scarcely assures systematic *expansion* in per capita growth rates, an essential mark of continuous development in a nation's economy.

Plan experience has not in itself shown the progressive expansion of successful development. This is true even though rates of increase in the major economic input factors — capital formation and labor force creation — have both expanded more or less systematically since 1950. But productivity per unit of factor input, a key of economic progress, grew but slowly over the two decades; indeed its growth rate declined. The record of actual growth did not parallel the output paths in the official long-term growth perspectives. Thus *actual* increments in output constituted a *diminished* ratio of *planned* increments in output over successive past plans. Also incremental capital-output ratios *increased* over these plans, in marked contrast to the constant or even diminishing relationships built into the plans. However crude these coefficients and ratios as barometers of economic change, they do suggest that by the late 1960's the economy had yet to begin systematic expansion in the pattern of India's long-term growth perspective.

Presumably it was this very record that made India's planners themselves decide that after two decades of planning, new directions were needed, that the old plans should be held in abeyance until the reformulation of a new fourth plan for 1969-74. Despite an impressive total output record, despite the diversity and modernity of India's post-independence economic life (particularly in industry), a newer and still different agriculture, industry, and trade are to provide augurs for the desired future. It took experienced and expert government officials to formulate these new directions, particularly for an agriculture which intimately involved most of the people of India. In this important sense, new actions did grow out of past experience. Yet the many decisive changes in inputs and anticipated outputs need to be related to earlier development actions. What expectations do basic aspects of post-independence development experience provide for India's new programs?

Investment

Plan experience with investment in India has not justified the emphasis given this input in the development schemes. Actual new capital formation was generally larger than planned in money terms and probably in real terms also. Domestic savings and foreign assistance may each have been above plan. Actual investment traced a pattern different from the plans, as to private and public uses and as to different industrial sectors. The binding forces that were to integrate sectoral investment did not bring about that end. The investment dimension of the development experience suggests that capital shortage in India was a lesser deterrent to India's economic expansion than is suggested by official literature and policy.

This possibility is also supported by the persistence of inadequate records on actual investment. Were planned capital formation, its level and pattern, so decisive to progress, it is not likely that successive plans would proceed with such incomplete information on what was actually happening to this basic item. Similarly, lack of official interest in capital formation outside of the monetized sector also testifies to a more relaxed position on investment flows than the official posture indicates. This last factor limits the state of knowledge of the level and importance of actual investment, as well as knowledge of the economic dynamics of the entire rural sector.

The past experience with investment under planning in India provides support for theories of development that place prime emphasis on factors other than capital formation. This conclusion has major significance for future plans.

Labor

India's labor force still retains its long-time rural and agricultural predominance. More than 80 percent of all Indians continue to live in rural areas; 70 percent of all workers continue to be committed to agricultural activities. The modernization trends in the economy and the structural change accompanying them have had but marginal effects on the occupational classification of the labor force. In particular, modern industry has not provided ready employment outlets for the new and the rural labor force. Officially India's labor force is still characterized as underutilized in economic activity; there is no official acceptance of any reversal in the growing degree of underutilization. This means that there has been limited effectiveness in programs to match available man hours in rural areas, with labor intensive opportunities in various kinds of needed construction. This situation takes on added significance from the evidence that growth in agricultural output has long been lagging in some regions of India, especially on larger farms; additional manhours could have been applied profitably from a private and social viewpoint. The situation in agriculture remains one of ample (excess?) labor supply along with economic opportunities for greater use of labor.

The record also points up the proposition that national well-being has been intimately related to the degree of productive use of India's labor force, since India's factor endowments still continue to favor labor-intensive economic activity. Past plans have not addressed this proposition squarely. In the short run this circumstance nurtured the underutilization position we now find and the foregone product associated with it. Over a longer period, it delays universal involvement of India's working people in the tasks of nation building. We must remember too that public policy and action on degree of use of labor pertained also to matters of technical training, higher education, and the development of managerial and entrepreneurial skills.

India's past experience with the problems of fuller labor force commitment underscores the limitations of a policy emphasis on capital expansion as the basic input requirement for accelerated use of labor. There is no longer room to question that employment creation, in rural areas especially, is an essential priority in official programs over the next decades. The primary need is the determination to organize and establish incentives for the additional work activities that are essential *both* to greater equity and more rapid economic expansion.

National Product

We note the internal patterns within the total product and in agricultural and industrial output — all with a slower rate of growth than anticipated. Contrary to the expectations of theory and of the plans themselves, agricultural product as a ratio of total product fell by a few percentage points only. It persisted close to 50 percent, significantly lower projections notwithstanding. Presumably this higher ratio will need to be built into policy and programs for plans into the 1970's at least.

We recall again that the product of India's tertiary activities grew rapidly, relative to growth of goods output and of course relative to plan estimates. Plans were explicit about a pattern of expansion that favored growth in industrial and agricultural products. It is hard to interpret this shift as a higher welfare output alternative. Were it so, this would be reflected in studies of demand elasticities. Similarly it is hard to visualize such an output pattern as a consequence of relative supply elasticities: is capital so productive in these service sectors? Further study needs to determine how gains in output over the next decades can contribute a relatively larger share to the material needs of a population with a very low level of consumption expenditures, and to the physical expansion of the nation's plant and equipment.

Agriculture

Most striking here is the diversity of performance within a middling over-all achievement. Particularly noteworthy are performance characteristics separable on a scale-of-enterprise and again on a regional basis. Output per acre tended to vary inversely with scale of operation. Small farms had large labor supply relative to land; capital inputs were small but still high relative to farm size; fertilizer use was low per farm but high per acre as compared to the larger farm position. On the whole, with these inputs and with familiar technology, gross returns *on small farms* tended to reach a maximum level. In marked contrast was the generally less intensive resource use on the larger farms; additional inputs, including man hours of labor, would seem to have been profitable. This contrast has become increasingly apparent over past plan years. However, the development programs did stimulate output differentially in those regions where operational holdings tended to be larger (10 acres or more); this was true before the advent of the new agriculture which intensified the trend to larger output growth on the larger farms. Since farmers on larger holdings had been less efficient but still wealthier, the forces toward increased productivity served to accentuate existing agricultural income inequalities. The past development experience in agriculture was aggravating social and political forces in the nation.

The new agriculture does not yet provide promise of mitigating these pressures inherited from past efforts. The green revolution may well solve the old problems of level and rate of growth of output, but it can complicate other economic problems rooted in India's agriculture. The shift of output to larger, more commercial farms, with proportionately less output from subsistence-type producers, means that India's agriculture may move increasingly toward a reduction in its labor-intensive character. The seeming private gain to the larger farmers through this shift may be self-defeating. In any event, this private gain can be more than offset by social costs of further underemployment among small farmers, former tenants, and landless workers. Recent trends in output have not been serving the closer integration of India's economy and society that is essential for continuous national progress in the decades ahead. New programs must cope with the continuing distributive aspects of India's agricultural efforts. They must at least undertake programs for absorbing and relocating as necessary the significant share of India's rural labor force that is adversely affected by agricultural progress.

Modern Industry

The amazing characteristic of India's growth in this sector — in parallel with developments in other new nations — is the relative straightforwardness of the process of creating modern facilities. Despite its seeming newness and despite a modernity in sharp contrast to India's long familiarity with agricultural activity, for example, the spread of industrialization posed few technological problems — fewer by far than did any comparable spread of output in traditional agriculture. Major shortfalls in industrial capacity *creation* arose for administrative reasons; major shortfalls in use of capacity arose from such economic factors as shortage of effective demand. In part this last problem was a function of government-induced expansion without sufficient concern about the forces that influence total demand. In part limited output was due to systems of control of prices and of basic inputs (capital allocation, foreign exchange regulation) that did not substitute adequately for the equilibrating forces of a market. However socialistic India's economy, most national product by far — at least 85 percent — continues to be generated from activity of the private sector. While structural imbalances within industry are inevitable in a newly modernizing land, they were accentuated by inflexibility of the control system. Pressure-induced responsiveness could at best only partially offset the rigidities in the system.

However rapid the growth of modern industry, India shared with other countries the disappointment of much slower growth in industrial employment. The reasons are also associated with slow growth in demand for industrial output: internally because sectors other than industry (especially agriculture) governed the level of total demand; externally because new industries can long remain high cost (and low quality) producers if they remain sheltered from competitive supply.

Plan experience emphasizes the need for improved plan integration of expanded industrial output with output expansion in agriculture, the major sector of the economy. Past experience suggests causes for underutilization of new productive facilities in industry.

Continued analysis is also needed on the role of improved decision-making mechanisms, including the market, in the effective demand that does in fact materialize.

Import Substitution

A modernizing economy anticipates domestic production to substitute for products imported at an earlier level of national development. The early emergence of a heavy industry emphasis in India's industrial plans and programs is of special interest. Import substitution was linked specifically to replacement of foreign supplies of capital goods more than to some optimum budgeting of probable foreign exchange supplies over the long term. This emphasis has probably delayed India's industrialization progress. Problems of demand loom large in connection with major industrial equipment. Domestic purchases are therefore encouraged; there are alternative supply sources available to foreign users. High costs built into user industries in the developing country spread price disadvantages through the economy. India's heavy capital goods enterprises have stepped up India's demand for imports of essential component inputs. Growth of final output in this sector has thus been accompanied by limited (if any) foreign exchange savings at stipulated levels of production (or supply). It is hard to see continued expansion in heavy machine capacity over the next decades except as part of an increasingly high cost, less competitive industrial structure.

Foreign Trade

A program for imports and exports, for both goods and services, was a feature of all India's plans. The long-term perspectives indicated a diminishing role for international trade as India attained status as a developed nation. Both imports and exports are understandable components of planning, given the role that a net import surplus played in India's development scheme. Past programs have not made a determinable contribution to a higher degree of international balance. That rests upon policies and programs for the current and future plans. Indian experience shows that it is the state of its domestic production that governs foreign trade; the important exception to this proposition lies in the need for a special domestic program with high priority for production and distribution of export-oriented goods and services. Import restrictions in themselves may not spur domestic product. On the other side, vigorous output will not tend to be associated with low imports. In an economy where private enterprise can exert itself, import trade tends to expand, perhaps more rapidly than total domestic product; but with export encouragement, international balance at a high level can be achieved. High trade interdependence between India and its trading partners can best assure a self-sustaining India. Given India's international indebtedness, the case is stronger yet for a vigorous policy toward the export stimulation and the domestic expansion consistent with high levels of foreign trade.

In Sum

Upward movement of India's economy over the past two decades has not been accompanied by patterns of internal change that assure dynamic expansion in the future. Past progress has exploited the more straightforward opportunities provided by a new nation, new government, and new world environment. It did not uncover ever-expanding opportunities. Thus, for example, whatever the specific area, public policy did not evolve a clear position on the relative importance of expansion in the more advanced sections as against catching-up in more stagnant sections. Progress in both directions is of fundamental importance in a nation like India. Today structural imbalances and non-functional inequalities persist and grow. Motivating the forces to overcome them still remains an important future task. The possibilities for rapid future growth depend upon strategies of development that have yet to emerge clearly in policy and plan, to say nothing of action.

The fundamental responsibility here is governmental — whether the programs are explicitly those of public agencies or, more important even, whether the programs are the responsibility of the private sector. Persistent and expanding economic progress provides a positive environment for changes in government's skills and effectiveness in growth activities. What has been achieved in this direction of public effectiveness is revealed to some degree in the new programs in agriculture, modern industry, and trade. As we indicate in the next chapter, major new tasks are involved in the problems of achieving closer integration of the separate lines of progress.

It now appears that India will confront those economic challenges under government leaders aware of the importance of stepped-up participation of the citizenry in the nation's development activities. Also, the election of March 1971 offers that government a relatively long period of strong political support throughout the land. In the earlier development decades, no government in India had both these attributes. Their presence now must be termed favorable for India's development outlook.

Future Tasks and
Further Gains

7

Past and Future

India's development experience since 1950/51 does not warrant
the judgment that habits of growth have been built into the ways
of the land; nor do India's recent efforts at expansion — those undertaken through 1970 at any rate— assure it will attain developed-
nation status. The potential for such achievement certainly exists,
but it will be realized only through further actions by India's leaders. The development experience suggests the nature of such actions, but it can offer no assurance that they will in fact be taken.
The prospect for continuous growth in India, however realizable,
is not certain.

These statements rest upon the analysis of the preceding chapters. During three plans, output grew on the average about 3.3 percent annually. This provided growth of some 1 percent in income
per person; the distribution of this increase aggravated the relative
position of most of India's poor people. Internal imbalances were
accentuated during the plans; productive potential and even actual
output failed increasingly to be matched by the growth of total
demand. The patterns in labor force utilization, in labor-capital

ratios, in capital-output coefficients, and in total productivity of factor inputs give little evidence of the structural shifts that usually accompany continuous economic progress. While past development achievement probably does rule out the possibility of any significant backward movement in output per capita, it does not assure the type of aggressive forward movement anticipated in the government of India's long-term plan perspectives.

On the other hand, in the past five years or so, significant changes in official plan emphasis yielded output and input developments markedly different from those of the first three plans. The new strategy for agriculture seems indeed to have brought a precipitous shift in output in this sector of India's domestic product. Since the technological bases of this program may well permit reasonably persistent application, this new force could in itself augment the nation's annual rate of national income growth by one percent or so for the next decade. Similarly, the Indian government's new sympathy for a greater degree of market guidance in modern industry —a shift with parallels in the greater reliance the new programs in agriculture place upon the market mechanism — could complement agriculture's new advances.

There are those who believe these two new directions in Indian planning and policy provide the means for a significant expansion in the rate of growth of national product per person.[1] The output potential of these programs is real, but they will need major reenforcement if adequate levels of total demand are to be assured. Without a conscious and deliberate program that broadens the participation of India's labor force in the additional output, the new directions in agriculture and in industry will be self-defeating on both economic and political account. The record of the past decades, we have seen, provides ample evidence that agricultural progress involving India's rural population broadly is the prerequisite on the demand side for growth in the modern sector, and indeed in the economy as a whole. Ample *supplies* of agricultural products are in themselves no substitute for this wide-scale participation of India's farm population in expanded output. Similarly the experience of the past few years points to the disruptive political potential inherent in the obvious unevenness of gains from the new programs. The entire plan period has provided evidence of differential gains for the larger farm units. So dramatic were these new advantages during the new agricultural revolution that rural India

---

[1]Thus see John P. Lewis, *Wanted in India: A Relevant Radicalism*, Policy Memorandum No. 36, Center of International Studies, Princeton University, December 1969.

was rocked with resentments of major social and political dimension. Apart from violence itself, a new political radicalism may indeed be extending to the many millions of rural poor.

The new directions in India's agriculture and modern industry continue to be focused mostly on supply of output. There is as yet insufficient concern for the infrastructure of the nation's product, for the actual flows of inputs and the demand for outputs, within and among sectors. The programs must be geared specifically to achieve technological linkages especially within the rural sector, and between modern activities with their limited labor inputs and more traditional activities with their high labor components in rural areas and throughout the economy. It is precisely this linkage phenomenon that is served by the directive mechanisms considered to be important in the fourth plan.[2] They were essential cogs in the conversion of the technical relationships of even a carefully-articulated plan into the operating reality of a growing economy. To date this recognized need has not yet been converted into new policy goals or tools for development.

We repeat the theme on which we opened this chapter. India's development achievement in the years ahead depends upon new actions by government to bring the more backward parts of the economy into the new programs for growth. Other additional inputs may also serve development objectives: more local resources for public sector use and perhaps even more foreign resources for public and private use. But these can be effective only *within* an effort in which there is broad-based participation of the labor force. *Without this*, additional foreign assistance, additional taxation and public savings may aggravate instead of ease the prospects of expansion. Before moving to consideration of program dimensions of future progress, we relate this internal theme to familiar conceptual schemes for growth and discuss the political framework in which these new directions must now be formulated.

Theory and Reality

The actual record of India's development performance over the sequence of three plans provides limited support for plan goals of

---

[2]This emphasis is seen in the 1966 draft, pp. 29–38, but it receives particular attention in the 1969 draft and in the fourth plan proper. "All strategic economic decisions [will be] made by agencies informed with a social purpose . . . [so that] agriculture and industry . . . private and public . . . will assure both future technological advance . . . and [increased] immediate employment and future employment potential." *Fourth Plan*, pp. 25–28.

continuous growth in later years. Performance contrasts with the sophistication of India's planning process and procedures. As we saw in Chapter 3, planning authorities used the best methods, some pioneered in India. By and large each plan reflected this front-line knowledge, whether in the form of the early Harrod-Domar model underlying the first pian, the more complex multi-sector formulations of Feldman and Mahalanobis particularly relevant to the second plan, or the yet more advanced maximizing propositions, based on interindustry flow coefficients and capital coefficients, that were available for the third and fourth plans. These permitted ever greater detail in projecting sectoral breakdowns and interdependencies of the total product. They indicated optimum timepaths for consumption and investment *within* a five-year interval, as distinct from earlier reliance only upon initial and terminal values of the various policy and instrument variables.[3] These ever-improving schemes for one development plan are applied to a next plan with mathematical and economic precision and sophistication. But these are in contrast to the essential neglect in the theoretical discussions of the relevance of that plan to actual happenings in the economy. We have seen that successive plans departed by increasing margins from their output objectives. Improvements in the conceptual schemes of each plan have been more or less directly matched by shortfalls in plan performance.[4]

Formal doctrine in Indian planning derives from the objectives of optimum use of scarce input factors in generating target levels and patterns of output. The planning assumes that both the relative stagnation of the pre-plan years and the below-target performance of successive plans are consequences of shortages, notably

---

[3]For a comprehensive, yet succinct account of these theoretical developments *and* India's plans, see Bhagwati and Chakravarty, *op. cit.*, pp. 3–29.

[4]See the ratios on p. 133 (Chapter 5) above. We have had ample occasion in this study to note that successive plan documents do not dwell upon actual performance in the preceding plan, or upon the relevance of past performance to the prospect of the current program. It is also interesting to observe that this gap between plan development and real development is not considered noteworthy even by students concerned with relevance of doctrine as well as with theory. Thus Bhagwati and Chakravarty discuss many real counterparts of economic propositions relevant to India's development policy and program, as in agriculture's responsiveness to price stimuli, or as in the extent and importance of disguised rural unemployment. But in their comprehensive review a reader could miss entirely the remoteness of plan development from real development. He certainly would not suspect the existence of an inverse association (for whatever causes) between *advances* in the conceptualization of successive plans (discussed at length) and the relative *declines* in achievement over the sequence of plans (discussed not at all).

capital and foreign exchange. Limited domestic savings are the classic core of the resource deficit; an ever larger foreign trade deficit means persistent shortage on international account. In fact, neither of these shortages was so pervasive over these years. As we indicated (Chapter 4 especially), levels of actual investment appear generally to have at least matched corresponding plan levels. Actual shortages of capital were not real enough to bring careful measurement and reporting of the new capital formation that in fact occurred; and shortages did not encourage exploitation of feasible domestic savings and investment possibilities disclosed in the actual record (Chapters 3 and 4). Similarly, foreign exchange shortages did not deter major imports not anticipated in the plans, nor was India's export potential developed in a spirit consistent with a priority need for foreign exchange. We have noted the course of real imports, as we have the degree to which conventional assumption was allowed to be substituted for hard fact in target levels of export trade, except perhaps in very recent years. The point again is simply that however expert and sophisticated the plans, they were not addressed to India's real shortages. Plans rested on the assumption that India's low-level equilibrium economy could grow only through eliminating factor shortages beyond the economy's own capacity to fill. India's actual position, we have argued, was one of disequilibrum, trapped by *internal* deterrents to economic adjustment. These internal factors are major concerns of a development plan, more so even than an initial concern about *external* factors like supplementary resources and foreign exchange.

It is noteworthy that the spectrum of problems that dominate planning doctrine and programs seems to neglect at least two areas directly relevant to the actual scene in India, as in other poor lands. First is the persistent underutilization of a relatively large amount of labor, largely but not entirely unskilled. The other is extensive regional diversity within the land, not only in resources and in output level and structure, but especially in product per worker in similar economic activities.[5] These two omissions in themselves go a long way to explain why so much growth theory seems not to pertain to actual India. Both revolve around the economy's and the society's limited adaptability to the equilibrium forces of economic doctrine. Labor in India wants and needs more employment, but the rigidity of the production functions and the forms of capital

---

[5]Both these are mentioned as "omitted areas" in Bhagwati and Chakravarty, *op. cit.*, pp. 19–20, 28–29.

use (or perhaps the rigidities people assume exist) deter adjustments that would prompt higher rates of labor utilization. Technological possibilities for this do exist and are used in India. Price relationships have on the whole not served to push adaptations in this directon, despite the needs and the gains from greater product with existing factor supplies. Indeed many recent shifts in production processes have been toward capital substitution for labor, partly because price relationships did serve such labor displacement for individual employers. Similarly, there is both room and need for narrowing internal differences, among regions and among productive units, as a basic element of India's growth process. Regional differences persist, economic opportunities for movement of people, goods, or techniques notwithstanding.

These neglected areas constitute in themselves much of the real content of India's economic imbalance. At the least they illustrate the internal factors that impede economic gains consistent with available resources. Their persistence constitutes a dramatic index of the limited relevance in India of forward or backward linkages in the maximizing propositions of economic theory. Yet while these two areas are consciously omitted from consideration, doctrines of growth for India persist toward greater sophistication, yielding answers that are increasingly dependent upon the interindustry and intersectoral allocations of conventional economic stimuli.

During the plans the actual economic system did respond partially at most; internal disequilibrium became more acute; and on the basis of the record the prospect for subsequent expansion became less certain. However there has been an improvement in India's growth rate in the recent past, especially in 1967–70. But this change is the consequence of special programs in agriculture and, in lesser degree, in modern industry. It is *not* a change brought through the application of India's sophisticated planning doctrines. In contrast to the greater sectoral and product articulations of the comprehensive national plans, the green revolution had a *project-type* orientation. Project integration into a comprehensive, national effort did not characterize this new program. Rather it focused intensively on a relatively restricted series of non-agricultural inputs—from the laboratory and from agro-industries. Indeed, it made only limited demands on India's farm enterprise itself, since by far the bulk of the new product arose from a small percentage of farmers, primarily those with large holdings. On the other side, with respect to the forward-linkage possibilities so important in this major component of total consumption, little consideration has yet been given to the relationships between expanded agricultural output and total demand. In 1971 there is already some evidence that this growth in output potential is self-defeating; in any case, it has not stimulated the needed demand for the product of modern industry. The new program for agriculture is not yet concerned with product utilization. The main development on the Indian planning scene, the development opening the door to a needed shift in national output, is far removed from the type of comprehensive program that evolved as India's plan structure over the entire planning period.

The new emphasis in modern industry does not go far enough in complementing the new agriculture in this regard. Industrial growth offers limited additional employment off the farms. Also, the higher degree of market dependence in the new industrial emphasis will mean better integrated industrial development. Backward linkages are relatively more important here than in agriculture, but the forward linkage is relatively smaller. In any event, even more rapid growth in modern industrial enterprise will not provide much of the important demand stimulus needed by the new agriculture. On the contrary we can expect that the cross-demand flow will for decades continue to be greater in the reverse direction: a vigorous agriculture, one with material gains throughout the very large agricultural labor force and rural population of India, can assure continuous demand for the expanded output in modern industry.

In total then, the new directions in industry as in agriculture will not suffice for sustaining Indian growth. They need to be supplemented — not by doctrine that assumes there will be interdependences throughout the economy, but by actions that are directed to assure a sufficient level of total demand and that affect directly the needed link areas of the economic structure. The present new agriculture offers product more than it does labor participation. Only such participation will make success in agriculture spread beneficial effects to other sectors, through its demand for products in these sectors. The pressing need is thus for a special program to expand use of labor primarily in rural areas, where 80 percent of India's workers live. It is not likely that this ratio will decline significantly for the next decades. Some work programs also make sense for urban areas, principally in the towns and small cities where population and economic growth have not expanded as much as in larger centers over the past 15 to 20 years.

Any special employment effort will have additive influence; it will not substitute for those benefits from the new agriculture and modern industry. In fact, the three efforts need to play complementary roles if India is to achieve impressive rates of growth in output. Growth is *aided* by broader participation in the program. The inverse expectation—the greater the inequalities the more the growth — stems from theoretical doctrines that have limited relevance in view of the underutilized resources in India today.

The mechanics of a major push to create supplementary jobs *beyond* those generated by the rest of the development effort will take many specific forms. All rest on a theoretical consensus that India's underemployed workers constitute a social cost to the society and economy — at least as large for each worker as the gap between his level of consumption and his actual contribution to output. Any additional product he generates can thus be considered primarily an increment to society's savings and capital formation. Theoretically the new employment effort need not add to the society's total wage bill. In practice, some activities in the supplementary programs will demand wage payments, although even these should in theory be offset at least in part by additional tax and revenue yields. Additional outlays for domestic and foreign goods will obviously involve inputs other than labor. These could be kept small, depending upon the specific tasks and upon the locations where additional labor was employed. In an economy like India's, with its resources not fully utilized, a special direct employment program offers unusual opportunities for social gain, provided the specific schemes are carefully selected and implemented.

Several key areas constitute priority directions for the new emphasis. The green revolution needs conscious extension to smaller-size farm enterprises. The scope for improvement in yields in dry-farming areas needs continuous reappraisal: here may be major opportunities for stepped-up utilization of rural manpower. Outside of agriculture directly, the key area is construction, where low-cost labor's contribution is technologically a ready alternative for high-cost capital inputs. The scope for specific activity extends broadly from public buildings for administration, education, and health to highways and rural roads. There are important possibilities also in India's private investment needs: small irrigation works, storage facilities, and of course rural housing. A third key element lies in the expansion of rural town complexes of complementary agricultural and industrial (especially small industry) activities. With the gradual expansion of industrial inputs into agriculture, *e.g.* chemicals and machinery, opportunities grow for a market-processing-manufacturing nexus in the agricultural hinterland.

All these types of programs have often been presented, with careful and relevant argument, as natural cogs in direct labor-using complements to the indirect employment effects of programs for a better agriculture and modern industry. What we stress here is the role such activities might play in broadening the motivating mechanisms in India's economic structure, so that stimuli for growth will be more readily linked to adjoining sectors and regions. The difficult input is the leadership and directive force for such activities. Obviously these must be primarily local: the objective in general is to expand the product from underutilized workers more or less *in situ*. This also offers the best means of reducing extra costs in a direct-employment effort. Focused on local benefits, the energies and enthusiasms of the workers may be greater. Furthermore, local planning and direction might well provide opportunities that appeal to the talents of the more educated among the underemployed workers. As we stressed earlier (in Chapter 4, especially) the tasks for expanding the use of labor merge intimately with the important tasks for expanding India's corps of trained, educated, and enthusiastic leaders in public and private activities.

It is absurd to think of such an effort, throughout the nation, as one which will be essentially costless in terms of resources that might have alternative uses, as for example, equipment, machinery, and raw materials. On the other hand, it is destructive to consider the special effort on anything near a full cost basis. Not only does this second view miss the economic opportunity provided by India's internal disequilibrium position; it also brings to the fore orders of magnitude for special-program expenditures that pose them as competitors, not complements, of the other parts of the development effort. This only serves to deter the adoption of an effort essential to continuous expansion in what are today the most hopeful directions in Indian economic activity — the new agriculture and the new modern industry emphases. The appropriate approach is for national leadership to proceed in the expectation that the new effort can succeed without significant change in the cost of the total development effort. Adjustments will need to be made, but this is the correct starting point.

The idea of work cadres is not new in India. As we saw earlier, all the plans made some special efforts to reach India's underemployed or unemployed. By the early 1960's these were even presented as an essential complement to the major development effort with its indirect employment emphasis, much as the theme presented here. The direct employment effort was to serve to maximize output from India's resources, currently and progressively through the more intimate involvement in plan activities of a growing percentage of the labor force. Even the scale of the effort envisaged (2,500,000 additional workers within the five-year span) could be justified as a reasonable minimum. But India's official planning groups seemed to have limited appreciation of the potential and the significance of such a program. Official doctrine as well as expert guidance leaned in other directions. Plans for large-scale work-cadre programs were essentially lost in the prevailing effort. Less than 500,000 additional workers may have been added to some employment listing, and this was during five years when the need for additional workers was expanding at rapid rates. By now, however, the gap between these official doctrines and India's development problems may be narrowing. New emphases in planning and in programs have appeared.

Over the next decade, work opportunities could be created for millions of persons who would be underutilized with present theories and plans for growth. Such a venture is required if the economy is to progress continuously. The program will complement major supply-oriented efforts in agriculture and in modern industry. It will constitute a major new effort, but it must not alter appreciably the scale of endeavor now visualized for India's development programs. The total bundle of activities — project approaches plus resource-utilization emphases — rests on a different theoretical structure from what has governed India's past plan efforts. But the new theory, in contrast to the old, has some basis in the reality of India's economic position and potential. Moreover, recent political developments in India may themselves mandate shifts from past approaches and achievements. These political developments could even assure enactment of main lines of this new economic effort.

The Political Scene: An Input for Growth?

Our assessment of India's present economic position points anew to the important role to be filled by the poorer people in the nation if the Indian economy is to move forward persistently. Economic pressures on behalf of the multitudinous poor in India need no longer be motivated simply by humane and socialistic concerns. The pressures are hard economic complements of such existing efforts as the green revolution and the greater freedom from overregulation in modern industry. Thus our argument was *not* that economic benefits had to be shared, grudgingly if necessary. Rather we stressed that unless there were accelerated rates of gain in the presently disadvantaged sectors of the nation, the entire economy, including its wealthier components, would suffer. The need was for an additional effort, supplementary to current scales of development activity, with a near-term goal of bringing at least ten million workers more effectively into the active labor force. These are mostly in rural areas, but not entirely so. Gains from the new agriculture need to be extended to the millions of operational units which are small-scale enterprises. Under existing policy, benefits might gradually extend to only 20,000,000 households or so, less than one-third of India's total.

One would expect political developments in India over the past decade to facilitate the adoption of an economic effort to this end. Take, for example, the emergence of a more alert and discerning voting public. Voting has become more popular; almost 60 percent of the eligible voters participated in the 1967 election, a much larger ratio than in earlier years. State and local elections have been educational with regard to political styles and party flexibilities. Rural voters in particular have been exposed intimately to political-administrative activities under panchayati raj; they have seen political power created and conducted. There is evidence that the Indian voter has developed a consciousness of the privilege and the power of his right to vote. Despite the traditional class order of Indian society, the individual voter may have begun to see elections as a means for replacing officials who fail to fulfill commitments. And the voter may now be more alert to issues rather than to individuals. He is more prepared to shift from his own class and caste identifications in pursuit of what he considers his own best interest.[6]

These are emergent more than actual forces. The relevant issues are not so readily isolated. Thus there certainly is no clear record that the votes of India's poor majorities have benefitted them relative to their situation at independence. Rather, the years since 1947 have provided dramatic illustrations of the nation's unfilled — sometimes unfillable — promises toward the poorer components of India's economy and society. "Land for the tiller," "ensurance of minimum consumption . . . for the entire population" — these

---

[6]These general statements are taken from D.L. Sheth, "Political Development of Indian Electorate," *EPW*, Annual Number, 1970, pp. 137–48. This article is a preliminary report of new studies undertaken at the Centre for the Study of Developing Societies, Delhi.

slogans as well as political and social equilization remain far short of promise, the voting-strength of the millions of disadvantaged notwithstanding. Indeed our earlier discussion suggested growth of inequality in rural and urban India over the development decades. Growing *comparative* disadvantage of the poor as the national economy expanded can not even be paralleled with unequivocal evidence that there was *absolute* improvement in their economic position. The decisive gains of development appear to have gone to those who already had incomes well above the national average; for the rest, gains remained promises of benefits to be derived after still more benefits to the wealthier parts of the society.

The political development of the Indian electorate stands in contrast to its economic achievement. Important changes did occur over the past decades in structure, composition, policies, and alignments of India's political parties. But no major party sought consistently to identify India's voters with a deliberate economic program dedicated to more jobs, greater popular involvement in the economy, and a larger labor share in total output. This can be attributed to developments on both the economic and the political side of the Indian situation. Nonetheless the nation's position today may well offer an opportunity to merge economic and political factors to that end. With a sensitive awareness of the problems of India's poor and with skillful management of economic tools, public policy could bring large gains to the economy and the society.

On the economic side the policy change is already in process. Where planners have long deprecated the goal of differential economic advantages for India's poor — most of the labor force and their families — rapid growth in employment has acquired a new priority. In past plans, the route to progress emphasized indirect benefits for the work force. Policy now seems to favor direct action. Where reliance was earlier placed on comprehensive and integrated development schemes to achieve progress throughout the system, the most hopeful output developments seemed to be associated with new project-type efforts in agriculture and in modern industry, although output increases here have tended to broaden the internal gaps in the economy. Perhaps a new project-type emphasis on greater employment could be implemented so as to link India's disadvantaged millions of people into a comprehensive economic structure. In any case, the economic state of the nation and its prospects at the end of the 1960's were clear testimony of the inadequacies of past approaches to the critical early stages of India's modern economic growth.

Will a new economic emphasis combine effectively with new political pressures to mobilize the productive efforts of the people? This study has neither place nor competence for analyzing the basic political forces on the Indian scene. It seems clear, however, that neither Mahatma Gandhi nor Jawaharal Nehru had felt it necessary to create in India a political structure able to serve the nation's modern development needs. In the economic area both men proceeded on the assumption that there were two viable alternatives for the Congress Party. They hoped that their programs and policies might directly benefit most of India's people, but they were also confident that the advantaged groups and the higher classes would always be able to retain sufficient economic and political power to assure cooperation on the part of the less privileged groups in the nation. Furthermore, the political strategy of the Congress Party over the past decades did not permit the emergence of a competitive national party that might better serve changing development needs. The philosophical boundaries of Congress policy were so flexible that the party could essentially absorb — and dilute — serious pressures from right or left. This course of political development served to deter the Congress from an ideological commitment to real improvement in the economic well-being of the mass of India's people.[7]

It may long have been Mrs. Indira Gandhi's resolve to transform the Congress Party into an "instrument of revolution and change," but neither the Party's image nor its parliamentary position served that end when she became Prime Minister after the death of Lal Bahadur Shastri in January, 1966. By then any revolutionary dimension that the Congress may originally have had in the economic area had aged and perhaps disappeared. To India's poor, the Party's limited identification with their needs had succeeded only in creating a record for its facility with words more than with deeds. In addition, the conditions of succession after Shastri stressed the image and the reality of internal conflict among Party leaders.[8] The next two or three years were in fact marked by a long and bitter series of central-state controversies — in West Bengal, Madhya Pradesh, and Tamil Nadu, especially. These meant real costs to the nation from poor administrative performance, so clearly mani-

---

[7]Thus, see Rajni Kothari, "Towards a Political Perspective for the Seventies," *EPW*, Annual Number, 1970, pp. 101–16. See also his *Politics in India* (Boston: Little, Brown and Company, 1970), especially pp. 152-70.

[8]Michael Brecher, *Succession in India* (Toronto: Oxford University Press, 1966), pp. 190–241.

fest in the abortive follow-up machinery for bank nationalization over the second half of 1969. The conflict also impaired the status of the Party by providing obvious evidence of its inability to co-ordinate ministerial responsibilities.

In 1969, even before the Party split, Congress had the lowest legislative majority in its history. And Mrs. Gandhi's parliamentary independence was restricted still more by that division. It separated off the Syndicate bloc into an opposition party, the Old Congress. Her New Congress made policy and survived as long as it did only through the temporary support of other socialist and also commu-nist parties, including occasionally Swatantra and even Jan Sangh, two conservative parties basically hostile to planning and to social reform. This period did not serve the image of a strong political organization; nor did it provide much evidence of any dynamic and liberal policy orientation of her government. Implementation even of the formal economic policy doctrine of the government (as re-leased after the December, 1969, meeting of the New Congress in Bombay) would have required an impossible compromise between its own conservative and radical parts, between its supporters from privileged and wealthy classes and its supporters among the poor in both rural and urban areas. Basic policy positions on land re-forms were again left for future implementation by state govern-ments; ceilings on urban property ownership and extension of state trading to include wholesale trade in important farm products were noted without official commitment. These were matters too close to the private interests of well-to-do New Congressmen. On the other side, an expansion of public ownership of the import trade, further extension of nationalization in insurance, and reduced public sup-port for former ruling princes were all measures that scarcely im-pinged on the power of Congress constituents, although they did appeal to the "Young Turk" followers of Mrs. Gandhi. But what was feasible (before the new election) fell far short of the dramatic and revolutionary changes — like real land reform or actual reduc-tion in inequality of property ownership — sought by these more radical groups.

The election results suggest strongly that the conservative roots of the Congress, especially in rural India, had been overestimated by the previous parliament. Policies for significant economic and social change may well be adopted, in spite of their limited progress either on the policy or action fronts in the period through 1970. Similarly, the new government should be able to establish again a workable pattern of center-state party relationships. Without the need for its tenuous accommodations with the Swatantra and Communist parties, the Congress re-emerges as the only source of strength at the center. Other parties continue to have strong regional pockets — in Bihar and the Punjab as well as in West Bengal and Kerala — but their local effectiveness requires that the Congress in New Delhi provide functioning machinery for interparty relationships and state-central coordination. In other words, it should be possible for the Prime Minister to lead a government that does appeal to the common man and that can bring to India's poor and disadvantaged, as to India as a whole, a new prosperity in a functioning democracy.

Specific directions for economic policy in such a program might still take quite different courses, all consistent with government's commitment to absolute and relative improvement in the economic status of most Indians. The redistribution could emphasize changed flows of current incomes. Thus greater income equalization might be sought through restrictions on high incomes or through more or less direct transfers from higher to lower income recipients. This objective could also be approximated by redistribution of factor ownership, thus altering the level of returns from these factors — or so it is generally argued, presumably on the assumption of more intensive use by the new owners.[9] Another range of policies attacks incremental flows more directly. Thus expansion of relative income in the public as against the private sector might offer greater gains to the less advantaged parts of the nation and society through greater public consumption, factor payments, or income transfers. Finally, policy might seek maximum expansion of total product primarily through increments in output generated from expanded use of underutilized resources.

While it is this last range of policies to which the present analysis has pointed, the ideology of public economic policy in India has long favored other categories. Apart from sporadic attention to income ceilings, and other more or less direct actions upon income, interest has long focused on land redistribution schemes and on fixed limits on property ownership. There are pressures for establishment of a cooperative society, at least for large parts of agriculture, small industry, and some related services. Nationalization and a wide range of less direct measures to expand the public sector

---

[9]This possibility is well illustrated in statistics of output per acre in Indian agriculture. For many years, larger holdings in the same crop were utilized less intensively than were smaller units of operation. See above, Chapter 5, pp. 149–51.

also have histories in India's socialistic doctrine. Higher taxes, price controls, capital rationing, profit restrictions — all have been advocated as tools for transferring the locus of rapid expansion from private to public parts of the nation. Many of these, if applied in limited measure, could well contribute to accelerated growth in national income, and perhaps differentially in the poorer parts of the nation. There is room for more complete implementation of ceiling legislation in some areas where land is farmed inefficiently; some cooperative services still have large scope in rural India both for agriculture and household industry. On the whole, however, further restrictions on market decisions will probably impede an already limited set of response mechanisms in the economy; there is rather some need for *reducing* the extent to which legislation or edict presently alters the economic counterpart of the technological interdependences of modern enterprise. Experience, as indeed new policy, already testifies to the advantages of less rather than more public involvement in economic decision making at or near the firm level. Public enterprise cannot continue to expand broadly except at very high costs to India's economic and social structure. The internal deterrents to such expansion are well illustrated by the actual difficulties already experienced in efficient implementation of plans for rapid growth in India's public sector.[10]

Indeed many of the guides for economic policy in the next decades will need to lean heavily on insights gained from the entire Indian development experience. New economic programs must consciously augment the thrust now given the nation by the two hopeful directions of action already in process — the green revolution and the new concern with the decision-making mechanisms in the organized parts of private activity. As we indicated above, these new directions have a project dimension; policy needs now to focus on gains both from additional direct employment activity (more output, more capital formation) and from expanded output per unit of present inputs through greater interdependences throughout the productive process. The present fourth plan has renewed (and perhaps made more realistic) the emphasis of the third plan upon work cadres, for construction especially, and in the rural areas in particular. There seems also to be a greater awareness among Indian officials of the importance of better use of underutilized resources, particularly manpower. Without doubt the prospect of

---

[10]Thus see the discussion above on actual experience with investment allocations and sectoral output, Chapter 4, pp. 86–96 and Chapter 6, pp.166–74.

easier food supplies encourages such an approach.[11] Very important also is a growing appreciation of the role that leadership in public and private activity plays throughout a growing economy. Committed and involved worker-participation is also an essential ingredient for growth.[12] On all these accounts the Indian scene may be more receptive to such new directions than at any earlier time. But at best it will take persistent guidance from high officials to make the requisite shift in policy directions. And this in turn could be helped by political pressures toward the improved well-being of India's many millions of poor people.

Development Activity in Prospect

In the 1970's most of the world's people still live in nations where levels of consumption, education, and health make mockery of the world's growth in wealth and of man's scientific, technological, and organizational miracles of the past century. By and large output per worker in these lands has increased over the past two decades but not as rapidly as in the rest of the world. There is general recognition that progress in the developing lands was below expectations; less general is consensus on the explanation for this record. The high priority tasks of development seem less straightforward now than they appeared to be in the early 1960's and certainly in the 1950's. Today the promise and prospect for future growth remain elusive. The reasons go far beyond level of capital supply or pattern of capital formation. They certainly embrace entrepreneurship, public leadership, and the participation and commitment of the total labor force. The extensive record of development experience since 1950 defies interpretation primarily in terms of capital and its allocation; it points up the roles of level and quality of labor.[13]

---

[11]Thus see J.P. Lewis, *op. cit.*, pp. 31–33.

[12]See Wilfred Malenbaum, "Government, Entrepreneurship and Economic Growth in Poor Lands," *World Politics*, 19:1 (October, 1966), pp. 52–68. Also see *Fourth Plan*, pp. 429–34.

[13]Thus see U.N., *World Economic Report 1967*, New York, 1968. Also see a UN Economic Commission for Asia and the Far East (ECAFE) *Report* (April, 1970) that indicates growing support for the "idea that development is a process in which social progress is not only a 'factor' but . . . an arbiter and prerequisite of economic growth." There is "belated recognition that existing patterns of development have in many instances failed to promote integration of national societies . . . ," that the need now is "for major efforts to reduce the glaring inequalities of income distribution."

In this study we have examined India's growth experience com-
prehensively. India did attempt to meet the challenge of its persistent poverty in an expanding world by mounting an ambitious and
aggressive development effort. In the wide range of its growth activities India relied upon the most sophisticated theoretical analyses
and empirical studies known to social scientists anywhere. These
doctrines and the parameters associated with them were built upon
a system of more or less immediate, short-run patterns of internal
adjustment and supply response; such patterns do not yet pertain
in most of the country. Capital inputs often created capacity that
had low rates of utilization: marginal capital coefficients turned out
to be unexpectedly high. Technological interdependencies were not
matched by actual balances. Economic disequilibrium as measured
by unequal returns per unit of comparable input characterized parts
of the economic structure. Such internal imbalances did not of
themselves set in motion forces to create better balance. The result
was loss of product from available input in an already low-income
and low-productivity land. These inefficiencies did not tend to dis-
appear with additional capital goods inputs; the reverse seemed to
be true.

Only with additional efforts in specific directions will economic
development be attained in India. The first need is for political commitment with appropriate organizational structure to step up the
degree of use of the factor supplies already in the economy. "Additional efforts" are to involve additional persons in effective output;
"specific directions" can assure an integrated use of available facilities. Public and private actions should serve to tie the poorer
components of the labor force into parts of the economy that are
physically or functionally nearby *and* are more modern and progressive. Only as these activities begin to lessen the nation's internal
maladjustments will capital supply and its allocation attain priority
in the development process. Capital inputs do have to grow steadily
as a poor country develops. Once problems of resource use are in
hand, even very rapid capital growth can be straightforward. New
investment resources at higher levels are more readily attracted
where existing production is efficient.

On the basis of our analysis of the past record and its implications for subsequent growth, we conclude this study with some
observations on new development targets and activities over the
next decade or two. These observations assume a total development
effort, as in the present fourth plan, for example, which already
incorporates expansion of the new agriculture and expansion of

greater market orientation for India's enterprises, especially those in the modern industrial sector. The major addition of course is a program for *supplementary employment*. An appropriate goal is two to two and one-half million additional jobs per year at least for the next five years; this is employment *beyond* the four or five million and more workers that would "normally" find new jobs over each of these plan years. The very scale of this effort demands a major political commitment. The program would seek to create employment for persons passed over in the nation's economic activities, whether these persons be among new members of the labor force, the unemployed, or those employed with productivity at very low levels. We are uncertain about the magnitude of the unemployment and underemployment labor reserve, but a work effort on this scale would permit more precise program definition over its first five years. On the other hand, the evidence already presented prompts an expected supplement of at least ten million workers over these years. The objectives of the additional employment effort are expanded output, greater interdependence within the economic structure, and a larger total effective demand — year in and year out — for national product. The major program areas of the economy are agriculture, construction, and other small-scale enterprises; benefits from these would be made to spread throughout the entire structure.

The problems of *output* are the main concern of current efforts in agriculture. We know the HYVP, IADP, and IAAP activities have operated primarily on large-scale enterprises; yields per acre are already increasing. We noted the political difficulties created by this aspect of the new agriculture as well as the economic setbacks inherent in growing inequalities of income. Can the new agriculture benefit the landless in the rural areas, and operators of holdings below five acres, for example?

The techniques for intensification of production and for multi-crop cultivation require ample water supply; there is also some premium to scale of enterprise, to capital supply, and to technical knowledge. The larger operations by wealthier farmers in the wet areas of the nation will continue to benefit the most. The tendency on these farms to intensify through seeking tractors to substitute for labor will not in general serve national economic and social objectives over the next decade. Labor per acre on India's smaller (and higher-yielding farms) has been two or three times the ratio on farms with more than 7.5 acres, for example. Increased labor use by these farmers would accomplish their own intensification goals while it also contributed to the output, spread, and demand objectives that the nation seeks through its supplementary employment emphasis. Even a relatively modest expansion in the labor-land ratio on India's larger farms might achieve half or more of the new-productive-job effort.

Indeed, in the near future the employment potential here could be substantially greater. Water supply of the requisite level is now found on some ninety million acres, less than one-fourth of India's net cultivated area. In part this is attributable to rainfall; for the most part it reflects the gradual extension of various kinds of irrigation. India's "ultimate potential" with all known forms of irrigation is estimated to be some one hundred million additional acres. This essential doubling of present levels of acreage with sufficient water could be attained over the next 15 to 20 years, provided a big enough supplementary irrigation effort were undertaken, beginning now. (This, of course, also opens the possibilities for additional labor use in construction activities.) There may now be about twenty-five million acres in the new agriculture. Included here are relatively few small farmers; these tend to be in selected areas, like Cuttack District in Orissa and Kolab District in Maharashtra, to which we have already referred. The new agriculture is expected to extend to sixty million acres by 1973/74, expansion that would require considerable progress in seed adaptation. Still, the present type of program has considerable scope for output expansion without special efforts to reach the smaller farmer in the wet areas. We have already noted that new irrigation has tended to move increasingly to areas of larger-farm size. Greater labor use on farms will depend increasingly on the greater use of labor — as worker or tenant — on the large-scale enterprises.

On India's 340,000,000 acres there are some 50,000,000 operational holdings, 63 percent of these cultivating less than 5 acres altogether on a total of less than 65,000,000 acres. So parcelized are Indian land holdings that one has to reach operational holdings that total at least 7.5 acres before the individual parcels average one acre in size. Most farmers by far work on unit plots well below ½ acre. These already use high labor inputs per acre; scope for additional man-hours of work here is small. Still, within the wet areas the exclusion of the small farmer from the new agriculture is due less to his scale limitation than to his limited resource position. India's new plans call for pilot experiments in twenty districts under a Small Farmer's Development Agency. The objective is to help narrow the big farmer advantage with respect to credit and efficient use of capital equipment. Still, the new agency does not expect to reach more than 1,500,000 small farmers over the fourth plan years. Unless major emphasis is given such programs, that objective may be high, given what appear as easier alternatives for attaining targets through the rich farmer.

The outlook is even less certain for small farmers in the dry-land parts of India. Here there are at least 140,000,000 acres under cultivation, about 40 percent of the total. Perhaps 10,000,000 operating units, and an even larger number of households, earn livelihoods on five acres or less. The new agriculture can only pass these by; it takes the larger holding and richer farmer to provide a base for the livestock and dairying to which these areas need to turn. More research efforts are being devoted to dry-farming problems by the Indian Council of Agricultural Research. It is a subject that continues to prove unrewarding as it has to admittedly limited research efforts elsewhere.

In any perspective time horizon, the prospect is small for absorption of India's millions of small farms into the current new agriculture. At the least, the small farmer in the wet areas must have new goals of higher subsistence levels if he is not absorbed as a laborer on the larger and commercialized new agriculture. At the least, the small-farmer effort in the dry areas needs to recognize the scope for part-time agriculture, with larger income shares from non-farm activities, including, of course, the construction and small industry opportunities in rural India.

India's construction industry offers possibilities for new additions directly to national product. It also offers indirect additions in other sectors through external economies both from new overhead facilities and from higher productive status of the total labor force. We have already noted in Chapter 4 the important role that the Indian economy on its own has given to the construction sector, beyond what was in official plans. With special organization, a nation like India offers great potential for construction of local roads, irrigation facilities, agricultural structures, public school and health facilities, and even housing, to say naught of additional and comparable needs in small urban parts of the nation. Construction complements efforts to expand rural industry, in the new opportunities and needs for storage, transport and agricultural processing and agro-industries generally. If small urban centers can take root along with India's growing agricultural potential, they provide obvious opportunities for greater use of labor in activities where our output, spread, and demand objectives can be fulfilled.

This merges readily with labor-intensive industry generally. In India small-scale industry has long been important; in some products particularly — bicycles, sewing machines, a wide variety of small industrial components, and traditional handicrafts — the possibilities for expansion are promising both for domestic consumption and export. This diversity in small-scale enterprise can in itself serve the objective of additional employment, for it permits local production of needed inputs beyond labor. Although a society like India's is committed to feed and maintain its workers, the newly employed (and the more fully employed) will increase their food consumption above subsistence levels. Domestic food output will be expanding. There will also be new demands for consumer goods and for some of the capital goods required in labor-intensive construction activities. New outlays will be needed for intermediate goods such as the pipes and fixtures in construction output, for example. These are small parts of total value, but they must still be purchased. In other words, the creation of additional employment on a large-scale will require some additional outlays, perhaps even abroad. But we recall the difficulties India has encountered through under-use of its own capital plant. The new employment push will thus serve to stimulate internal interdependences. There will need to be additional public outlays, but we have noted the potential for additional internal resource mobilization, particularly in the rural household sector, where in fact so much of the additional labor use and output are to take place.

The point it is very important to stress is that for India a supplementary employment program requires primarily one costly input: daring, determined, and imaginative public leadership. With such a commitment, additional resources will be found. We saw that past efforts to bring together India's potential for "extra" product have not moved far; invariably the required inputs of skill and imagination were not made available. Moreover, the specifics of a major program for additional employment and output must be engineered at local levels throughout the land, wherever more output can be obtained from India's resources. The program needs not only unskilled labor but also the special talents of the educated, including those skilled in the mechanical and engineering arts. In other words, a major work-cadre effort provides a unique opportunity for using the technical skills and the advanced training for which demand in India has been declining, as we noted earlier. Some additional public outlays will be needed if the unemployed and underemployed educated groups are to be used. But these are low-cost outlays, reimbursed in resulting short-run gains as well as long-run benefits from an economy and society that have made the transition to persistent growth.

On another matter, Indian development obviously demands continuous *expansion of its modern industry*. While this is well treated in current plans, we note that the additional employment emphasis above will create an environment for more rapid industrial expansion. What must be assured is that the plans serve increased industrial efficiency. It is important that current trends toward more market-oriented policies on licensing and pricing be maintained and indeed be accelerated, subject to feasible adjustment requirements and realistic restraints on international trade and exchange account. Impressive progress has been made over the past year in liberalizing India's basic industrial policy. Early in 1970 licensing requirements were eased significantly both for new industrial undertakings and for substantial expansions of existing enterprises. One important area that remains unhappily restricted concerns protective devices for established industry. Import substitution, we have noted, often tends to raise domestic costs and prices. In India it has precluded the effective export stimulation so important to India's new trade policy. We suggested earlier that a less restrictive import policy might actually help India's international competitive position. An industrial expansion that is almost completely isolated from world market pressures is more apparent than real. Not only does it reduce the nation's productivity; it eventually undercuts effective resource utilization. India's expanding industry is generously interspersed with protected infant industries, now ten and more years old. A matter of high priority over the next five years or so is the systematic reduction of their dependence upon import quotas and upon comparable restrictions on the domestic availability of lower-cost or better quality foreign products.

While problems of foreign trade go well beyond the modern-industry sector, we emphasize here our earlier conclusion on the importance of a high import level (of non-grain products) for a vigorous Indian industry and economy, and for a high-export level that can sustain import growth. Exports of agricultural products, traditional and new, are important as are the varied outputs from small-scale and handicraft industry. But the most elastic supply component of exports lies in India's modern industries. We have noted recent export developments in this regard. But the gains from exporting underutilized industrial capacity are not readily maintained, and domestic consumption will compete effectively with exports that can be sold abroad only at prices that fail to meet capital costs. Some export stimulation schemes may actually constitute net drains on foreign exchange, a situation which can at best be tolerated as a short-period interlude to actual (net) earnings. Again the specifics are complex and varied; but there is no question that India's export expansion warrants continuous and imaginative action on the part of planning officials, as well as private and public industrial enterprises.

What levels of foreign exchange availability are reasonable for India to anticipate over the next five to ten years? This question concerns not only possible export levels but also the level of foreign assistance. And it is intimately related to total investment and product in India over this period. Brief observations on these matters constitute our end notes on development activities in India over the next plans.

In May 1970, India's planners projected foreign exchange resources for the new fourth plan period, 1969–74, as Rs 12,330 crores; Rs 8300 crores were to be met from export earnings, and Rs 4030 from foreign assistance (less than 10 percent of which would be PL 480 food aid).[14] More than half of this foreign aid will be offset by debt servicing obligations. A net aid figure of only Rs 1750 crores was assumed available to help meet new foreign assistance needs. We did argue (Chapter 6) that the Rs 12,330 crores figure might be considered somewhat optimistic. This was particularly so on the export side, given the doldrums of India's export levels through most of the 1960's. The gross aid level and special arrangements for debt servicing did not seem promising in the recent foreign aid "weariness" of many donor lands. In any event, India adopted a deliberate policy to achieve marked reductions in imports. For the two years to April 1, 1970, these were actually 15 percent below the two previous years' level. On the whole these represent the effects of good harvests, with significantly reduced imports both of foodgrains and some agricultural raw materials (*i.e.* raw cotton in 1969/70). Industrial imports have for the most part been maintained. With favorable exports, India's position on international account has benefitted. The government has taken the opportunity to strengthen its external reserve posi-

---

[14]The Rs 4030 apparently also includes a new inflow of Rs 30 crores on private enterprise account. Gross private investment from abroad was projected at Rs 300 crores, but capital repayments on foreign investment are anticipated to take 90 percent of the total over the five years. See *Fourth Plan*, 1969 draft, pp. 90–94.

tion. For the first time in nearly two decades, foreign exchange reserves exceed one billion dollars, an expansion of more than 50 percent from June 1966, when the rupee was devalued.

Government's opting to build up its reserve position at the start of the new plan reflects uncertainty about foreign assistance; more fundamentally also it reflects government's determination to seek its development objectives while its dependence on foreign aid does, in fact, decline. This has been an early and persistent target, but it is a target on which little progress has been made over past plans. Foodgrains and agricultural raw materials apart, further import reductions might impair India's output performance, at least for some years. Moreover, the supplementary employment effort could provide new justification for additional imports, as we indicated above. Indeed, Indian officials might well argue that in the present trade position such additional imports would need to be financed externally if the new effort is to be made at all. Our study suggests that pressures for further aid for this purpose be resisted: the nature of the supplementary employment program places a premium on maximum fulfillment of its input needs through indigenous activities. With government determined to lower foreign aid ratios, the prospect for such indigenous achievement is enhanced. And this also provides a real possibility that aggressive export expansion, including exports of products encouraged by the new effort, could gradually offset present emphasis on reducing nonfoodgrains imports.

In India's plans, investment over the 1969–74 years is projected at Rs 22,600 crores, which implies that domestic savings would be of the order of 12.5 percent of national income over those years. This is high by past standards and cannot be considered probable even were less conventional forms of savings tapped more systematically, as suggested above.[15] But savings rates could expand during these years when more workers were finding effective employment and were also making larger gains through the improved interdependences in the economy. The total effort outlined here can be expected to lower significantly the past relationships between new capital investment and additional output in the economy. Thus with an incremental capital-output ratio close to the 2.5 level, even lower investment during 1969–74 might be consistent with income increases at rates *above* 5 or even 6 percent annually. Such an order of magnitude for growth in the economy

---

[15]Pp. 100–102.

is certainly possible; with the program indicated, it could well be higher and also be followed by progressive expansion in later plans.

Finally, with respect to individual well-being, we feel this total product will be somewhat more equitably distributed than in earlier years. On the other side, there is no real possibility of appreciable reductions in the rates of population growth over the next decade or so at the least. India is striving to lower this rate through measurable declines in the birth rate. Its comprehensive efforts to this end have recently been assessed by an expert UN Advisory Mission.[16] Important recommendations of the Mission rested on the multi-faceted nature of the family planning objective. Population control is viewed in the context of a human improvement effort that alerts man to his potential and his importance for his world, his nation, his family, and himself. Over the next decade, India's success in turning output trends upward persistently may not be aided by any "numbers" effect of slower population growth. But the new development emphasis in our study emerged from the concern for human transformation essential to structural change.[17] It would thus serve the human changes that affect decisions on size of family. Output growth, a better interrelated economy, expanded total demands for goods and services — these can eventually proceed toward a higher per capita achievement to which slower population growth will also contribute.

---

[16]See U.N., Commissioner for Technical Cooperation, *An Evaluation of the Family Planning Programme of the Government of India*, TAO/IND/50, November 24, 1969, especially pp. 7–8, 54–68.

[17]Above, pp. 48–50 and 205–10.

Index